Congress and Diaspora Politics

Congress and Diaspora Politics

The Influence of Ethnic and Foreign Lobbying

Edited by

James A. Thurber, Colton C. Campbell,
and David A. Dulio

Published by State University of New York Press, Albany

For information, contact State University of New York Press, Albany, NY
www.sunypress.edu

Library of Congress Cataloging-in-Publication Data

Names: Thurber, James A., editor. | Campbell, Colton C., editor. | Dulio, David A.,
    editor.
Title: Congress and diaspora politics : the influence of ethnic and foreign
    lobbying / edited by James A. Thurber, Colton C. Campbell, and David A.
    Dulio.
Description: Albany : State University of New York Press, 2018. | Includes
    bibliographical references and index.
Identifiers: LCCN 2017044277 | ISBN 9781438470870 (hardcover : alk. paper) |
    ISBN 9781438470894 (ebook)
Subjects: LCSH: Lobbying—United States. | Pressure groups—United States. |
    Minorities—Political activity—United States. | Foreign agents—United
    States. | United States—Foreign relations. | United States. Congress.
Classification: LCC JK1118 .C58 2018 | DDC 328.73/078—dc23
LC record available at https://lccn.loc.gov/2017044277

10 9 8 7 6 5 4 3 2 1

Contents

Tables and Figures

Tables

Figures

Acknowledgments

As with any collaborative project, this book would not have been possible without the cooperation of many people. We must first thank Michael Rinella at SUNY Press for agreeing that a better understanding of ethnic and foreign lobbying in Congress was worth publishing. We also extend special thanks to Eileen Nizer, who shepherded the book through the production process. Our academic colleagues who contributed chapters deserve particular mention for committing to this novel project and for delivering such insightful works in an efficient and professional manner. A special thank you goes to the reviewers, who provided thoughtful and timely input. We would also like to thank our colleagues at American University, the National War College, and Oakland University for their continued guidance and support. Finally, we would like to acknowledge our families whose support and patience remains constant. Jim Thurber would like to thank his wife Claudia and his family. Colton Campbell would like to thank his wife Marilyn and son Caden. Dave Dulio would like to thank his wife Adrianne and daughters Abby and Sophia. To all these individuals we express our deepest appreciation.

Chapter 1

Congress and Diaspora Politics

The Influence of Ethnic and Foreign Lobbying

JAMES A. THURBER, COLTON C. CAMPBELL,*
AND DAVID A. DULIO

The Obama administration's push to approve a nuclear accord with Iran in 2015 captured the attention of many Americans, especially those of Jewish descent, not just because of its potential security implications for Israel, but because of the American Israel Public Affairs Committee's (AIPAC) inability to corral lawmakers on both sides of the aisle to produce their desired policy result. The lobbying powerhouse, which some argue has undue influence over Congress,[1] was offset by J Street, a liberal lobbying group that advocated support of the nuclear deal.[2] The opposing sides waged dueling campaigns to persuade undecided lawmakers that they best represented the concerns and views of pro-Israel voters.[3] AIPAC spent tens of millions of dollars in television and social media advertisements against the deal, mobilized grassroots opposition rallies, steered activists to meetings and town-hall gatherings with lawmakers around the country, formed a tax-exempt group—consisting in part of former lawmakers—to educate people about the "dangers" of the deal, and led two congressional trips—one with Democrats, the other with Republicans—to Israel during the sixty-day period in which Congress had to consider the agreement.[4] In turn, J Street executed its own multi-million-dollar media blitz, as well as deployed former military officials and diplomats to Capitol Hill to assuage those members of Congress, particularly Democrats, who feared a backlash from Jewish voters and donors for supporting the deal.[5]

*The views expressed in this chapter are those of the author and not the National Defense University, the Department of Defense, or any other entity of the U.S. government.

1

While few political observers see AIPAC's failure to block the nuclear deal with Iran as an end to its political sway on Capitol Hill, the setback does represent an important and emerging trend, as different ethnic lobbies have been able to argue that their positions are part of the American national interest. Historically, some ethnic groups have exercised more influence in Congress than others, especially those with large blocks of unified voters.[6] Yet success is no longer limited to just a few. The number of ethnic groups now lobbying the U.S. government has increased significantly in recent years, as has the political skill and electoral clout of those groups. Indeed, the importance and power of diaspora politics has never been greater. Whereas ten years ago, for example, Armenia was of little concern to most members of Congress, today the Armenian-American lobby is one of the most active ethnic lobbies on the Hill, a power that stems from the heavy concentration of Armenian Americans in states like California, Massachusetts, New Jersey, and New York.[7] Working with key lawmakers and the ninety-five-member Congressional Caucus on Armenian Issues, they have successfully lobbied for a steady stream of foreign aid to Armenia,[8] although they have fallen short of their goal of getting the United States to formally recognize what they refer to as the "Armenian genocide." Likewise, the emergence of black ethnic Congressional Member Organizations (CMOs), such as the Congressional African Immigrant and Diaspora Caucus and the Congressional Ethiopian-American Caucus, have provided African immigrant communities with a legislative voice in ways they have not seen before.[9]

Foreign governments also are increasingly relying upon hired lobbyists—often former lawmakers and their staff—rather than just their diplomats to promote their policies with members of Congress and officials of the executive branch.[10] This practice is nothing new to Washington, DC, however. Starting in the 1970s, many nations began to work directly with Congress by having their ambassadors and other representatives meet directly with members of the House and Senate to advocate for policy alternatives important to their home countries. Of course, many of these meetings were arranged by American lobbyists paid by those foreign governments. In addition, countries well-known to Americans including Germany, France, and the United Kingdom had begun to spend large sums on lobbyists by the 1990s. Other countries even closer to home—Canada and Mexico—spent millions to lobby on U.S.–Canadian Free Trade Agreement and the North American Free Trade Agreement, respectively. These practices have only been expanded in recent years. Millions of dollars are spent each year on hired guns. In 2015 alone, Saudi Arabia hired eight different American lobbying firms and spent more than $9.4 million in an effort to block legislation that some said could potentially expose the Arab kingdom to litigation over the 9/11 terrorist attacks.[11] According to OpenSecrets.Org, from 1955 to May 2017, Saudi Arabia paid millions of dollars annually to 1,281 top lobbying organizations, recently including Hogan & Hartson, Podesta Group, Squire Patton Boggs, Glover Park Group, and Hill & Knowlton. Even nations that do not have strong diplomatic ties with the United States are looking for outside help.[12] As an example, several Washington, DC lobbyists were paid more than $500,000 in 2014 to counsel the small, West African nation of Gabon on a potential bilateral investment treaty between it and the United States.[13] Foreign government lobbying became front-page news in early to mid-2017 during the controversy over Russian interference in the 2016 U.S. presidential election. Amid several investigations (by congressional committees, a special prosecutor in the Department of Justice, journalists, and others) into the matter, the activities of some Russian lobbyists were brought to the fore. In particular, the activities of Rinat Akhmetshin, a Russian-American lobbyist, and his partner Robert Arakelian were reported. Lobbying reports showed the pair's work on behalf of The Human Rights Accountability Global Initiative Foundation totaled roughly $50,000. Akhmetshin and Arakelian "reported lobbying on adoption issues related to the Magnitsky Act, a U.S. law reviled by Vladimir Putin that sanctioned Russia for human rights abuses in the death of a Russian whistleblower named Sergei Magnitsky."[14]

Congress first regulated lobbyists for foreign governments in 1938 with the Foreign Agents Registration Act (FARA) in an effort to curb growing Nazi influence within the United States. FARA, however, has evolved over time. The first focus after World War II was communism and secret agents inside the United States. In the mid-1960s, FARA was amended to move away from hidden agendas and toward agendas that were arguably more transparent—those of governments more friendly to the United States who would try to influence U.S. policy. An additional evolution was the addition of provisions that call for the criminal prosecution of foreign agents who make campaign contributions to federal candidates in the U.S. Today, any foreign agent who lobbies and conducts political activity on behalf of a foreign government must register with the Department of Justice, detailing the extent of their relationship with the foreign nation, how much they are paid, etc. Even so, FARA has seen relatively weak enforcement and few prosecutions. However, FARA in general and its criminal provisions in particular came into greater focus during the first months of Donald J. Trump's presidency with investigations, indictments and guilty pleas surrounding accusations made against the 2016 Trump campaign. In December 2016, a bipartisan group of members of Congress introduced legislation to strengthen FARA, to ensure that the American public knows who is trying to influence their policy.[15]

The lobbying efforts of ethnic groups, particularly ethno-national diaspora, at times combine with and promote the interest of a homeland government, especially in the area of U.S. foreign policy.[16] An increasingly professional and well-funded Indian diaspora, for instance, lobbies on issues of concern to the nation of India.[17] In 2008, working both through the U.S. India Political Action Committee (USINPAC), the most influential Indian-American lobby, and through lobbying firms retained by the Indian government, Indian Americans helped shepherd through Congress the India-U.S. Civil Nuclear Agreement.[18] Taking a page from AIPAC's lobbying playbook, USINPAC created a strong foundation for its organizational strength by starting a national outreach program that coalesced different viewpoints within the Indian-American community, particularly those in politically influential states such as California, New York, Texas, and Illinois.[19] It also initiated a youth committee to "perpetuate the new vision of Indian-American leadership, and starting a national outreach program to bring together different Indian-American viewpoints."[20] It built a large funding base by soliciting donations from its members, and encouraged them to write letters to lawmakers urging them to support the deal. A tracking system was designed to closely monitor lawmakers' sentiment toward the nuclear agreement. This, in turn, informed campaign contributions to key lawmakers who represented areas with significant Indian-American populations.[21] USINPAC framed its message in a way most likely to obtain congressional approval by linking the agreement to other goals in U.S. policy related to India. Through issue briefs to members of Congress and staff, office visits, and receptions it framed the deal in terms of economic and environmental goals as well as trade potential in the civilian nuclear sector.[22] When progress on the deal stalled in India, USINPAC met with senior leaders in the Indian legislature to understand their differing perspectives on the issue.

At other times a diaspora's interests might diverge from its home government.[23] This sort of cleavage was on display in 2006 when Vietnam joined the World Trade Organization (WTO). Although Congress had no direct role in the country's accession to the WTO, as with other communist countries, U.S. trade relations with Vietnam were subject to the so-called Jackson-Vanik amendment. As such, Congress needed to enact legislation to grant permanent normal trade relations (PNTR)[24] status to Vietnam if the United States was to benefit fully from the terms of its WTO membership. The Vietnamese embassy in the United States retained three different Washington, DC lobbying firms to help obtain a clean (i.e., free of amendments), stand-alone bill extending PNTR for Vietnam by conducting various meetings with congressional members and staffers.[25]

Lawmakers whose constituencies had large diasporic communities of Vietnamese, however, opposed granting PNTR status to Vietnam on the basis of poor human rights and religious freedom conditions in Vietnam. "Just two months ago, the Vietnamese government arrested my constituent, a U.S. citizen, Cong Thanh Do," declared Representative Zoe Lofgren (D-CA). "Mr. Do had posted comments on the Internet while at home in San Jose, California advocating that Vietnam undergo a peaceful transition to a multiparty democracy. For exercising his U.S. Constitutional right of free speech, the Vietnamese arrested him and held him in prison for 38 days in Vietnam without charges."[26] Lofgren further stated: "Other U.S. citizens have been imprisoned in Vietnam for what appear to be political reasons, including the sister of another one of my constituents, Thuong Nguyen "Cuc" Foshee.[27] Similarly, Representative Loretta Sanchez (D-CA), a member of the pro-trade New Democrat Coalition CMO, but whose district includes Little Saigon, home to approximately 10 percent of the entire Vietnamese-American population, voiced opposition to normalizing trade relations with Vietnam without "mandating essential human rights protections."[28]

To the surprise of House leadership, congressional opposition stymied its initial attempt to expeditiously consider PNTR as a stand-alone measure under Suspension of the Rules.[29] The measure had majority support, 228 to 161, but it failed to muster the two-thirds needed to pass under the suspension procedure. Leadership subsequently had to fold PNTR into a larger measure, invoke marshal law, and bring it to the floor under a closed rule, with no opportunity for amendments.[30]

In another example, at the start of the new Obama administration, Afghanistan increased the amount it paid lobbyists by more than 205 percent compared to previous years during the Bush administration.[31] It also spent $324,000 and retained five different lobbying firms in the first half of 2015 to persuade President Obama and Congress to delay the planned troop withdrawal from Afghanistan.[32]

This volume addresses several themes related to the topic, including the strategies and tactics employed by ethnic groups in the United States and foreign nations abroad, a range of issues—in both domestic and foreign policy—that are of interest to foreign governments and ethnic groups in the United States, and the successes (and failures) of these efforts. Before turning to more details on the volume, we examine ethnicity and lobbying in a broader context. These examples of only a few recent instances raise questions about the general practice of lobbying by different ethnic groups and foreign nations who have interests being considered by the U.S. government, and Congress in particular.

Ethnicity and Lobbying

Ethnicity, as an agent of change on Capitol Hill, is afforded an underappreciated role in the study of Congress. Moreover, the importance of lobbying is either derided[33] or given relative little attention compared to other topical areas, such as congressional elections, partisanship and polarization, and members' voting patterns, to name just a few. Yet lobbying is an invaluable and constitutionally protected right found in the First Amendment: "Congress shall make no law . . . abridging the . . . right of the people . . . to petition the government for a redress of grievances." And growing ethnic populations and their political goals are shaping the congressional landscape through sophisticated lobbying campaigns that include direct lobbying, grassroots and "grasstops" mobilization, advertising, social media, coalition building, survey research, supporting think tanks, involvement in election campaigns and other advocacy tactics.[34]

While an exhaustive review of literature on ethnicity and lobbying is beyond the scope of this book, providing some context of how these two topics come together is important.

Scholarly examination of these combined topics has been arguably inconsistent over time. Studies of ethnicity and lobbying or ethnicity and foreign policy more generally have not been as numerous as other topics covered in political science. There are, however, some noteworthy aspects to the study of ethnicity and lobbying. First, this is not a new field of inquiry. Scholars were examining the impact of ethnicity and lobbying as early as the 1950s and 1960s.[35] However, the bulk of the work has been more recent. Even with this more recent work, much of it is dated given how politics and policy have changed generally in the United States, how Congress has evolved in its consideration of policy alternatives, and how issues confronting the United States—and the world, for that matter—have developed over time. For instance, early works on immigration policy in the United States[36] are helpful to understand where policies have come from but are focused on decades-old political contexts. Additionally, even though those that are more up-to-date have come to include arguments on what immigration means for America's political identity and its public policy choices, including its foreign policy, that are outdated given more recent political dynamics that have appeared in the United States.[37] In short, an updated examination of some of the most current and pressing issues in American politics affected by ethnicity is needed.

Another characteristic of much of the literature at the intersection of ethnicity and lobbying is that it is segmented. For instance, much work has been done on the impact of ethnicity or ethnic groups on U.S. foreign policy in particular.[38] However, other areas of policy also merit study and attention. There are also excellent volumes full of case studies that pick up on themes explored in this volume.[39] Some studies focus on the impact of ethnicity on member behavior, but these are typically part of a larger study on Congress and are inconclusive about the impact of ethnicity on member behavior.[40]

Few scholarly works exist that center directly on ethnic lobbying and fewer still focus specifically on Congress, as we do here.[41] However, as Lindsay and Ripley have noted previously when suggesting future research directions in the area of ethnic lobbying and Congress:

> We know a reasonable amount about the impact of interest groups in U.S. politics. But we know least about interest group influence on foreign and defense policy. Part of the problem lies in the diversity of groups lobbying on foreign policy issues. Some lobbying efforts, most notably those involving defense contracting and trade policy, involve the same politics that surround domestic distributive policy, a domain that has received ample scholarly attention. Others, however, look quite different. Numerous groups are organized around ethnic ties (e.g., the Jewish lobby or the Greek lobby) or specific policy issues that are not primarily economic in content (e.g., arms control or U.S. relations with individual countries in Central America). Ethnic and policy lobbies also differ from each other: most ethnic lobbies are well institutionalized and wealthy, while policy lobbies (especially on the left) often are not.[42]

Many of these same observations can be made today. In addition, Lindsay and Ripley's description of the work on ethnic lobbying being anecdotal also still holds today. Their important work that describes some possible future research in the area identifies several areas that we hope are somewhat addressed in this volume. For instance, Lindsay and Ripley suggest studying the tactics groups use in their attempts to influence members of Congress. In addition, they urge scholars to study the conditions under which lobbies succeed or fail when it comes to influencing U.S. foreign policy.

DeWind and Segura adeptly showcase the policy convergence/divergence between the U.S. government and different diaspora in shaping of foreign policy.[43] There are two basic analytical approaches to understanding this dynamic predominate, they argue. One sees policy convergence "as a result of diaspora and government representatives' identification of overlaps between what seem to be essentially objective, preexisting national and group interests and goals." The other views convergence and divergence "as the result of a shaping of national interests in the give-and-take of democratic processes, including lobbying, and sees them as involving compromises and/or the predominance of one side over the other."[44] Through their collection of essays they conclude that "the influence of diaspora and the U.S. government on one another in shaping foreign policy increases when convergent interests and goals become recognized, whether these are preexisting or constructed, and decreases when interests and goals are seen to be divergent."[45]

And in their comprehensive study, Paul and Paul skillfully shed light on the influence of ethnic lobbies and U.S. foreign policy by examining what factors attribute to their success and why.[46] As with other domestic interest groups, ethnic lobbies confront the same obstacles on Capitol Hill. Their strategies therefore may include *direct* lobbying methods, such as information or electoral support in terms of votes and/or campaign contributions, or *indirect* efforts such as grassroots lobbying, coalition building, advertising, social media, and monitoring of legislative activity.[47] Paul and Paul further compare the influence of ethnic lobbies against other actors, including business groups, the media, and foreign lobbyists. Larger ethnic groups, such as the Jewish or Israeli and Cuban lobbies, for instance, are able to affect the course of U.S. foreign policy relative to smaller ethnic groups because they are well organized and better positioned to identify members of their ethnic community across congressional districts to wage grassroots lobbying campaigns.[48]

This volume is at the confluence of two important areas of study: ethnicity and lobbying. We intend to help further bridge this gap, thereby contributing to the dearth of research on the subject by exploring and analyzing not just the effectiveness of various ethnic and foreign interest lobbies, but to better understand how these very important constituencies attempt to persuade Congress. Where other studies on ethnic lobbying confine their focus primarily to foreign and trade policy, or frame their theoretical discourse through the interest group literature, our goal is to enhance the understanding of ethnic and foreign lobbying in the legislative arena and to enrich the literature on Congress. This is done in several ways. First, various case studies examine interest groups that form around a particular ethnic community, including Muslim Americans and Cuban Americans. Second, policy areas with domestic implications are addressed. Third, the focal point throughout the collection of essays is Congress and the lobbying efforts—including strategies and tactics employed—of both ethnic groups and foreign governments. Lobbying can and is commonly done by nations that have interests in policy outcomes, and this dynamic is examined through different policies that are lobbied. Finally, the volume features cases in which a diaspora and its home government were intractably juxtaposed to one another on an issue, highlighting an age-old dilemma of representation—legislating between local interests and national needs.

The chapters that follow cover a wide-ranging number of issues and parts of the world. This is by design. The number of issues that can be lobbied either by ethnic groups in the United States or foreign governments is vast. So, too, are the number of groups and nations that are interested in trying to influence U.S. policy. The chapters are essentially case studies of either ethnic groups in the United States or foreign nations and their efforts to influence an area of U.S. policy. Issues range from those related to immigration, trade, defense, foreign policy generally, and others. Different areas of the world are well represented, including Latin America, the Middle East, the Far East, and Europe. While no one volume can cover every issue or all parts of the globe, this volume begins to fill gaps in the literature and address many parts of the world and interests of the peoples from those areas.

Themes and Structure of Volume

The chapters that follow are a collection of essays that connect in myriad ways to the topic of ethnic and foreign lobbying in Congress. The volume begins with some foundational information, first from two different perspectives on questions such as who, what, where, when, and how ethnic groups and foreign interests lobby in the United States. Following this introductory material, chapters on specific lobbying efforts by specific interests are considered. However, we also add a practitioner perspective with chapters from those who have worked on both sides of the lobbying equation—A View from K Street (the lobbying side) and A View from the Hill (the government side). Additionally, we include chapters on nations, interests, and ethnicities from across the globe. Chapters that address interests and nations from the conflict in the Middle East are the first to be considered. It is natural to include back-to-back chapters on Israel and Jewish Americans, and Muslim Americans. After those chapters, however, comes a chapter focused on issues related to another nation close to the region: Turkey. Questions centering on Hispanic Americans are also grouped with chapters on Mexico and Cuba. Finally, a chapter on a less-familiar, but sometimes-powerful, group of Americans—Asian Americans, and specifically Vietnamese Americans—is provided.

Some shared themes appear across chapters. These include how domestic ethnic groups, foreign governments, and other interests employ strategies, tactics, and resources to influence policymaking. Also covered are challenges lawmakers face when diaspora interests collide and intersect with national interests. Finally, we include chapters that illustrate how and where foreign interests affect the legislative process.

As noted above, foreign governments spend millions each year to influence opinions and policy on a range of issues, such as military and economic aid, bilateral relations, trade development, immigration, public relations, and tourism. This is done informally through personal meetings and foreign-sponsored travel, and more formally through legislation, floor statements, and CMOs concerned with improving relations with another country or region of the world. In the 114th Congress (2015–2017) alone, for instance, seventy-three House congressional caucuses—nearly one quarter—were country-specific. Lobbying efforts may be narrowly focused, such as when the embassy of Ecuador hired a Washington, DC-based lobbying firm for $300,000 to help counter growing congressional criticism against the South American country for refusing to rule out asylum for Edward Snowden, the computer programmer who copied and leaked classified information from the National Security Agency in 2013.[49] Or they may be part of a country's broader attempt to gain long-term influence in Washington, DC. As an example, Algeria spent slightly more than $86,000 in 2006 for strategic advice on ways to support "legitimate interest and policy goals." It then paid the same lobbying shop another $150,000 to assist coordinating meetings with members of Congress to discuss trade and foreign policy affecting Algeria, as well as facilitating the creation of an "Algerian Caucus" of those members with special interest in the North African country. Since then, the same lobbying outfit has received more than $400,000 a year from Algeria to maintain access to policymakers and congressional staff to promote Algerian-U.S. relations and respect for human rights.[50]

Chuck Cushman leads off the volume by addressing three key questions that help provide foundational information for questions addressed in later chapters. First, what can foreign governments legally do to shape American policy decisions? Second, which nations make the main efforts at influencing Congress, and why? And, third, how do they do it?—who meets whom, and how do they target their lobbying efforts? These fundamental questions are examined through the lens of how defense and foreign policy issues generally are lobbied by foreign governments on Capitol Hill.

Patrick Griffin and William Danvers also provide an examination of fundamental questions but do so in an analysis derived from their many years of experience on K Street and in government in both the legislative and the executive branches. They examine the players and issues central to many lobbying campaigns foreign interests, including governments, corporations, and non-government organizations. As Griffin and Danvers contend, the practice of lobbying on behalf of international interests and issues has similarities to more traditional domestic lobbying. It is about getting the facts to the right people on Capitol Hill or in the executive branch at the appropriate time and in the right context. Successful lobbying campaigns by international interests, as is also true of domestic lobbying, requires crafting message-tested arguments, constructing winning coalitions with like-minded stakeholders, and employing communications outreach efforts, both in Washington, DC and beyond.

As noted above, this volume includes chapters on traditionally ethnically based lobbies and how they have used their resources (including wealth, influence, votes on Election Day, and political connections with key members) to advocate for their agendas. The first two chapters that strike this chord come next, focusing on an oft-studied part of the world: the Middle East. The effectiveness of Jewish efforts in advocating pro-Israel foreign policy positions on both sides of the partisan aisle is frequently viewed as a textbook example of how particular ethnic groups successfully influence lawmakers. AIPAC, for instance, coordinates Jewish lobbying activities on virtually all issues related to Israel and vigorously supports sympathetic legislators as well as backs challengers of unfriendly incumbents. In short, they have been a lobbying juggernaut in previous years. To this end, Kirk Beattie examines various approaches used by Jewish-American individuals, lobbyists, and interest groups to influence Capitol Hill and the legislative process. Techniques involved include the use of campaign finance donations throughout the electoral process, direct and indirect contacts with members of Congress, provision of information, talking points, policy preferences, drafts of legislation, encouragement and threats, as well as the application of pressure to determine memberships of important committees and subcommittees, the selection of "expert witnesses" for briefings and hearings. There is great diversity of positions and approaches adopted by a large number of predominantly Jewish-American groups, Beattie argues. These groups, of course, vary tremendously in their resources, staff sizes, and experience. The chapter also assesses which groups are described as most successful, and why, in the eyes of congressional staffers.

Khalil Mousa Marrar examines the impact of the Arab Spring turned Winter on Arab- and Muslim-American interest groups and the concomitant interaction between them and U.S. policy toward the Middle East and North Africa. It does so through a series of related questions: How did Arab- and Muslim-American organizations see the Arab Spring and the U.S. reaction to it as relevant to their larger agenda? How did they attempt to influence members of Congress by entering into the discourse about the Arab Revolts? In what way did the Arab revolts figure into the activities of Arab and Muslim groups on Capitol Hill and elsewhere? And how did U.S. diplomatic, economic, military, and political actions toward the revolts in the Middle East and North Africa influence Arab and Muslim lobbying efforts? Marrar addresses these questions by examining the positions toward the Arab Spring of the following organizations: the American-Arab Anti-Discrimination Committee (ADC), the Arab American Institute (AAI), the American Task Force on Palestine (ATFP), and the Council on American-Islamic Relations (CAIR). While all of these organizations supported the aspirations underlying the Arab Spring in some manner, their lobbying on and off Capitol Hill varied across different revolts, their consequences, and American policy reactions to both. They were also forced to adapt to the rapid evolution of U.S. national interests in the broader region as mass protests gave way to Islamist violence, embodied by ISIS and other terror militias.

The book continues with a chapter centered on the lobbying efforts over another longstanding debate and disagreement that is not far in geographic terms from those covered in the previous two chapters. Julien Zarifian examines the political struggle between Armenian Americans and Turkey—their strategies, their successes, and their failures, over the course of these past few decades—to get Congress to recognize the Armenian massacres of 1915 to 1917, perpetrated by the Ottoman Empire, as genocide. His chapter begins with background on the state of the Armenian genocide recognition in the United States, discussing which national institutions and political figures have recognized the Armenian genocide and which have not. It then turns to the U.S.-Armenian lobby and its activism and the (non-)progress of the genocide recognition by the United States. It concludes with an analysis of how Turkey lobbies Congress and interacts with the executive branch to incite it to pressure the legislative one, evaluating its successes and failures.

The volume then moves across the globe and examines lobbying efforts affecting Hispanic Americans. Walter Clark Wilson and William

Curtis Ellis explore the increasingly interwoven histories of U.S.-Mexico policies on immigration and trade. Drawing on archival research and first-hand accounts from policymakers and lobbyists, their analysis illustrates the complex interests that determine whether Mexico assists or opposes the initiatives of Latino advocacy organizations, and reveals the extent to which cooperation between Mexican-American interests and those of Mexico often ends, and conflict begins, at the border.

Next, Patrick J. Haney analyzes the dynamics between Congress and the executive branch over the end of the Cuban Embargo. Similar to the Jewish-American community and AIPAC, the Cuban American National Foundation (CANF) and its Free Cuba PAC regularly flexed its muscles in American foreign policy toward Cuba by getting Congress to pass restricting legislation in the area of trade. After a brief recap of the working parts of the embargo from the 1980s and the emergence of the Cuban American National Foundation, he focuses attention on Congress: its rise in embargo politics in the 1990s, particularly in the Cuban Democracy Act and Helms-Burton, the way Presidents Bill Clinton and George W. Bush fought back to retain control over policy, and into the Obama era. Ultimately, a fast-evolving Cuban-American community that was also rapidly receding in political clout; shifting national opinion on the embargo; a divided Republican Party on the issue; and a second-term president not beholden to the embargo brought the embargo into question—something not seriously considered beforehand.

Yet Congress still has a key role to play thanks to its efforts in the 1990s to codify the embargo into law.

The final chapter examines a small but sometimes influential group in the United States—Vietnamese Americans. Christian Collet's chapter discusses the conflict between Vietnamese Americans and the Socialist Republic of Vietnam (SRVN) in contemporary Washington, DC. It begins by considering the transformation of Vietnamese Americans as a group and voting bloc and explains how issues related to Vietnam have been a core element of their political identity across two generations in U.S. society. It then moves to a discussion of a parallel transformation in the SRVN. The strategy and tactics of both sides are considered and compared. The chapter then includes the results of an empirical analysis of Vietnam-related legislation in Congress and an evaluation of the effects of Vietnamese Americans and partisanship on legislative action. It concludes with an evaluation of "who's winning" in the conflict, explaining that while Vietnamese Americans have had considerable success in winning advocates and attention for human rights issues in Congress via the democratic process, they have struggled to exert any strength among

Washington, DC's foreign policy elite to disrupt the momentum toward closer trade and diplomatic relations with the SRVN.

The volume concludes with another practitioner perspective. A long-time Hill staffer, Gregory C. McCarthy, indicates that the influence of ethnic lobbies, particularly in foreign policy, crosses both sides of the political aisle and is often unpredictable in its political effect. From his congressional perspective, several examples over the last two decades demonstrate how ethnic lobbies are received by their target audience, which is frequently through former lawmakers, constituent mobilization, and issue interest. Despite the potential liability of objectionable characteristics or political embarrassment, he argues, members generally subject themselves to ethnic lobbies, most of which are supportive allies, others less obviously so.

Members of Congress are regularly pulled in many directions. One of the great tensions in representative government is the relationship between the legislator, who might be hearing from his or her party leaders about a critical vote, and the representative, who might be hearing a different message from his or her constituency. Although individual legislators do not necessarily mirror their constituents in terms of demographic characteristics, the electoral process yields many who favor local views and prejudices, including those who live in their district or state who do not share the member's ethnic background. Members also serve the nation, however, and are expected to keep the national interest in mind when legislating. Yet they frequently are influenced by local attitudes, even when those attitudes conflict with the national interest. The result is a constant tension between the demands of representation and those of legislating. The former requires advocacy. The latter requires accommodation of differing views and interests. These cross-pressures can be difficult for members to balance when they are centered on a domestic issue. The tension can become greater when it involves an issue that influences foreign policy or is centered on a foreign government or interest. Our hope is that the chapters in this volume help to shed light on some of the central issues surrounding this tension, where they stem from, how they are manifested in lobbying efforts, and how the actors on both sides of the issue handle them.

Notes

1. John J. Mearsheimer and Stephen M. Walt, "The Israel Lobby," *London Review of Books* 28(6) (March 23, 2006): 3–12.

2. The founders of J Street formed the group to counter, in their view, the influence by neoconservatives and evangelical Christians on U.S. policy toward Israel. See Michael Abramowitz, "Jewish Liberals to Launch a Counterpoint to AIPAC; Political Funds, Lobbying to Promote Arab-Israeli Peace Deal," *Washington Post*, April 15, 2008, A13.

3. Julie Hirschfeld Davis, "Pro-Israel Group Creates Plan to Lobby Against Iran Deal," *New York Times*, July 18, 2015, A3; Julie Hirschfeld Davis, "Fierce Lobbying, Even on Vacation, for Iran Accord," *New York Times*, August 18, 2015, A10.

4. Karoun Demirjian and Carol Morello, "How AIPAC lost the Iran deal fight," *Washington Post*, September 3, 2015, https://www.washingtonpost.com/news/powerpost/wp/2015/09/03/how-aipac-lost-the-iran-deal-fight/; Scott Wong, "Lawmakers to meet with Netanyahu in Israel," *The Hill*, July 28, 2015, http://thehill.com/homenews/house/249497-lawmakers-to-meet-with-netanyahu-in-israel

5. Alexander Bolton, "Nuke deal strains relations with big Jewish donors," *The Hill*, November 26, 2013, 1.

6. Patrick J. Harvey and Walt Vanderbush, "The Role of Ethnic Interest Groups in U.S. Foreign Policy: The Case of the Cuban American National Foundation," *International Studies Quarterly* 17 (Dec., 2002): 343; John F. Stack, Jr., and Colton C. Campbell, "Congress: How Silent a Partner?" in *Congress and the Politics of Foreign Policy*, ed. Colton C. Campbell, Nicol C. Rae, and John F. Stack, Jr. (Upper Saddle River, NJ: Prentice Hall, 2003), 22–43; David King and Miles Pomper, "The U.S. Congress and the Contingent Influence of Diaspora Lobbies: Lessons from U.S. Policy Toward Armenia and Azerbaijan," *Journal of Armenian Studies* 8(1) (Summer, 2004).

7. John Newhouse, "Diplomacy Inc.," *Foreign Affairs* 88(3) (May/June, 2008): 10; Stack, Jr., and Campbell, "Congress: How Silent a Partner?" 37–40.

8. Michael Dobbs, "Foreign Aid Shrinks, but Not for All; With Clout in Congress, Armenia's Share Grows," *Washington Post*, January 24, 2001, A1.

9. Menna Demessie, "Congress from the Inside: U.S.-Africa Foreign Policy and Black Ethnic Politics," *PS, Political Science & Politics* 44(3) (July, 2011): 685–687; Jim Snyder, "Ethiopian-American group tries to raise profile on Capitol Hill," *The Hill*, September 21, 2006, 3.

10. Aaron Kessler and Wanjohi Kabukuru, "Shadow Diplomacy: African Nations Bypass Embassies, Tap Lobbyists," *Huffington Post*, July 30, 2013, http://www.huffingtonpost.com/2013/07/30/african-lobbyists_n_3676489.html; Colby Itkowitz, "Which foreign countries spent the most to influence U.S. politics?" *Washington Post*, May 14, 2014, https://www.washingtonpost.com/blogs/in-the-loop/wp/2014/05/14/which-foreign-countries-spent-the-most-to-influence-u-s-politics/; and Ari Rabin-Havt, "Bipartisan Agreement: Foreign Governments Pay Former Senate Leaders to Sell TPP," *Observer*, June 11, 2015, Lexis-Nexis, accessed May 5, 2016.

11. Megan R. Wilson, "Saudi Arabia has lobbying muscle for 9/11 fight," *The Hill*, April 19, 2016, 11. See also Mark Mazsetti, "Saudi Arabia Warns of Economic Fallout if Congress Passes 9/11 Bill," *New York Times*, April 15, 2016, http://www.nytimes.com/2016/04/16/world/middleeast/saudi-arabia-warns-ofeconomic-fallout-if-congress-passes-9-11-bill.html?_r=0

12. Itkowitz, "Which foreign countries spent the most to influence U.S. politics?"

13. Data derived from U.S. Department of Justice, *Report of the Attorney General to the Congress of the United States on the Administration of the Foreign Agents Registration Act of 1938* (Washington, DC: 2014).

14. Jonathan Easley and John Solomon, "Russian lobbying that touched Trump tied to Moscow figures," The Hill, July 14, 2017, http://thehill.com/homenews/administration/342097-russian-lobbying-that-touched-trump-tied-to-moscow-figures

15. The "Disclosing Foreign Influence Act" (S. 2039 and H.R. 4170), sponsored by U.S. Sen. Charles Grassley (R-Iowa) and U.S. Rep. Michael Johnson (R-La.), would provide the U.S. Department of Justice with enforcement tools to help ensure full disclosure of activities by foreign governments and foreign entities designed to influence American public policy.

16. John DeWind and Renata Segura, "Diaspora-Government Relations in Forging U.S. Foreign Policies," in *Diaspora Lobbies and the U.S. Government: Convergence and Divergence in Making Foreign Policy*, eds. John DeWind and Renata Segura (New York: NYU Press, 2014).

17. Mira Kamdar, "Forget the Israel Lobby, The Hill's Next Big Player is Made in India," *Washington Post*, September 20, 2007, B3; Adam B. Lerner, "The New Indian Lobby," *Politico*, December 14, 2014, http://www.politico.com/magazine/story/2014/12/indian-americans-113546_Page2.html#.VyinTqpf3cs

18. Kathleen Newland, *Voice After Exit: Diaspora Advocacy* (Washington, DC: USAID, 2010), 6; Jason A. Kirk, "Indian-Americans and the U.S.-India Nuclear Agreement: Consolidation of an Ethnic Lobby?" *Foreign Policy Analysis* 4 (2008): 275–300; Mike McIntire, "Nuclear deal tests Indian-Americans' lobbying skills," *The International Tribune*, June 6, 2006, 1.

19. Allison Freedman, "USINPAC and the U.S.-India Nuclear Deal: Lasting Influence or One Shot Victory?" CUREJ—College Undergraduate Research Electronic Journal, University of Pennsylvania, College of Arts and Sciences, 2009

20. Ibid., 32.

21. Ibid.

22. Freedman, 33.

23. DeWind and Segura. "Diaspora-Government Relations in Forging U.S. Foreign Policies."

24. By authorizing PNTR status, formerly known as "most favored nation" status, the United States agrees not to discriminate trade arrangements between trading partners.

25. *Report of the Attorney General to the Congress of the United States on the Administration of the Foreign Agents Registration Act of 1938, as amended, for the six months ending December 31, 2006*, p. 242, United States Department of Justice, https://www.fara.gov/reports/December31-2006.pdf, accessed August 5, 2006.

26. Representative Lofgren, speaking on legislation to extend PNTR status to Vietnam, 109th Congress, 2nd session, *Congressional Record* 152, pt. 17: 21844.

27. Ibid.

28. Representative Sanchez, speaking on legislation to extend PNTR status to Vietnam, 109th Congress, 2nd session, *Congressional Record* 152, pt. 17: 21843.

29. Marshal Law bypasses the procedural requirement to wait a day after the Rules Committee passes a special rule establishing floor debate parameters before voting on a piece of legislation after it has been reported out of committee.

30. Suspension of the Rules is a procedure the House uses to expeditiously consider legislation—routinely non-controversial and non-complicated measures.

31. Percentage increase calculated by authors. See *Report of the Attorney General to the Congress of the United States on the Administration of the Foreign Agents Registration Act of 1938, as amended, for the six months ending June 30, 2009 and December 31, 2009*, https://www.fara.gov/annualrpts.html.

32. Ibid. See *Report of the Attorney General to the Congress of the United States on the Administration of the Foreign Agents Registration Act of 1938, as amended, for the six months ending June 30, 2015.*

33. Tal Kopan, "Poll: Lobbyists rank last on ethics," *Politico*, December 16, 2013, http://www.politico.com/story/2013/12/lobbyists-ethics-gallup-poll-101187

34. For a description of all the elements of congressional lobbying campaigns, see Patrick Griffin and James A. Thurber, "Teaching Public Policy Advocacy by Combining Academic Knowledge and Professional Wisdom," *Interest Groups & Advocacy* 4(1) (March 2015): 40–52.

35. See, for instance, Lawrence H. Fuchs, "Minority Groups and Foreign Policy," *Political Science Quarterly* 74 (1959): 161–175; and Joseph P. O'Grady, ed. *The Immigrants' Influence on Wilson's Peace Policies* (Lexington: University of Kentucky Press, 1967).

36. See, for example, Robert A. Divine, *American Immigration Policy, 1924–1952* (New Haven, CT: Yale University Press, 1957); and John Higham, *Strangers in the Land: Patterns of American Nativism, 1860–1925* (New York: Atheneum, 1971).

37. See, for example, Samuel P. Huntington, *Who Are We? The Challenges to America's National Identity* (New York: Simon & Schuster, 2004); Leonard Dinnerstein and David M. Reimers, *Ethnic Americans: A History of Immigration.* 4th ed. (New York: Columbia University Press, 1999); Alejandro Portes and Rubén G. Rumbaut. *Immigrant America: A Portrait.* 3d ed., rev. and enl. (Berkeley: University of California Press, 2006); and John Gerard Ruggie, "The Past as Prologue? Interests, Identity, and American Foreign Policy," *International Security* 21(4) (1997): 89–125.

38. See, for instance, Laurence Halley, *Ancient Affections, Ethnic Groups and Foreign Policy* (New York: Praeger, 1985); David M. Paul and Rachel Anderson Paul, *Ethnic Lobbies and U.S. Foreign Policy* (Boulder, CO: Lynne Rienner, 2009); Tony Smith, *Foreign Attachments: The Power of Ethnic Groups in the Making of American Foreign Policy* (Cambridge, MA: Harvard University Press, 2000); and Will H. Moore, "Ethnic Minorities and Foreign Policy," *SAIS Review* 22(2) (2002): 77–91.

39. See, for example, Mohammed E. Ahrari, ed., *Ethnic Groups and U.S. Foreign Policy* (Westport, CT: Greenwood Press, 1987); Thomas Ambrosio, ed., *Ethnic Identity Groups and U.S. Foreign Policy* (Westport, CT: Praeger, 2002); Hélène

Christol and Serge Ricard, eds., *Hyphenated Diplomacy: European Immigration and U.S. Foreign Policy, 1914–1984* (Aix-en-Provence, France: Publications Université de Provence, 1985); and Stack, John F., Jr., ed. *Ethnic Identities in a Transnational World* (Westport, CT: Greenwood Press, 1981).

40. Sophia J. Wallace, "Representing Latinos: Examining Descriptive and Substantive Representation in Congress," *Political Research Quarterly* 67(4) (Dec., 2014): 917–929.

41. See, for instance, Tevor Rubenzer, "Ethnic Minority Interest Group Attributes and U.S. Foreign Policy Influence: A Qualitative Comparative Analysis," *Foreign Policy Analysis* 4(2) (2008): 169–185; and Stephen M. Saideman, "The Power of the Small: The Impact of Ethnic Minorities on Foreign Policy," *SAIS Review* 22(2) (2002): 93–105.

42. James M. Lindsay and Randall B. Ripley, "Foreign and Defense Policy in Congress: A Research Agenda for the 1990s," *Legislative Studies Quarterly* 17(3) (Aug., 1992): 417–449.

43. DeWind and Segura, "Diaspora-Government Relations in Forging U.S. Foreign Policies."

44. Ibid., 6.

45. Ibid.

46. Paul and Paul, *Ethnic Lobbies and U.S. Foreign Policy.*

47. Ibid. See chapter 3.

48. Ibid. See chapter 7.

49. Kevin Bogardus, "Ecuador inks $300K lobbying contract amid Snowden asylum fight," *The Hill*, July 17, 2013, Lexis-Nexus.

50. For data, see United States Department of Justice, Foreign Agent Registration Act (FARA), http://www.fara.gov/. The FARA requires agents lobbying on behalf of a foreign client to register with the Justice Department and to file semiannual reports disclosing the issues they work on, the lawmakers and staff they meet with, and the amount of money they are paid.

Chapter 2

Foreign Government Efforts to Influence Congressional Foreign and Defense Policy

CHUCK CUSHMAN*

Recent years have seen many examples of visits to Washington, DC, by high-ranking foreign dignitaries intent on getting Congress to support foreign policy choices advantageous to their countries, particularly in the area of defense. Israeli Prime Minister Binyamin Netanyahu gave an address in 2015 to a joint session of Congress describing his country's concerns about the international agreement with Iran that was then about to be completed. In 2016, newly appointed Saudi Deputy Crown Prince Mohammad bin Salman bin Abdulaziz made a visit to Washington, DC that coincided with a ferocious public relations blitz of Capitol Hill by the Royal Saudi embassy; his focus was securing support from the United States for the ongoing Saudi war in Yemen against Iran-backed rebels, and for the Saudi's approach to dealing with the rise of the Islamic State; his visit also coincided with votes on Capitol Hill to approve a bill allowing U.S. citizens to sue Saudi Arabia for damages due to the September 11, 2001, attacks on New York and Washington, DC.[1] These examples could give the impression that this is how foreign governments seek to influence Congress: premiers and princes come to Washington, DC to woo members of Congress, while savvy diplomats who have lived in Washington, DC for decades wine and dine them at amazing parties in their multi-million-dollar mansions just across the Potomac River in Maclean, Virginia, as Yousef Al Otaiba, ambassador of the United Arab Emirates,

---

*The views expressed in this chapter are those of the author and not the National Defense University, the Department of Defense, or any other entity of the U.S. government.

is famous for doing.[2] But that is not the whole story—or perhaps even the important part of the story.

The real story is far less posh. It is really a story of the same kind of slow, grinding work that has to be done by anybody who wants to influence policy outcomes on Capitol Hill. And this work must be done whether a foreign country is working to maintain current U.S. policies, or if they are trying the much harder task of changing U.S. responses to their nation.[3] Another widely reported example offered another glimpse of how foreign governments seek to influence U.S. foreign policy—and how such efforts can actually influence American politics. In August 2016, reports surfaced about lobbying, done on behalf of ousted Ukrainian president Viktor Yanukovych, by Paul Manafort, then chairman of GOP presidential nominee Donald J. Trump. These reports indicated that Manafort had led Yanukovych's efforts to improve his image in Washington, DC policymaking circles following the uprising that toppled his pro-Russian government in February 2014. Manafort's lobbying firm, DMP International, worked through a recently founded nonprofit think tank called the European Centre for a Modern Ukraine, hiring top GOP and Democratic lobbying firms to work on Capitol Hill and with Obama administration officials to burnish Yanukovych's reputation in Washington, DC, spending $2.2 million on the effort.[4]

The reports also noted that Manafort and his firm were under investigation by the U.S. Department of Justice for failing to report these activities as required by the Foreign Agents Registration Act (FARA), passed in 1938 to track the actions of foreign countries in influencing U.S. policy and ensure such actions were clearly identified to American audiences. Manafort and his lawyers had reviewed the work and judged they did not need to make such reports because they had reported their work under the much less onerous Lobbying Disclosure Act (LDA), which did not require as extensive a report as FARA did.[5]

Manafort resigned from the Trump campaign to avoid having this investigation damage the electoral prospect of the candidate. Regardless of how the investigation ultimately plays out, Manafort's case underscores the complexity, uncertainty, and confusion that attach to the laws covering foreign lobbying, as well as how they are enforced. This makes it difficult to craft a complete picture of the scale, cost, methods, and effectiveness of foreign lobbying efforts on Capitol Hill. But what we can learn makes it clear that these efforts look a lot like any other lobbying campaign in Washington, DC, making foreign countries competitors to companies, trade associations, local and state governments, unions, and interest groups in seeking audiences among members of Congress to shape how they think about important policy topics.

In this chapter I will sketch out how foreign nations play the influence game in Washington, DC, so we can understand better how they seek to shape U.S. foreign policy. We must answer three questions to do this. First, what can foreign governments legally do to influence congressional action? Second, who are the key players in this conversation? Finally, how do they actually work to influence outcomes on the Hill—what does foreign lobbying look like?

What Can Foreign Powers Do in Washington, DC?

Fear about foreign influence on U.S. policy is not a new feeling. The generation of the Founders broke down into competing factions supporting British and French interests from the end of the Revolutionary War, which contended with each other for control over U.S. foreign and trade policy until after the end of the Napoleonic wars in Europe.[6] The first influential foreign-born group to influence U.S. politics emerged in the 1840s to 1850s, with the arrival of waves of Irish immigrants fleeing the famine. As their numbers grew, Irish political leaders[7] emerged first at the local level, and as they rose to national prominence, Irish Americans would urge U.S. foreign policy toward Great Britain to focus on nationalist goals for Ireland.[8]

But the first time foreign influence raised serious concerns for policymakers was in the 1930s, with the rise of German-American organizations that sponsored clubs, demonstrations, and rallies in support of the new German government under Adolf Hitler—enough concern that in 1938 Congress passed a law requiring agents of foreign powers to register and report their activities in the United States. The act does not prevent foreign actors from taking part in U.S. policymaking, but it does require that they report their actions. The FARA requires foreign agents to submit reports to the Department of Justice (DOJ) every six months. Whenever they conduct public relations campaigns (the law specifies any activity when they share information with two or more U.S. citizens), agents must submit a report within forty-eight hours of any sharing, such as a mailing or a meeting. In addition, agents must submit any notes or testimony they share with Congress if they hold a meeting on Capitol Hill.[9] Stiff penalties follow from prosecution over failure to report meetings, and foreign nationals can be deported for a violation of FARA rules. These rules apply only to persons hired by foreign entities to work on political or policy issues—purely business activities need not be reported, nor do activities by official staff of foreign countries (e.g., accredited embassy officials), and charitable work and fundraising are also exempt from reporting under FARA. These exemptions mean that FARA compliance reports, even if they were perfect, would still not give a complete account of what foreign actors might be doing in Washington, DC.

In 1995, Congress added a new regulation for lobbying efforts with the passage of the Lobbying Disclosure Act (LDA), which requires lobbyists to submit reports to the House and Senate twice a year covering their activities. The LDA allows agents to report under it instead of the FARA system, as well, as long as their foreign clients are not governments or political parties.[10] And the LDA's reporting requirements are not as detailed as FARA calls for. Because of the concern of many lobbyists that registering as foreign agents could harm their business, many agents switched their reporting to the LDA system and no longer submit anything to the FARA office at the DOJ.

With two sets of rules to choose from, which exempt many actors, and which require limited information in their reporting, it should be clear that the system has limitations that prevent a comprehensive analysis of foreign lobbying efforts in Washington, DC. Although there are sanctions in FARA for late or incomplete reporting, the DOJ rarely prosecutes violations, seeking rather to use notices of infraction to educate agents and teach them to do proper reporting in the future.[11] With the passage of the LDA, many agents chose to report under it to Congress rather than to the DOJ under FARA, making the FARA database an incomplete record of foreign lobbying efforts; in addition, recent reports indicate that the loopholes in FARA, and lax enforcement of its requirements, have led to poor overall compliance with the law's reporting rules.[12] The FARA data are not available in an easily searchable, digital format, making it difficult to do searches or to collate any statistics about foreign lobbying efforts in Congress, leading the Sunlight Foundation, a major government transparency watchdog, to create its own foreign influence database by reviewing the DOJ's files and compiling them into a useable format.[13] And since the official activities of foreign government officials in Washington, DC are not subject to any reporting, it is not possible to capture what is likely to be the main effort of most countries to influence policymaking on Capitol Hill.

Even with the limits on data available for analysis, we can still discern the scale and basic features of the foreign effort on influencing Congress, and analyze that effort *in toto* as part of the broader lobbying effort that occurs in Washington, DC. So how does lobbying on foreign policy shape up as a part of the whole lobbying industry in Washington, DC?

The American political system is complex, made up of many participating—sometimes competing—parts. Students of the system have long referred to the American way of conducting politics as *pluralism*—many groups, with different interests and goals, interacting with the organs of government to influence the laws that get made in Washington, DC.[14] The pluralist description of American politics has always noted the presence of business voices in the mix, and has regularly noted that business interests seem to outweigh other potential voices.[15] Businesses usually have much clearer goals, and much clearer targets for their efforts, such as tax breaks, or regulatory changes favorable to a particular business sector.[16] And businesses also tend to have more resources to expend in seeking influence over political decisions. In other words, *lobbying*.

Lobbying is a distinctive feature of American politics, with historical records of lobbying efforts recorded as far back as 1832.[17] Lobbying came under sustained study, and sustained attack, in the 1920s and 1930s, and was a regular subject of serious political science research by the 1950s.[18] But the golden age of lobbying kicked off in the 1970s, when lobbying became big business.[19] In that decade, American business leaders, worried about new regulations coming out of Washington, DC, realized that they had no real voice in Washington, DC. Spurred by the Chamber of Commerce, big companies started opening Washington, DC, offices to communicate with federal agencies and Congress, and numerous industries organized trade associations to press for their interests.[20] By the end of the decade, the lobbying industry grew to become an integral part of how major American businesses operate. The industry has continued to grow since then, spurred especially by the pro-business environment of the Ronald Reagan years. Where once business considered Washington, DC to be the enemy, lobbyists have helped business to see that Congress and the executive branch could be partners in economic growth, if business leaders remain engaged in their policy advocacy.[21]

The lobbying industry today is a major feature of Washington, DC's landscape, connecting businesses, interest groups, labor, federal agencies, and Congress in a vast and highly interlocking network of information sharing—and jobs. Many former Hill staffers, elected officials, and administration figures move off the public payrolls into well-paying lobbying jobs. Policymaking is so complex that their inside knowledge of how the system works, and their networks, are highly valued in the lobbying world.[22]

Several organizations study lobbying and report on the scale of the industry, as well as on analyzing lobbying across multiple issues and business sectors. Among the most well-respected efforts is the research conducted by the Center for Responsive Politics, who report their findings regularly on their "Open Secrets" website (www.opensecrets.org), updating as new data are reported. Using their database, and the database on foreign influence efforts maintained by the Sunlight Foundation, we can see a clear picture of the lobbying industry, and see how it acts over time. Table 2.1 compares the lobbying industry at three different points: 2006, 2010, and 2014 (all midterm election years, so the political context is the same in each example). The table lists total lobbying spending, and the top five industry sectors in each year. Of interest here is the massive scale of the whole industry—it is a $3 billion-plus market, and the same three sectors (miscellaneous business, health care, and finance/insurance/real estate) make up the top three in each year, although they change specific spots. The same areas, natural resources/energy and communications-electronics, hold the fourth and fifth slots each year, trading spots in each year. Defense holds ninth place in overall ranking each year, and foreign/defense policy is unranked each year—and represents a significantly smaller level of effort compared to the highest-ranked sectors. Table 2.1 shows how large the industry is, and how small a piece of it is made up of lobbying on foreign and defense policy topics.

Looking at the major players in lobbying, using the same years for comparison, we see an interesting pattern develop (table 2.2 on page 26 summarizes the top lobbying players across the three years). The U.S. Chamber of Commerce is the leading lobbyist every year, with a significantly increasing effort over time. There is a growing gap between their lobbying effort and that of the second-place player, and another gap between number two and everyone else. The only other repeating member of the top five players is the American Medical Association, in fourth or fifth place each cycle; more interesting is that every other top-five player is different in each of the three years. This suggests that lobbying is episodic—if a bill or a regulatory action is under debate in Washington, DC, interested parties increase their spending to help shape policymaking, and then fade back into the pack as other issues become prominent.

Foreign policy simply does not generate the same lobbying effort that business does. An examination of the big players in defense and foreign policy lobbying show just how much smaller this sector of lobbying is, and how much smaller the individual efforts of advocacy organizations are, as compared to the major business lobbies reviewed above. Table 2.3 on page 27 reports on the top foreign and defense policy lobbying players in the comparison years. The Citizens' Educational Foundation, which works on Puerto Rican independence, was the top spender in the sector in 2006. The Ploughshares Fund was the top in 2010; they work for a world without nuclear weapons. In 2014 the top figure was the American Task Force Argentina, which works for legislation requiring Argentina to pay back debts from financial restructurings in the past. Several players repeat in the ranking over time, particularly the U.S. Fund for UNICEF

Table 2.1. Top-Ranked Lobbying Sectors, Cross-Year Comparison

	2006 Total Spending $2.63 Billion		2010 Total Spending $3.52 Billion		2014 Total Spending $3.26 Billion	
Rank	Sector	Spending	Sector	Spending	Sector	Spending
1	Health	$385,286,861	Misc. Business	$581,349,208	Misc. Business	$555,417,154
2	Finance/Insurance/Real Estate	$380,051,885	Health	$527,668,881	Finance/Insurance/Real Estate	$500,216,442
3	Misc. Business	$368,964,061	Finance/Insurance/Real Estate	$479,215,686	Health	$491,375,462
4	Communications/Electronics	$355,452,978	Energy/Nat. Resource	$454,202,925	Communications/Electronics	$380,731,558
5	Energy/Nat. Resource	$245,365,623	Communications/Electronics	$363,442,657	Energy/Nat. Resource	$347,905,791
9	Defense	$118,893,909	Defense	$148,731,343	Defense	$128,597,939
—	Foreign/Defense Policy	$5,190,812	Foreign/Defense Policy	$6,490,365	Foreign/Defense Policy	$6,218,783

Source: The Center for Responsive Politics' Lobbying Database, housed at opensecrets.org, hosts the data from which this table comes. Webpages consulted:
https://www.opensecrets.org/lobby
https://www.opensecrets.org/lobby/top.php?showYear=2014&indexType=c
https://www.opensecrets.org/lobby/top.php?showYear=2010&indexType=c
https://www.opensecrets.org/lobby/top.php?showYear=2006&indexType=c
https://www.opensecrets.org/lobby/indusclient.php?id=Q04
https://www.opensecrets.org/lobby/indusclient.php?id=Q04&year=2014
https://www.opensecrets.org/lobby/indusclient.php?id=Q04&year=2010
https://www.opensecrets.org/lobby/indusclient.php?id=Q04&year=2006

Table 2.2. Top Lobbying Spenders, Cross-Year Comparison

	2006		2010		2014	
Rank	Sector	Spending	Sector	Spending	Sector	Spending
1	U.S. Chamber of Commerce	$72,995,000	U.S. Chamber of Commerce	$132,067,500	U.S. Chamber of Commerce	$124,080,000
2	AT&T Inc	$27,445,497	PG&E Corp	$45,510,000	National Assn. of Realtors	$55,057,053
3	AARP	$23,160,000	General Electric	$39,290,000	Blue Cross/Blue Shield	$22,168,774
4	American Medical Assn.	$19,880,000	FedEx Corp	$25,582,074	American Hospital Assn.	$20,773,146
5	U.S. Telecom Assn.	$18,380,000	American Medical Assn.	$22,555,000	American Medical Assn.	$19,650,000

Source: Opensecrets.org, specific webpages consulted:
https://www.opensecrets.org/lobby/top.php?showYear=2014&indexType=c
https://www.opensecrets.org/lobby/top.php?showYear=2010&indexType=c
https://www.opensecrets.org/lobby/top.php?showYear=2006&indexType=c
https://www.opensecrets.org/lobby/indusclient.php?id=Q04
https://www.opensecrets.org/lobby/indusclient.php?id=Q04&year=2014
https://www.opensecrets.org/lobby/indusclient.php?id=Q04&year=2010
https://www.opensecrets.org/lobby/indusclient.php?id=Q04&year=2006

Table 2.3. Top Spenders in Foreign/Defense Policy, Cross-Year Comparison

Rank	2006 Sector	Spending	2010 Sector	Spending	2014 Sector	Spending
1	Citizens' Educational Foundation	$530,000	Ploughshares Fund	$855,000	American Task Force Argentina	$1,490,000
2	Better World Fund	$500,000	U.S. Fund for UNICEF	$800,000	Better World Fund	$720,000
3	U.S. Fund for UNICEF	$400,000	American Task Force Argentina	$740,000	U.S. Fund for UNICEF	$684,000
4	Alliance for a New Kosovo	$380,000	Better World Fund	$640,000	Trident Foundation	$570,000
5	National Dialogue Party of Lebanon	$320,000	International Rescue Cttee	$500,648	Puerto Rico Statehood Council	$500,000

Source: Opensecrets.org, specific webpages consulted:
https://www.opensecrets.org/lobby/indusclient.php?id=Q04&year=2006
https://www.opensecrets.org/lobby/indusclient.php?id=Q04&year=2010
https://www.opensecrets.org/lobby/indusclient.php?id=Q04&year=2014

and the Better World Foundation (which lobbies for support of the UN). A new entrant in 2014 was the Trident Foundation, which hired an ex-congressman to lobby on behalf of Ukrainian business interests.[23]

Just like American and international business leaders, foreign countries have many reasons to want to talk to the U.S. government and try to shape U.S. foreign policy. Many countries appear to rely completely upon their embassies to do this. Others have significant numbers of their countrymen now living in America, allowing them to rely on these citizens for grassroots pressure on Congress (as evidenced by the examples contained in some of this volume's other chapters). But even with a good staff and a well-organized ethnic interest group ready to help, it is sometimes necessary to hire professionals to aid in deciphering the complex policymaking system of Washington, DC, and get their message to the right policymakers in time to make a difference.[24] Enter foreign policy lobbyists.

What Countries are the Key Lobbying Players?

Who wants to influence Congress, and who is willing to put in the work (or pay for the lobbyists to do it)? A first take on the answer to these questions might send you to the list of countries who receive the most foreign aid, or the most military aid, from the United States. A quick review of top recipients makes is clear that aid receipts have little or nothing to do with which nations lobby Congress most intently. The top receiver of American aid, Israel, receives over $3 billion annually in economic aid, and another $3.1 billion in military aid, but does not show up in lists of major foreign countries seeking to influence Congress.[25] Second-place Egypt ($1.5 billion in economic support; $1.3 billion in military aid) is also absent, as are third-place recipients Afghanistan ($1.1 billion) and Jordan ($1 billion). All of these countries have been key partners of the United States for many years (decades in the case of Israel and Egypt), and have received extensive aid from the United States for long periods of time. Why do they not show up in the leading ranks of foreign lobbyists of Congress?

One immediate reaction to a review of top lobbyists in a few selected years makes it clear: lobbying is not a sustained activity as much as an episodic one, where maximum effort is not necessary unless issues of specific interest to a nation appear on Congress's policy radar screen. Foreign policy lobbying is a small issue compared to domestic topics, generating a total of $6.3 million in paid lobbying efforts in 2014. But foreign countries do lobby on a multitude of topics, not just foreign and defense policy; they have business interests and regulatory concerns, as

Table 2.4. Top Foreign State Lobbying Spenders, Cross-Year Comparison

Rank	2007		2013	
1	United Arab Emirates	$10,914,002	United Arab Emirates	$14,186,622
2	United Kingdom	$6,105,200	Germany	$12,008,299
3	Japan	$4,231,656	Canada	$11,246,019
4	Iraq	$3,708,368	Saudi Arabia	$11,101,041
5	Turkey	$3,524,632	Mexico	$6,132,132
6	Morocco	$3,337,392	Morocco	$4,052,857
7	Saudi Arabia	$3,308,285	South Korea	$3,920,616
8	South Korea	$2,941,004	Republika Srpska	$2,397,650
9	Netherlands	$2,694,604	Georgia	$2,358,938
10	Equatorial Guinea	$2,408,168	Azerbaijan	$2,298,339

Source: ProPublica, Sunlight Foundation. 2007 data reported in Anupama Narayanswamy, Luke Rosiak, and Jennifer LaFleur, "Adding it Up: The Top Players in Foreign Agent Lobbying," August 18, 2009, https://www.propublica.org/article/adding-it-up-the-top-players-in-foreign-agent-lobbying-718; 2013 data reported in Sunlight Foundation, "2013 Location lobbying totals," http://foreign.influenceexplorer.com/lobby-location2013

well. Table 2.4 lists top foreign lobbying for two years, 2007 and 2013, noting the total spending by each of the top ten nations in each year. The United Arab Emirates is the lead player in each year, with Morocco, South Korea, and Saudi Arabia also appearing in both year's lists. While the list indicates significant money being spent by foreign *governments* to lobby in Washington, DC, it is important to compare the scale of these efforts to those of foreign *business* lobbying. The real heavyweights in the lobbying industry pursue economic or industrial interests rather than policy outcomes. While the United States does have a foreign aid budget and an extensive foreign military aid program, the real money is in pursuing economic ties to the United States. Key foreign players seem to be economic entities rather than countries, which is similar to lobbying in general. For example, German telecommunications giant Deutsche Telekom alone spent $11,858,343[26] in 2013 to lobby for mergers being pursued by its American subsidiary, T-Mobile, which spent $5.2 million itself that year.[27] The shifting membership of the top players' list indicates that foreign lobbying is just as episodic as lobbying by U.S. participants.

A second reason many foreign governments might not show up in the lists is that they can do all the necessary contacts themselves, and therefore do not need to hire lobbyists to help them make their case to Congress. However, since no embassy reports its contacts publicly, researchers cannot accurately assess how much effort they may be making. Longstanding allies like Great Britain, France, or Israel have many diplomatic staff with extensive experience in the United States; their understanding of American politics and their networks of contacts in the U.S. governments, developed over many years of service in Washington, DC, give them sufficient in-house talent to meet all of their lobbying needs without having to hire experts to help them. A former British ambassador pointed out that he devoted much of his energy to meetings with Congress, where he would discuss politically sensitive matters such as defense policy directly with the key policymakers, leaving the less sensitive, day-to-day meetings with the Department of State, Pentagon, and other key agencies to his staff; these meetings are not reported publicly because they fall within the normal business of conducting the United Kingdom's diplomacy here in America.[28]

Israel has another key advantage, as well as its dedicated and experienced staff: a huge network of well-informed, well-financed interest groups made up of Jewish Americans, who have a natural interest in supporting a strong U.S.-Israel relationship (see chapter 4). The Jewish-American community has been politically active in the United States for most of the country's history, and activism in Washington, DC has been part of the community's strategy since the 1930s. The community has the "size, commitment, unity, resources, and most important, its political skill or ability to make effective use of the first four qualities" to make their case powerfully in Washington, DC.[29]

So, in short: foreign lobbying efforts tend to be episodic rather than sustained, and driven by what is on the Washington, DC policy agenda at any given time. Most paid efforts on behalf of foreign actors come from smaller countries, not necessarily the longstanding allies of the United States, most of whom have enough talented and deeply knowledgeable staff to do all of their lobbying for themselves. Some foreign countries also benefit from domestic interest groups who lobby Congress on their behalf. And much more than policy advocacy, economic or industrial interests drive the bulk of foreign lobbying, given the relatively large scale of business interests in expanding trade with the United States as compared to the modest scale of the space covered by U.S. foreign policy, even including economic and military aid to other countries.

How Foreign Governments Lobby Congress

Now that we have a sense of the scale of foreign lobbying efforts, as compared to the massive lobbying industry that targets Capitol Hill, and recognizing the limitations of the data in helping us to complete a full picture, we can still develop a solid portrait of the efforts that foreign countries make to influence Congress on foreign policy issues. Any lobbying campaign designed by advocacy professionals in Washington, DC will consider how to manage four lines of effort aimed at supporting the client's desired policy outcomes: *direct* lobbying, which brings participants (whether foreign officials themselves, or hired lobbyists carrying out the client's plan) into meetings with policymakers in Congress, Administration offices, and federal agencies; *indirect* lobbying, where affiliated grassroots groups communicate or meet with government officials to support the foreign nation's goals, or where influential press outlets carry op-eds or articles favoring the foreign nation's goals; *coalition-building*, where a foreign country might reach out to other nations with similar interests in Washington, DC, or with industry, to work together for mutual support in their lobbying efforts; and *monitoring*, where an allied interest group, think tank, or influential expert tracks behavior of public officials on specific issues, as when a think tank issues voting scorecards on members of Congress.[30] Not every lobbying campaign would necessarily include each element, but a well-financed effort on a key issue might contain every line of effort outlined here. In this section, we will compare the recent efforts of two nations to shape U.S. foreign policy. Both Saudi Arabia and Israel have longstanding and significant diplomatic relationships with the United States, and both devote energy and serious resources to managing those relationships. From their efforts, we can draw a sense of what it takes to lobby Congress.

Direct lobbying is the basis of any lobbying effort, and the point of a lobbying campaign: to get the spokesperson for an interested party into meetings with U.S. officials. This involves both a country's own efforts and using paid lobbyists to connect with Congress and executive branch officials. Saudi strategy over the past several years has been to develop the military, intelligence, and command and control capabilities that enable it to accomplish the many military tasks it now relies on Western (mainly U.S.) partners to provide. As part of its overall effort to be the leader of the Arab countries, Saudi Arabia wants to add other tools of state power to its religious centrality (as the home of the holiest Muslim cities, Mecca and Medina) and economic heft. At the same time, its new leaders are working hard to develop plans to diversify the Saudi economy, to get beyond overreliance on oil revenues. Key to these efforts, however, is to maintain strong relations with the United States. Thus, lobbying is a major component of Saudi Arabia's national security strategy.

The Royal Saudi Embassy in Washington, DC sends staff to meet regularly with the Department of Defense, the Department of State, and the White House on issues important to the country. Key activities involve purchases of U.S. military equipment.[31] In addition to staff work, in 2015–2016 the embassy played host to several high-level delegations from Riyadh. These state visits included a state visit to Washington, DC by King Salman in September 2015, followed up by a trip by the newly appointed Defense Minister and Deputy Crown Prince, Mohammad bin Salman bin Abdulaziz, in June 2016.[32] These visits allowed the highest level of Saudi officials the chance to meet with senior U.S. officials to press their case personally. The Saudis also received visits from Secretary of Defense Dr. Ashton Carter and Secretary of State John Kerry, and President Barack Obama made his fourth state visit to Saudi Arabia in April 2016. Such reciprocal visits allow Saudi officials to continue conversations and discussions from their Washington, DC trips.

The Saudis make extensive use of professionals for their efforts to lobby Congress. Saudi politics is so different from the style of interaction on Capitol Hill that reliance on professional lobbying advice is a sensible, sound approach. Saudi Arabia retains as many as eight Washington, DC–based lobbying forms to handle its communications with Congress and the executive branch.[33] The approach they have taken brings officials into contact with Hill staff and members on several key issues, including U.S.-Saudi military and intelligence cooperation, Saudi purchases of U.S. military equipment, supplies, and maintenance/logistics support contracts, and ongoing Saudi efforts to combat extremism and terrorists in the Middle East. Saudi communications efforts are designed to retain support for the Kingdom on Capitol Hill, among administration officials, and within the Washington, DC policy community.[34]

In support of the June 2016 visit of Prince Mohammad bin Salman bin Abdulaziz, lobbyists delivered to key Hill offices copies of a 104-page report on recent Saudi counter-terror actions.[35] No other communications effort revolved around the publication of the twenty-eight-page section of the 9/11 Commission's report that had been classified over fears of implicating Saudi government officials in support of the hijackers who committed the attacks; the publication of those pages in July 2016 was occasion for pro-Saudi pundits, think tank researchers, and former U.S. officials, such as former George W. Bush homeland security adviser Frances Townsend, to argue that Saudi officials were now finally freed of suspicion.[36] The prince also released his strategic plan for diversifying the Saudi economy, called *Saudi Vision 2030*, before his visit.[37]

One powerful means of establishing good relations, which can enhance a country's direct lobbying efforts, such as Saudi Arabia's program just described, is to engage in indirect lobbying, as well. The indirect approach builds support via grassroots activism and the media to shift U.S. public opinion as well as move Congress. A key advantage in this tactic is if a country has a significant ethnic community in the United States. If that community is well established, politically active, and committed to support of the home country, activism by those U.S. citizens can be decisive in gaining congressional support for a foreign country's lobbying goals. Several nations have this advantage today, including Ireland, India, Armenia, China, and Israel.[38] Saudi Arabia does not have the benefit of a large, coherent body of *Saudi* Americans to call upon in the same way: Arab Americans are a smaller population, and since they come from so many different countries, it is harder to get them to collectively support issues important only to one or a few Arab countries.

Israel's national security strategy has relied on sustained military preeminence over their neighbors. Part of staying much stronger militarily than these neighboring countries is the longstanding U.S.-Israel security agreement, which not only allows Israel access to high-tech U.S. weapons, but also supports Israeli defense budgets with the largest foreign and military aid package the United States offers to any nation. In addition, Israeli leaders work to ensure that their relationship is the paramount one for the

United States in the region—if preeminence is to be sustained, no other Middle East countries can have the same kind of strong relationship that the United States and Israel share. Like Saudi direct lobbying of Congress, Israeli indirect efforts are a major feature of the nation's security strategy.

Many observers of U.S. interest group politics look to the American Israel Public Affairs Committee, AIPAC, as the quintessential grassroots lobbying organization in the country.[39] And they may be right. AIPAC's focus is narrow; its mission "is to strengthen, protect and promote the U.S.-Israel relationship in ways that enhance the security of the United States and Israel."[40] AIPAC produces action items on key legislative topics for its members, most of whom are Jewish Americans, who have a natural interest in support of the State of Israel. AIPAC action agendas help citizens know what legislative action of interest is taking place, how to contact their elected officials in Washington, DC to urge them to support such actions, and talking points for the messages they send to those officials. In addition, AIPAC hosts a well-attended Policy Conference, which brings together interested citizens, key Israeli political figures, and U.S. government officials. The conference culminates in a series of lobbying visits by AIPAC members to their elected officials' offices on Capitol Hill (see chapter 4). These visits have a major impact; they are numerous, the AIPAC members are well briefed, and their message parallels the messages that the Israeli government shares with U.S. officials. Thus, the grassroots meetings reinforce the message that the United States and Israel are strong partners for democracy and peace in the region. The Policy Conference was also where Prime Minister Netanyahu previewed his speech on Iran to Congress in 2015, and where he made a speech in 2016 on the continuing strong U.S.-Israel relationship.[41] But AIPAC is only one of many influential Jewish-American groups that lobby Congress on behalf of Israel. The seventeen most important of these groups work together under an umbrella organization called the Conference of Presidents of Major Jewish Organizations. The member groups and the Conference of Presidents make regular visits to Capitol Hill, and their memberships are engaged and active in speaking to their elected officials. With such a large number of grassroots activists helping them to lobby Congress, it should be obvious why Israeli officials do not spend much money on professional lobbying.[42]

In addition to grassroots lobbying, two other indirect methods deserve attention. The first is support for informal groups of members of Congress, called caucuses. In the 114th Congress (2015–2017), the caucus list is eighty-nine pages long, covering every conceivable topic or reason for joining a club.[43] Many caucuses center on foreign policy interests; for example, the Congressional Caucus on India and Indian Americans—

which has only one member who is actually an Indian American (the remaining 100-plus joined the caucus because their districts are home to large communities of Indian Americans, one of the more politically active diaspora communities in the United States). Caucuses are a powerful indirect lobbying mechanism—members hear from other elected officials, and from interest group and foreign officials who communicate directly with caucus members.[44]

Among others, the Saudis have effectively used their lobbyists for a second indirect approach: placement of supportive articles and op-eds in key newspapers, journals, and television programs. Even the online news site *Huffington Post* got into the action, inviting Saudi Ambassador Prince Abdullah bin Faisal to pen an op-ed on Saudi anti-extremism initiatives.[45] Of course, this is a double-edged sword, as other countries also actively pursue this tactic; witness the Iranian foreign minister, Mohammad Javad Zarif, who wrote an op-ed in the *New York Times* entitled "Let Us Rid the World of Wahhabism," a very direct counter to the whole Saudi public relations message.[46]

Two final lines of effort conclude a lobbying strategy: building coalitions and monitoring the activities of targeted officials. Even the most powerful players sometimes look for allies to help win a legislative battle. The Saudi efforts to influence Washington, DC have been significantly reinforced by major spending on allied lobbying from the Gulf Countries, for instance. Working in concert, the Saudis and Gulf countries funded a think tank, the Arab Gulf States Institute in Washington, DC, which opened in October 2015, and has provided testimony to hearings on Capitol Hill, as well as published favorable articles and research.[47] Both the Saudis and Gulf countries have spent lavishly over the past several years on research institutes and other grants to established think tanks, as well. This effort is important because it reinforces a status quo assessment in the Washington, DC policy community, that Saudi Arabia and the Gulf Countries are good partners to the United States in its pursuit of security issues in the region—and the easiest lobbying to do is that which reinforces the status quo.[48] Another, simpler way of building coalitions is through social events, galas, and parties, which give foreign dignitaries multiple chances to build solid personal connections with U.S. officials in nonthreatening, informal settings. As mentioned at the start of the chapter, the United Arab Emirates' Ambassador Yousef Al Otaiba is recognized across the Washington, DC social, diplomatic, and policy spheres as the master of such events. His successful management of these social interactions has given him access and influence that many ambassadors of much larger countries could only dream of having.[49]

Monitoring is a tool for signaling to elected officials that their actions are being watched and evaluated by interested groups, and by the voters back home. This does not have to take the aggressive form of "voting guides" that many political action committees issue at election times, but can be simple action alerts, or calls for advocates to contact their elected officials on specific topics, and ask their representatives for their support. For instance, in February 2016, Americans for Peace Now (one of the members of the Conference of Presidents, mentioned above), called on its members to write their congressional delegations to oppose several resolutions and bills being introduced in the House and Senate that touched on the question of Israeli settlements in the West Bank; the Peace Now action alert informed advocates of the terms of the proposed bills, explained what the issues were, and asked that members tell their representatives that these bills did not help to advance a peace agreement between the Israelis and Palestinians. Such action alerts remind elected officials that they have interested constituents back home who track certain kinds of legislation—and that their votes on that legislation will have an impact.[50]

Conclusion

This overview of foreign lobbying on foreign and defense policy suggests that many countries take active roles in helping to shape American policy. By direct and indirect lobbying, and by monitoring U.S. officials' actions, these foreign countries help the U.S. government to make decisions. It is also clear that this effort, while substantial and expensive, pales in comparison to the massive efforts of business to influence Congress, the White House, and federal agencies.

But the story also makes it clear that the whole story may not be available for researchers, policymakers, and activists. Weak reporting requirements, loopholes, and lax enforcement mean that some unknown amount of this work is never reported, and is thus unavailable for review or study: how much do we miss because nobody reports the boring, everyday hustle that is the lifeblood of Washington, DC, or any major capital?

What could be done to make the system more effective in tracking what foreign entities do to influence U.S. policy? Obviously, the first step would be improved enforcement of the rules that do exist. Within the DOJ, several reforms make sense, including more oversight of the FARA office by senior DOJ officials; more resources for and devoted to compliance; and actual punishment of lobbyists who fail to comply, or whose actions are illegal under the law.

Legal reforms would also be necessary to really guarantee a comprehensive reporting environment. Congress could amend both FARA and LDA to require that all foreign entities must report under FARA. Congress could also add civil penalties for noncompliance that could be used to enforce better adherence to FARA reporting rules. Congress could also clarify the reporting requirements under FARA and make LDA reporting as comprehensive—as well as closing loopholes in both laws, requiring more timely reporting, and requiring both the DOJ and the House and Senate compliance offices to publish everything they receive from foreign agents and lobbyists in regularly updated, easily researchable data formats. Such changes would enhance the ability to know who is talking to government officials and what they are saying—and would give observers a better chance to understand the forces that influence elected officials' decisions.

Notes

1. Aron Heller and Deb Riechmann, "Netanyahu: Deal Would 'All But Guarantee' Nuclear Weapons for Iran," *PBS Newshour*, March 3, 2015, http://www.pbs.org/newshour/rundown/netanyahu-warn-iran-deal-today-visit-congress/; Julian Hattem, "Saudis scramble for Washington allies," *The Hill*, May 24, 2016, http://thehill.com/policy/national-security/280987-saudis-scramble-for-washington-allies; Felicia Schwartz and Margherita Stancati, "Saudi Prince Visits U.S. to Improve Kingdom's Image," *Wall Street Journal*, June 15, 2016, http://www.wsj.com/articles/princes-u-s-trip-aims-to-improve-saudi-image-1466025451

2. Ryan Grim and Akbar Shahid Ahmed, "His Town: Yousef Al Otaiba is the most charming man in Washington: He's slick, he's savvy and he throws one hell of a party. And if he has his way, our Middle East policy is going to get a lot more aggressive," *Huffington Post Highline*, September 3, 2015, http://highline.huffingtonpost.com/articles/en/his-town

3. James M. Lindsay, "Getting Uncle Sam's Ear: Will Ethnic Lobbies Cramp America's Foreign Policy Style?," *The Brookings Review*, 20(1) (Jan., 2002): 37–40; http://dx.doi.org/10.2307/20081021

4. Jeff Horwitz and Chad Day, "Trump Advisers Waged Covert Influence Campaign," *The Big Story*, AP Newswire, August 19, 2016, http://www.bigstory.ap.org/article/efb1cc930fc7488ebfa5a257ffa25347/trump-advisers-waged-covert-influence-campaign

5. Megan R. Wilson and Harper Neidig, "Manafort helped Ukraine party secretly pay U.S. lobbyists: report," *The Hill*, August 17, 2016, http://thehill.com/blogs/ballot-box/presidential-races/291680-report-manafort-helped-ukraine-party-pay-us-lobbyists

6. Sam W. Haynes, *Unfinished Revolution: The Early American Republic in a British World* (Charlottesville, VA: University of Virginia Press, 2010).

7. David Carroll Cochran, "Ethnic Diversity and Democratic Stability: The Case of Irish Americans," *Political Science Quarterly* (Academy of Political Science), 110(4) (Winter, 1995/96): 587.

8. David Sim, "Filibusters, Fenians, and a Contested Neutrality: The Irish Question and U.S. Diplomacy, 1848–1871," *American Nineteenth Century History* 12(3) (Sept., 2011): 265–287, http://dx.doi.org/10.1080/14664658.2011.626161

9. FARA website, FARA Enforcement office, U.S. Department of Justice, https://www.fara.gov/enforcement.html

10. The rules are well described in Jack Maskell, *Lobbying Congress: An Overview of Legal Provisions and Congressional Ethics Rules*, RL31126 (Washington, DC: Congressional Research Service, September 14, 2001), 4–5.

11. Lydia Dennett, "Justice Dept. Watchdog Confirms 'Unacceptable' FARA Compliance," The (POGO) Blog, September 8, 2016, http://www.pogo.org/blog/2016/09/justice-dept-watchdog-fara-unacceptable.html

12. Ben Freeman and Lydia Dennett, *Loopholes, Filing Failures, and Lax Enforcement: How the Foreign Agents Registration Act Falls Short*, Project on Government Oversight, December 16, 2014, http://www.pogo.org/our-work/reports/2014/loopholes-filing-failures-lax-enforcement-how-the-foreign-agents-registration-act-falls-short.html

13. See their Foreign Influence Explorer at http://sunlightfoundation.com/blog/2014/05/07/a-better-way-to-explore-foreign-influence

14. For an excellent overview of the theoretical explanations of American politics, with significant recent additions, see Frank Baumgartner and Bryan Jones, *Agendas and Instabilities in American Politics* (Chicago: University of Chicago Press, 2009, 2nd ed.).

15. An excellent consideration of business interests and their political efforts is E.E. Schattschneider, *The Semisovereign People: A Realist's View of Democracy in America* (Fort Worth, TX: Harcourt Brace Jovanovich, 1975 [1960]).

16. Frank Baumgartner and Beth Leech, "Interest Niches and Policy Bandwagons: Patterns of Interest Group Involvement in National Politics," *The Journal of Politics* 63(4) (Nov., 2001): 1191–1213.

17. The *Oxford English Dictionary* notes lobbying's first mention in a biography of President Martin Van Buren, and includes mentions in the press as early as the 1830s, with regular mentions by the 1850s. See entry for "lobby" at the OED website, http://www.oed.com/view/Entry/109496

18. Christopher Loomis, "The Politics of Uncertainty: Lobbyists and Propaganda in Early 20th Century America," *The Journal of Political History* (21)2: 187–213. Daniel Tichenor and Richard Harris, "Organized Interests and American Political Development," *Political Science Quarterly* 117(4) (Winter, 2002–2003): 587–612, make the argument that policy analysts have argued about the emergence of large-scale, organized lobbying in Washington, DC in several waves since the early 1900s, suggesting that business interests have long understood the need to work on influencing policy outcomes.

19. For a representative study from the 1930s, see Pendleton Herring, "Special Interests and the Interstate Commerce Commission," *The American Political Science*

Review 27(5) (Oct., 1933): 738–751. For an excellent source representative of lobbying studies from the 1950s on, see Raymond Bauer, Ithiel De Sola Pool, and Lewis Dexter, *American Business and Public Policy* (New York: Atherton Press, 1964).

20. The Chamber commissioned a report on what they perceived as an antibusiness political environment in Washington, DC, written by Lewis Powell in August 1971; the memo, "Attack on American Free Enterprise System," launched the Chamber's efforts to reinvigorate business involvement in lobbying the U.S. government. The memo can be found on Washington and Lee Law School's Lewis Powell Archive at http://law2.wlu.edu/deptimages/Powell%20Archives/PowellMemorandumTypescript.pdf

21. Lee Drutman, "How Corporate Lobbyists Conquered American Democracy," *The Atlantic*, April 20, 2015, http://www.theatlantic.com/business/archive/2015/04/how-corporate-lobbyists-conquered-american-democracy/390822/

22. The Center for Responsive Politics' Lobbying Database, housed at Opensecrets.org, reports that 61.9 percent of the pharmaceutical lobbyists they interviewed were former government officials, as were 68.4 percent of the electronics lobbyists, 65.7% of the manufacturers' lobbyists, and 52.7 percent of education lobbyists (https://www.opensecrets.org/revolving/top.php?display=I). And people also move in the opposite direction through the "revolving door"—over 120 lobbyists joined the ranks of Hill staff when the GOP regained control of the House in 2010 (https://www.opensecrets.org/revolving/reverse.php).

23. Megan R. Wilson, "Ex-Lawmaker Registers to Lobby for Ukrainian Businessmen," *The Hill*, May 5, 2014, http://thehill.com/business-a-lobbying/lobbying-contracts/205248-ex-lawmaker-lobbying-for-ukrainian-businessmen

24. John Newhouse, "Diplomacy, Inc.: The Influence of Lobbies on U.S. Foreign Policy," *Foreign Affairs*, May/June 2009, https://www.foreignaffairs.com/articles/2009-05-01/diplomacy-inc

25. In September 2016, the United States and Israel signed a new aid memorandum, increasing the package to $38 billion over ten years. Nicole Gaouette, "Largest-ever U.S. Military Aid Package to go to Israel," September 13, 2016, http://www.cnn.com/2016/09/13/politics/us-israel-military-aid-package-mou/index.html

26. Ryan Sibley, "What Foreign Interests Spent the Most to Influence the USA?," Sunlight Foundation Blog, May 7, 2014, http://sunlightfoundation.com/blog/2014/05/07/deutsche-telekom-lobbies-the-u-s

27. Allan Holmes, "T-Mobile's Lobbying Spending May Be Paying Off," Center for Public Integrity, January 23, 2014, https://www.publicintegrity.org/2014/01/23/14159/t-mobile-s-lobbying-spending-may-be-paying

28. Newhouse, "Diplomacy, Inc."

29. Lindsay, "Getting Uncle Sam's Ear"

30. Julien Zarifian, "The Armenian-American Lobby and Its Impact on U.S. Foreign Policy," *Society* 51 (2014): 503–512, published online August 19, 2014, http://dx.doi.org/10.1007/s12115-014-9816-8

31. Sunlight Foundation, Foreign Influence Explorer, Proposed Arms Sales, lists thirty-nine separate contracts for Saudi Arabia from 2009 to 2016, http://foreign.influenceexplorer.com/more-search?q=saudi%20arabia&armspage=1

32. David Ottaway, "Saudi Arabia's Wonder Prince Comes to Washington," Wilson Center, Jun 13, 2016, https://www.wilsoncenter.org/article/saudi-arabias-wonder-prince-comes-to-washington; Sami Aboudi, "Powerful Saudi Prince to Meet Obama, Ban on U.S. Visit," Reuters newswire, June 13, 2016, http://www.reuters.com/article/us-saudi-usa-visit-idUSKCN0YZ0MD

33. Max Fisher, "How Saudi Arabia Captured Washington," *Vox*, March 21, 2016, http://www.vox.com/2016/3/21/11275354/saudi-arabia-gulf-washington

34. Ibid.

35. Nahal Toosi, "Exclusive: In Memo to Congress, Saudis Insist They're Fighting Terror," *Politico*, May 19, 2016, http://www.politico.com/story/2016/05/congress-saudi-arabia-terror-fight-223383

36. Lee Fang, "Saudi Arabia's PR Machine Uses the 28 Pages to Blame Iran for the 9/11 Attacks," *The Intercept*, July 21, 2016, https://theintercept.com/2016/07/21/saudi-arabias-pr-machine-uses-the-28-pages-to-blame-iran-for-911-attacks/; Lee Fang, "Inside Saudi Arabia's Campaign to Charm American Policymakers and Journalists," *The Intercept*, December 1, 2015, https://theintercept.com/2015/12/01/inside-saudi-charm-campaign

37. Saudi Vision 2030 website, government of the Kingdom of Saudi Arabia, http://vision2030.gov.sa/en

38. See Newhouse, "Diplomacy, Inc.," and Lindsay, "Getting Uncle Sam's Ear" for a sustained discussion of the advantages these particular countries have because of their diasporas in the United States.

39. Kirk J. Beattie, "How Congress Shapes Middle East Policy, and How the American Israel Public Affairs Committee (AIPAC) Shapes Congress," Washington Report on Middle East Affairs, May 2016, pp. 15–19; http://www.wrmea.org/2016-may/panel-1-how-congress-shapes-middle-east-policy-and-how-the-american-israel-public-affairs-committee-aipac-shapes-congress.html

40. AIPAC, "Our Mission," http://www.aipac.org/about/mission

41. "Full Text of PM Netanyahu's Speech to AIPAC," *Jerusalem Post*, March 2, 2015, http://www.jpost.com/Israel-News/Politics-And-Diplomacy/Full-text-of-PM-Netanyahus-speech-to-AIPAC-392701; "Full Text of Netanyahu's 2016 Address to AIPAC," *Times of Israel*, March 22, 2016, http://www.timesofisrael.com/full-text-of-netanyahus-video-address-to-aipac

42. See the Conference of President's website (http://conferenceofpresidents.org/) for its political agenda, its messages on key issues of importance to the American-Jewish community, and its annual visit to Israel, where the prime minister met with the delegation in February 2016.

43. The list of caucuses is available at https://cha.house.gov/sites/republicans.cha.house.gov/files/documents/114CMOList%289.20.16%29.pdf; the Senate recognizes only one official caucus, the Senate Caucus on International Narcotics Control, and does not publicize its list of informal caucuses, although many listed by the House have members from both chambers.

44. Susan Webb Hammond, *Congressional Caucuses in National Policy Making* (Baltimore, MD: Johns Hopkins University Press, 2001).

45. Abdullah Al-Saud, "Confronting Extremism," *Huffington Post*, March 9, 2016, http://www.huffingtonpost.com/abdullah-alsaud/confronting-extremism_b_9420330.html?1457580232

46. Mohammad Javad Zarif, "Let Us Rid the World of Wahhabism," *New York Times*, September 13, 2016, http://www.nytimes.com/2016/09/14/opinion/mohammad-javad-zarif-let-us-rid-the-world-of-wahhabism.html?_r=0

47. Julian Pecquet, "Gulf-funded Think Tank to Make Capitol Hill Debut," *Al-Monitor*, October 5, 2015, http://www.al-monitor.com/pulse/originals/2015/10/gulf-funded-think-tank-capitol.html#ixzz4L1BevLFq

48. Fisher, "How Saudi Arabia Captured Washington"; Fang, "Inside Saudi Arabia's Campaign"; Nahal Toosi, "Saudis Try to Clean Up Image Ahead of Obama Visit," *Politico*, April 18, 2016, http://www.politico.com/story/2016/04/saudi-arabia-obama-visit-terrorism-221950; Akbar Shahid Ahmed, "How Wealthy Arab Gulf States Shape the Washington Influence Game," *Huffington Post*, September 2, 2015, http://www.huffingtonpost.com/entry/arab-gulf-states-washington_us_55e62be5e4b0b7a9633ac659; Dania Koleilat Khatib, "Arab Gulf Lobbying in the United States: What Makes Them Win and What Makes Them Lose and Why?," *Contemporary Arab Affairs*, 9(1), 68–81, http://dx.doi.org/10.1080/17550912.2015.1121647

49. Grim and Ahmed, "His Town."

50. Americans for Peace Now, "Tell Congress: Pro-Settlements is NOT Pro-Israel," APN Action Alert, February 8, 2016, http://peacenow.org/entry.php?id=16833#.V-RFRaJWJps

Chapter 3

A View from K Street

PATRICK GRIFFIN AND WILLIAM DANVERS

In this chapter we will examine lobbying on international issues, which, depending on the issue, can involve governments, corporations, ethnic diaspora, and non-governmental organizations. An analysis of the roles these four groups play will be included, as well as the issues that frame their advocacy and lobbying—economic, political, and security. This analysis is derived from our years of experience on K Street and in government—Congress and the executive branch—as well as from viewing lobbying as part of the academic study of American politics.

The popular TV show "The Americans" is set in the 1980s and based on the practice of the Soviet Union Americanizing some of its spies, planting them in the United States as ordinary citizens who secretly work on behalf of the Soviet Union. These illegals, as they were called, were engaged in dangerous business—working to advance the interests of their government but afforded no diplomatic cover and very little protection, and at constant risk in the land of their enemy. Espionage at this level was tricky, and the consequences for getting caught spying could be severe.

In 2010, the U.S. government uncovered a ring of eleven Russian illegals operating undercover in the United States. They were "Americanized" and trying to steal secrets for their country. As it turns out, no espionage charges were leveled against them. Instead, among other things, they were charged with the crime of violating the Foreign Agents Registration Act (FARA), a statute that, since the mid-1960s, has been used as a way to keep track of those who lobby on behalf of foreign governments.[1] A more recent example of alleged violations of FARA were the indictments of Donald Trump's campaign chairman, Paul Manafort, and his associate Richard Gates in late 2017.

FARA, passed into law in 1938, originally focused on stopping the spread of propaganda for foreign powers, especially Nazi Germany. It was particularly used during World War II to fight those who might want to aid the enemy and to keep the United States out of the war. In the mid-1960s, the focus of the law changed to those acting on behalf of a foreign principal, most often a government. The Act requires disclosure of money given to an individual or organization representing a foreign government, but it does not dictate disclosure for efforts related to representing a foreign company. While the Act does have criminal penalties, there have been no convictions under FARA since 1966.[2]

FARA is one way that foreign lobbying (*not* spying) is regulated in the United States. The other way is by registering via the Lobbying Disclosure Act (LDA).[3] The LDA requires lobbyists to register with both the clerk of the U.S. House of Representatives and secretary of the U.S. Senate on behalf of a client. It has civil but no criminal penalties. While it has loopholes and exceptions, it is the law that regulates most U.S. lobbying activity, including some working on foreign or international interests. The LDA is a less complicated standard to follow than FARA because clerks of the House and Senate do not have the enforcement capacity of the Department of Justice, which oversees FARA registration. FARA registration is also a clearer signal that one is likely working for a foreign government, which can make the lobbying more nuanced. The LDA is a more typical registration, and that can make it easier to identify the issue being lobbied with a domestic agenda. Either way, lobbying on international issues has similarities with domestic lobbying, but is also unique both in approach and appearance.

These two laws provide the framework within which international lobbying in the United States (lobbying on behalf of foreign interests, both political and economic) is carried out. This world of international lobbying has become big business and includes working for governments, political parties, businesses, and other economic interests and/or policies, specific causes, including security matters, as well as other large and small campaigns that involve clients and issues worldwide.

The real work of lobbying both from the vantage point of those who lobby—K Street—to those who are being lobbied—Congress and the executive branch—is determined both by practice and by issue. Experience helps guide the approach, but so does context. In that regard, lobbying on international issues, which has a unique context, is somewhat different from more traditional, domestic lobbying. FARA registration itself sets it apart from domestic lobbying, since individuals register as foreign agents, an uncomfortable term for some. More importantly, when one represents a government, they are potentially working with a complicated client, more complicated than even the biggest multinational corporation. It is also a client that has its own set of diplomatic relations across the U.S. government and with Congress. For example, if the work of the lobbyist is to lobby against a U.S. government policy, it becomes even more difficult, at the diplomatic, personal, and professional level. It is one thing to support or oppose, say, a trade deal, since there are clear economic considerations on both sides. It is another issue to oppose a treaty or an agreement that is part of U.S. foreign policy. An example of this would be representing the former head of the Philippines, Ferdinand Marcos, when it was clear the Reagan administration wanted him to relinquish power.

Experience demonstrates that another difference is who plays a role in the lobbying and who is lobbied. Experts in international affairs frequently are recruited from Capitol Hill and agencies such as the Department of State to help with these kinds of lobbying efforts. Their skills are often apolitical and more policy focused, making them somewhat unusual for lobbyists, who are often more generalists with strong political skills. In addition, lobbying the foreign affairs committees in the House and Senate is not typical in the lobbying world. These committees are not as accustomed to being approached by lobbyists as the tax and trade committees (who are also lobbied on international issues). Therefore, lobbyists who work on these issues need to have a slightly different approach, one that may emphasize policy more than straight economics or politics. If one needs to make an argument about a particular sale of arms, it can help to say, "when I served in the country in question," or "as a result of my work in the region," making the argument more substantive.

Lobbying on behalf of a foreign interest or issue sends a different signal than lobbying on behalf of a domestic interest. As an example, if a lobbyist works for the oil industry, he or she may get push-back from the environmental community, but if a lobbyist works on behalf of the government of the People's Republic of China, the push-back is likely to be much more intense, to come from multiple directions, and to sometimes go beyond simple economics and question whether the work he or she is doing runs counter to perceived U.S. interests or policy.

Foreign interests hire U.S. lobbyists because the U.S. government is unique. The U.S. president may speak for the government writ large, but most certainly does not speak for the legislative branch. Embassies have a direct diplomatic pipeline to the U.S. government through the Department of State. Most also have relations with other key government agencies and the White House. But those relations only get so far. In an era in which the only thing that stops at the water's edge is the coastline, engaging Congress is an important part of engaging the United States.

This maze of political players is as confusing to foreign companies as it is to foreign governments. They also need help in developing strategies that reflect the reality of how Washington, DC works—through relationships—rather than adopting a more theoretical approach, working through traditional governmental channels. Non-governmental organizations working in this sphere (most of which are American, but some of which are based in foreign countries) have a better sense of how to lobby Washington, DC, and often utilize grassroots, support of think tanks, advertising, publication of research, and so on to help them make their point.

The Actors Represented in Foreign Lobbying

A multitude of actors actively lobby or employ lobbyists on their behalf in the area of foreign lobbying, but three categories of actors are most prominent: governments, business interests (both foreign and domestic), and various diaspora and non-governmental organizations.

Governments

Close allies of the United States rely on their embassies for the most part to advance their agendas. For example, it would be unusual for the United Kingdom or France to hire outside lobbyists for general relationship-building purposes with the United States. That said, they might have a team of insiders, including American nationals, who help them navigate the complicated political waters of Washington, DC.

The reason some other embassies and many foreign firms hire lobbyists is because the U.S. political system is far different from anything they have seen at home. In a parliamentary system, political party loyalty is at a premium. If an elected official breaks from his or her party, that official is often penalized and may even lose his or her seat. That makes the prime minister a very powerful individual. She or he speaks for the government.

The president generally speaks for the U.S. government, at least in theory, but embassies and their lobbyists—sometimes in house, sometimes with outside firms—will lobby different agencies in order to have an impact on a White House decision. If a foreign government wants to see an arms sale completed, or a trade agreement enacted, it will hire outside lobbyists to work with embassy staff that follows Congress to work to achieve the desired result. In effect, the lobbyists will be an adjunct to the embassy team, working closely with them on a regular basis until the goal is reached. That would not happen in the same way in a parliamentary system where, again, party discipline is tantamount to party and personal success. Each House and Senate office is to a certain extent independent. Representatives and senators will follow the party line, but it is not as automatic as it is in some other systems. This is where lobbyists come into play. Since party discipline can be ephemeral, lobbyists will often focus on individual House or Senate offices as part of their strategy on a particular issue.

Lobbyists will often have relationships with particular offices, and they will use those relationships to try to persuade a representative or senator to support the position they are lobbying. A free trade agreement (FTA) is an example. Traditionally these are unpopular with Democrats, particularly in the House, but some Democrats are willing to support trade deals and become the focus of lobbying efforts to get the votes to get a trade agreement passed. These targets may be amenable to FTAs because they are in a safe district that does not threaten to produce an electoral challenge, so the member can more easily break with his or her party, because there is some element to his or her constituency that would lead to support for these agreements, or because of some other factor or dynamic. Those lobbying in these circumstances often specialize in working with these offices, helping them make the case for a particular agreement. In working for the government of Colombia, we met weekly to discuss strategy and tactics to get congressional support for the U.S.-Colombia FTA. This included trying to respond to concerns of organized labor and their Hill supporters. Eventually, those concerns were addressed, and the Congress passed the FTA in 2011.

Most embassies have staff that follow Congress for them. They may also establish relations outside the Department of State and U.S. government both to gather information and in some cases to attempt to affect policy. Embassies of smaller countries are often at a disadvantage because they lack the number of staffers necessary to keep track of the executive branch and Congress. They may, therefore, hire lobbyists to help them generally or for a specific issue.

Another scenario that would lead a government to hire U.S. lobbyists is when that country is having a difficult time with its relationship with the U.S. government. The government may hire a lobbyist to help manage its image by talking to administration officials, but more often it is to arrange meetings with Capitol Hill offices. Again, a key is the relationships the lobbyist has with those within the U.S. government.

Much of this is done at the staff level, explaining a complicated issue or problem between the United States and the government in question, so that if an issue comes to a head, there is potential political support for the government on the Hill or even at the working level of a particular U.S. government agency. For example, the now deceased military dictator and president of the Democratic Republic of the Congo from 1965 to 1997, Mobuto Sese Seko, hired lobbyists to help him with his image in the United States. Other governments have done the same from time to time. In addition, the government of Dubai, in the wake of the Dubai Ports World problems in 2006 and other issues, decided to hire outside help to assist them in developing relationships on Capitol Hill and with think tanks, and also to get a better understanding of how Washington, DC works. Eventually Abu Dhabi, capital of the United Arab Emirates (UAE), which included Dubai, brought in a new ambassador who in addition to being effective and well regarded changed for the better the perception of the UAE, including Dubai, in Washington, DC. The ambassador continued to use outside advisors to help promote his nation's relationship with the U.S. government and Congress.

Foreign governments, whose embassies may know the Hill but understand their reach is limited, often hire lobbyists to help push an agenda item across the finish line. The lobbyists may advocate for outright approval or simply to get the administration to make a favorable decision, which will get the clearance process started. An example is the sale of an Airborne Warning and Control System, or AWAC, to Saudi Arabia, which was a big issue during the Reagan administration (see below for more details). Another has been opposition at various times to arms sales or transfers to Turkey because of political concerns. The Turkish government has used lobbyists to make their case in these instances.

Business

U.S. and foreign businesses play an important role in the world of lobbying on foreign issues. This includes working with embassies, working with a coalition of domestic and foreign companies, working through trade associations, or working as an individual company. One key to having a foreign firm involved is making the case that it creates jobs and contributes to the U.S. economy. For instance, when Airbus is competing for a U.S. government contract, part of its strategy is to make sure Congress knows that it employs American workers when it builds aircraft. To underscore this point, consider the issue of parking spots on Capitol Hill, which have always been, and continue to be, a valuable commodity for staff. During the 1980s, Representative William D. Ford (D-MI), then chairman of the House Post Office and Civil Service Committee, did not give parking spots to staff who drove foreign cars. This was in the days before foreign automakers had plants in the United States, and Representative Ford was focused on jobs—union jobs, in particular. For our purposes here, Representative Ford was sending a signal to those lobbying on foreign economic issues that they had to fine-tune their arguments, connecting to local economic concerns as much as possible. While it may not have made a difference on who got what parking place, Representative Ford's action was a good reminder of the need for lobbyists when working on an international issue to talk to members (and staff) about why a policy being lobbied for is good for the United States, particularly the U.S. economy.

Many large corporations have full-time, in-house lobbyists who devote their time to international issues. Additionally, corporations will often augment the work of their in-house team by hiring outside lobbyists to help with a specific issue. These lobbyists are looked to for substance but also for the critical piece of lobbying mentioned above—the relationships they already have with those in government. Lobbyists can also provide more coverage for a firm if an issue is complicated and needs a lot of congressional support. In many cases, these outside lobbyists are former Hill staff who worked on the House and Senate Armed Services Committees, or Appropriations Committee staff who work on international accounts. For example, since defense spending determines the amount of money available for a particular defense contract, big defense contractors will often hire former congressional appropriations committee staff to help advocate for funding projects in which they are involved. These same corporations may also hire former government officials—having worked at the Department of State is often a good credential—to help in house or on a particular project. These hires are often seen as having a particular expertise useful in shaping arguments for or against a particular issue. What they might lack in political acumen they make up for with their background.

Trade associations are often used as organizing instruments in a particular lobbying campaign. For instance, the U.S. Chamber of Commerce plays an important role in shaping the debate with trade agreements. Regional business councils do as well. Since a number of trade associations often share a particular focus, they often will collaborate in a lobbying effort, combining resources and reach. There can be competition as well. Someone has to pay the bills, and associations are always anxious to prove their value.

Finally, trade unions play an important role in debate over trade agreements. They can stop an agreement from being considered, and they can play an important role as to what will be part of an agreement. For example, the U.S.-Colombia FTA did not pass until special provisions were added to protect labor rights in Colombia. Unions are also influential in seeing that legislation such as Trade Adjustment Assistance to help workers affected by a trade agreement is addressed before a trade agreement moves forward. Unions are almost always on the other side of a trade agreement from the business community, which means you cannot get a trade agreement passed unless the perspective of unions is accounted for or otherwise accommodated.

Diaspora and Non-Governmental Organizations

Various diaspora and NGO often play an outsized role in driving issues that are part of the world of international lobbying. They can represent specific causes such as human rights or advocate for support for refugees and/or a particular community or country. These groups might work to support or oppose U.S. policy in a particular issue area generally, or might simply want to change part of a particular aspect of a specific policy. They might be involved at a local, state, or national level. Diaspora and NGOs often work with their in-house lobbyists, but will from time to time hire outside lobbyists depending on the issue and what they can afford.

One of the most well known of such groups is the American Israel Public Affairs Committee (AIPAC; see chapter 4), which for decades has been involved with U.S. policy toward Israel. Its support for strong U.S.-Israeli ties reflects the views of some in the Jewish-American community. The group has been criticized for having more influence than is appropriate for an independent group—in many ways a tribute to its effectiveness—but it is always respected.

AIPAC wields influence because it has the active support of a large segment of the Jewish diaspora in the United States; it is also well organized and sustains its involvement in all issues concerning U.S.-Israeli relations. Like any outside organization, its success is measured by its ability to get support for a particular issue. And while it wins some issues, such as maintaining aid to Israel, and loses others, such as its opposition to the Iran nuclear deal, what is most important from a lobbying point of view is that it is always part of the legislative mix.

AIPAC has served as a model for how other organizations, such as the Cuban American National Foundation (CANF), can influence U.S. foreign policy. Under the leadership of Jorge Mas Canosa, CANF was successful in helping to shape U.S. policy toward Cuba for years. Like

AIPAC, Canosa organized a significant part of the Cuban-American community to play an important role in the discussion over U.S.-Cuban relations. After Mas Canosa died, and the perspective on what kind of policy toward Cuba makes sense in the twenty-first century changed, CANF's role became less central to U.S.-Cuban policy. President Barack Obama, backed by domestic economic interests, as well as some political leaders who saw the U.S. approach as outdated, opened up relations with Cuba. The lobbying by CANF and its supporters was no longer central to the debate. Other lobbyists with other interests became important players in the changing policy. Other powerful organizations saw their roles change as policies shifted.

There are other ethnic diaspora groups that play a role on issues of importance to them. While all of these groups are Americans first, they also support policies favorable to the countries of their heritage. Greek Americans routinely want to ensure that Greece is treated fairly by the U.S. government, particularly with respect to certain arms sales and arms transfers. The Armenian-American community lobbies hard on the Armenian genocide resolution (see chapter 8).[4] Even members of the Irish diaspora became involved in trying to secure a visa for Sinn Fein political leader Gerry Adams. As policies change, so can the importance of NGOs and the role of various diaspora connected with an issue.[5] Often if an issue is not hot the lobbying effort is less important. For example, as the United States' relationship with the People's Republic of China became more complex over time, human rights concerns remained part of the U.S. bilateral agenda but were not central to the conversation between the two countries. While human rights groups continue to lobby the executive branch and Congress, focus has diminished in part because other issues are considered more immediate and important. Groups such as AIPAC maintain their importance because there are always issues between the United States and Israel, and because the organization finds a way to always be heard on Capitol Hill. Other groups that work on relations with specific countries, such as the Greek-American community or Armenian Americans, as well as those who focus on human rights and development/refugee issues, will always have a role as well, albeit sometimes more important than others.

Major Issues That Come Up in Foreign Lobbying

Just as there are a number of actors who might get involved in foreign lobbying but three are most often the central focus, of the many issues ripe for international lobbying, most fall into three main categories: economic interests, security, and political issues and causes. Not surprisingly, overlap often occurs across these areas.

It's the Economy

Economic concerns drive governments and companies to try to secure an advantage, be it in the context of a trade agreement, a tax bill, or other legislation. The United States is the largest economy in the world, and having unfettered access to its market is essential for all nations and their economies, large and small. The legislative and regulatory process in the United States is byzantine, which would not matter except the smallest regulation or line in a trade agreement or bill can make a big difference to a nation's economy or a company's bottom line. That is why lobbyists who know their craft politically and substantively can be very valuable, although the best do not come cheap.

Tax and trade are the two primary areas that affect and interest governments and companies. Tax measures can open up markets or close down access to them for both U.S. companies looking to export goods and those abroad looking to bring them to the United States. Tariffs are also considered revenue, and if there is a pledge by, say, the president of the United States, not to raise taxes, then that is an argument that can be made by a lobbyist of a foreign interest. Tax reform for corporate interests can also set a precedent for how other governments will approach international tax issues. The Base Erosion and Profit Shifting (BEPS) project the G20 asked the Organization for Economic Cooperation and Development (OECD) to undertake is an example of this.[6] How the United States handles the issue—whether it embraces it, dismisses it, or somewhere in between—is key to how other governments will respond. Working with the administration, but also with the tax writing committees on Capitol Hill—Ways and Means in the House, and Finance in the Senate—must be part of any exercise of simply gathering information or trying to help shape U.S. position through the legislative process.

More often than not, a foreign government, such as those mentioned above, will hire U.S.-based lobbyists to help craft trade agreements. If it is an FTA, an embassy might hire one team to work Democrats and another to work Republicans. As mentioned, the Colombian government used lobbying firms that had relationships with congressional leadership and key Democratic and Republican offices to gain support for an FTA. The Andean nations did the same for the renewal of the Andean Trade Preference Act (ATPA).[7] It will expect one of the teams—the one whose party is in the White House—to work closely with the administration. It often takes several years to get a trade agreement approved, so a foreign government maintains lobbyists on retainers to sustain the effort until an agreement is passed. As an example, the Colombian FTA took several years to pass, and the government kept Washington, DC lobbying firms involved throughout. The government of El Salvador did the same during the debate over the Central America Free Trade Agreement (CAFTA).[8]

A more complicated endeavor is regional trade agreements, which can involve several governments. The ATPA is a good example of several governments hiring lobbyists to get the Act through Congress and then renewed as individual governments got their own FTAs. As the ATPA countries of Peru and Colombia received their own FTAs, support for a broader regional trade preference agreement lost momentum, since Colombia in particular was a key driver behind the ATPA.

Often in the context of an effort to get a trade agreement passed, embassies will coordinate with U.S.-based companies and trade associations, which play an important role in getting trade agreements passed. Embassy staff, association lobbyists, and lobbyists for different companies work together in their campaign efforts. This multiplier effect helps embassies and others cover more ground. During the debate over CAFTA, there were regular meetings of all the embassies involved to synchronize their lobbying efforts. The same was true with the ATPA, where affected South American nations worked together with business interests to gain support for the agreement. For example, as part of one effort to renew ATPA, the Peruvian Asparagus growers hired lobbyists to ensure their interests were represented.

While Congress is central to lobbying efforts on tax and trade issues, it is essential to engage the administration as well. The White House is at the center, but the Department of Treasury and the United State Trade Representative (USTR), which is part of the Executive Office of the President, are also key players on tax and trade issues, respectively. The Department of State plays a role but is not as pronounced in taxes and trade. A good lobbyist will touch all bases and focus efforts where they are most effective.

The range of international economic issues that the administration and Congress must deal with are numerous and complicated. Over the years, one of these—economic sanctions—has become an important foreign policy tool. For example, the U.S. government's use of sanctions with Iran and Cuba helped shape U.S. relations with those nations. While most would agree that it is better to accept an economic toll than to engage in warfare, this hardly means that sanctions are victim free. Businesses get hurt, and sometimes innocent populations do as well. Lobbyists make the point on behalf of both.

Indeed, foreign lobbying can make for strange bedfellows. For instance, a hypothetical situation could arise in which Quakers (a religious group who counted William Penn, founder of Pennsylvania, as one of their own) and General Electric (GE) join together in a common cause. In this hypothetical, GE could oppose an arms sale to a country on commercial or economic grounds (i.e., their business interests would be harmed), and the Quakers—through the American Friends Service Committee, which is a Quaker organization that focuses on changing a number of policy issues—could oppose it over human rights concerns.

The Department of Treasury's Office of Foreign Asset Control (OFAC) oversees what can or cannot be sold or traded with a sanctioned country. Before the loosening of relations with Cuba, there was often a backup and long delay at OFAC about whether a trip could be taken to Cuba (OFAC controls that kind of access as well) or if a product could be sold to Cuba and under what conditions. Lobbyists who work in this area are often engaged in explaining to clients how OFAC works and whether information can be supplied that would help lead to a favorable decision for a client. We represented a company that produced communication satellites. They wanted to explore doing work with Cuba and asked us to work with the Department of State and OFAC. This was a good example of an education effort. We understood that OFAC would rely on their colleagues at the Department of State to give them a better understanding of the status of U.S.-Cuban relations, even though OFAC was responsible for the final decision of whether to grant a license.

Arms sales is another dimension of foreign lobbying. The administration—mainly the Departments of State and Defense, as well as the White House—and Congress play significant roles in arms sales. These sales are obviously important to the livelihood of U.S. defense contractors. Most of the big defense firms have outside and inside lobbyists to help push sales, including Caterpillar, Proctor and Gamble, Boeing, and Airbus. However, for our purposes here, it is important to note the intersection of foreign and domestic lobbying. Indeed, foreign governments also get involved, sometimes in support of and sometimes against the sales. This is an example of a marriage of political and economic interests. For instance, Saudi Arabia might lobby on behalf of an arms control agreement in which economic interests and political considerations share a common cause. The ATPA, initiated by the George H.W. Bush administration, is an example of corporate interests supporting an agreement that was also seen as a policy tool to help nations of the region with their economies, and to fight illegal drug production.

The example of arms sales to foreign nations is complex. Some members of Congress oppose arms sales on principle, while others oppose sales to specific nations on human rights grounds. Other lawmakers support them for national security reasons or simply because of jobs for the U.S. corporations that are involved. Sometimes an administration will be on the fence as to whether or not a sale should go through in part because of political considerations, and in part because Congress, which has significant leverage over such sales, may oppose it. This single issue encapsulates not only how different elements of the U.S. government can see an issue differently, but how issues in foreign lobbying can become intertwined with others—in this case economics and national security.

Security

U.S. national security, economics, and politics regularly intersect when dealing with international issues. An example was shortly after President Ronald Reagan took office and announced that the United States would sell Airborne Warning and Control System (AWAC) planes—manufactured by Boeing—to Saudi Arabia, a controversial announcement that provoked many different reactions. The administration believed it was in the interest of U.S. regional policy to support the sale. The sale was opposed by many on the Hill, who thought it would give Saudi a political advantage over Israel.[9] Not surprisingly, and for the same reasons, the Israeli government vehemently opposed the sale.[10] At the same time, commercial interests converged in the debate over this issue, with industry pushing it to go through against many in Congress.[11] At the time, this was part of the largest-ever U.S. arms sale, totaling over $2 billion.[12] In the end, the administration prevailed, but this sale and the battle that surrounded it is a good example of how many issues can converge in a single lobbying effort.

The Iran nuclear deal that the Obama administration spearheaded in 2016 is another example of a battle over security concerns. The administration struck a deal it felt was fair and balanced, and lobbied Congress and the American people on behalf of the deal. Congress voted on a resolution of disapproval, which would not have stopped the agreement even if it had passed and a promised presidential veto was overridden.[13] While the White House did not hire lobbyists, it had plenty of its own internal lobbyists from the White House, as well as the Departments of State, Energy, and Defense, working with outside groups to rally support for the agreement.

In terms of foreign lobbying, AIPAC and a bipartisan group of members from both chambers who opposed the agreement worked hard to stop the deal. Millions of dollars (estimates range between $20 and $40 million) in advertisements, forums, and direct lobbying were part of the opposition's effort to kill the deal.[14] The Israeli government aggressively expressed its opposition, and Israeli Prime Minister Netanyahu spoke before Congress against the deal.[15] Republican lawmakers on the Hill were uniformly against it, as were some Democrats.[16] In the end, Congress could not stop it, and the deal went through, despite these aggressive lobbying efforts. A filibuster by Senate Democrats stopped a vote on the agreement, which meant the president did not have to use his veto.[17] All told, the Iran nuclear deal is an excellent example of a security-focused lobbying campaign on both sides of the issue. With the change in administrations, discussions have occurred on whether the Trump administration would try to reopen the Iran agreement—an example of an issue perhaps not being resolved even after it seemed to be.

It is easy to see how these two examples fit into the security basket, but trade agreements, which on their face seem to be much more economic, can have a security dimension as well. For instance, the connection between economics and security was emphasized by the Reagan administration during the debate over the economic trade agreement Caribbean Basin Initiative (CBI). The CBI was part of the effort to stop leftists from taking over Caribbean and Central American governments in the 1980s.[18] However, President Reagan employed the argument that economic development was an essential component for the country's national security by stopping the spread of communism in Central America and the Caribbean.[19]

Similar themes are also seen in a more recent example. Supporters of the Trans Pacific Partnership (TPP) often discuss it not only in economic terms but also as a way for the United States to offset Chinese influence in East Asia. The argument is that economic engagement is a way to make the nations of East Asia and the United States more secure, hedging against Chinese influence. It is unclear at this stage how much of an impact such arguments will have on the passage of TPP, which is much more a matter of economic concerns.

Political Issues and Concerns

While some issues are simply political in nature and do not involve economic or security considerations, for other issues, political, economic, and security considerations overlap. For decades, Congress has been asked to take up a resolution commemorating the Armenian genocide that occurred during World War I. The Turkish government has been unalterably opposed to the resolution, believing the resolution characterizes Turkish involvement in the tragedy. Needless to say, the Armenian community feels very strongly about the resolution and the need for closure of this tragic period. The legislation itself only acknowledges the event. It does not change law or call for policy action. Nonetheless, fierce lobbying has occurred on both sides of the issue. Every administration that has had to address this issue, as well as many in Congress, have been whipsawed between the two parties. The Turkish government has said such legislation would severely damage U.S.-Turkish relations, and some in the Armenian community reply angrily that they cannot support those who cannot support the resolution.

Human rights concerns are another good example of a purely political issue. For instance, there was a strong push during the Soviet era to free Soviet Jews, allowing them to emigrate. Those who were not allowed to leave the Soviet Union were called refuseniks. Legislation was passed— the so-called Jackson-Vanik bill—that prohibited the United States from having a trade agreement with Russia unless they allowed Soviet Jews to leave. Members of Congress were lobbied to take up the cause in general and also the cases of specific refuseniks. Eventually the Soviet Union collapsed and the issue of emigration became less important. Although Jackson-Vanik is no longer an issue with respect to trade relations, the concept of using trade agreements and economic relations as a way to address human rights concerns remains.

Human rights concerns, however, are also an issue that can mix with economic ones. The issue of human rights has often been front and center in any meeting between U.S. and Chinese officials. There has always been a strong push to release political prisoners. This was certainly true during the debate of whether to grant permanent trading relations (formerly known as MFN) with China. As China became more and more powerful economically, these issues had less prominence on the bilateral agenda, much to the chagrin of human rights groups and some members of Congress who lobbied on their behalf. Today, those supporting increased trade with China lobby to have human rights play a less important role in the context of U.S.-China relations.

Some political concerns are prominent for a time, involving lobbying, then fade because circumstances change. The Soviet Jew issue just described is a good example. The collapse of the Soviet Union and the opening up of Russian immigration policy made its effort to help refuseniks obsolete. The National Conference on Soviet Jewry (NCSJ) did, however, shift its focus to human rights rather than immigration. Another was the support for Baltic Freedom Day. Every year for a number of years, Congress considered nonbinding legislation in support of the Baltic States, which had been annexed by the Soviet Union, to declare Baltic Freedom Day. Despite little to no opposition to the legislation, lobbying occurred to get a high number of supporters in order to emphasize the importance of the issue.

Follow the Money

Election campaign fundraising is an important element of what lobbyists do. One side will support another. For example, when a lobbyist and an elected official support a common issue, it only makes sense for them to help one another in raising funds. To be clear, however, this is *not* a case of quid pro quo. If an issue is not sound substantively, no amount of money will carry the day for an elected official. Lobbyists must have good arguments and political support if they want their issue to be taken seriously. Note also that financial contributions are heavily regulated, with individuals permitted to contribute only $2,700 to candidates for the presidency, and U.S. House and Senate and political action committees (PACs) limited to $5,000.

Raising funds for international lobbying can be tricky. It is illegal in the United States for foreign persons, particularly those who work as part of a foreign government, to contribute to a candidate's campaign.[20] But while a president, prime minister, or sultan cannot directly help their preferred candidate, their U.S.-based lobbyists can and are often expected to do so, although they cannot make campaign contributions that are passed to them from foreign nationals.

Members of a foreign or ethnic diaspora, however, can fill the gap with contributions (if they are U.S. citizens), as can companies doing business in a country or on an issue that involves international lobbying. The Clinton administration successfully got the Senate to ratify the Chemical Weapons Convention (CWC),[21] which was opposed by the then-powerful chairman of the Senate Foreign Relations Committee, the late Senator Jesse Helms (R-NC). It did so by enlisting the help of the Chemical Manufacturers Association (CMA), which believed the treaty benefited the commercial interests of their companies. Certain NGOs also may help with political campaigns, although nonprofits cannot.[22] And U.S. citizens can always make contributions within the limits noted above.[23]

Because foreign nations and foreign nationals who follow their issues are not legally allowed to contribute to U.S. candidates, it can be more difficult for a member of Congress on a foreign policy-focused committee to raise money compared to a member on a committee that deals more in domestic issues (the House and Senate Armed Services Committees are exceptions because they work with the defense industry). Human rights groups are an excellent example of this. There is generally not a great deal of campaign money tied to these groups or in support of their issues. Commercial concerns tend to have more money, making it easier for them not only to hire experienced lobbyists but to influence campaigns for Congress. Social justice issues are another example; those who lobby in this area can be effective, but because of resource limitations, it can be harder for them to engage in a broad, sustained lobbying campaign.

Members of congressional committees that focus on these issues can, however, be creative in trying to use their position on the committee to raise campaign funds. In the 1980s, a member of the House Foreign Affairs Committee would send out newsletters to various ethnic communities, sometimes with a picture of himself in traditional garb, in efforts to gain support and raise money. (Note that this individual was also a hard worker and extremely thoughtful about the issues on which he and the committee worked.)

Fundraising surrounding trade and arms sale issues is much easier. With respect to trade issues, the House Ways and Means and Senate Finance Committees play a larger role in both helping to shape trade agreements once removed—fast-track or trade promotion authority procedures in which an agreement cannot be changed by Congress prevent direct involvement—by weighing in with the USTR and the White House. There can also be another opportunity to have an impact on an agreement through legislation that implements the agreement. Companies and others with vested interest in the agreements will use fundraising with members of key committees, as well as others who choose to play a role in the debate over the agreements, to help get their point of view across.

The Armed Services Committees in particular, but also the Senate Foreign Relations and House Foreign Affairs Committees, play a role in whether arms sales go through. Most of the sales are not particularly controversial and do not involve lobbyists, but the bigger and more politically controversial sales, like the AWACs debate during the Reagan administration, will involve lobbyists and fundraising.

Our Experience

There is always a gap between theory and practice. We have attempted to use our experience as a means to provide a framework for the theory of the case of international lobbying. International representation, as we have attempted to point out, is in a separate category both practically and culturally. On the practical side, as we mention, the registration process—FARA—is clearly different. It is a more rigorous and expansive undertaking. It forces you to reveal more about the relationship with the client, and the failure to register holds the threat of something greater than a fine. The LDA has its own rigor, but not to the level of FARA.

On the cultural side, several factors come into play. One is the interaction with the client. This includes everything from fees to expectations as to what the client gets in return for those fees. Sticker shock is not unusual with any client. Determining value for the intangible can be tricky, but with a foreign client it can move from tricky to disbelief. In addition, some governments in particular know they need help, but have a tough time justifying a monthly fee that is considerably larger than what is the norm back home. With many of our foreign clients, we did a lot of back and forth on fees before signing a contract. Tied into those fees were metrics that allowed an embassy, for example, to be able to justify to the government back home that the money being spent was necessary to getting the job done.

Even the richest clients do not always pay. If they feel they have gotten what they needed or want, they might not feel obliged to live up to the terms of the contract. That happened to us, and the cost of trying to force them to fulfill their obligation was not worth it. There is always that risk. Another cultural issue is understanding on the part of a client as to what you can and can't do for them. For example, a client we were helping with a trade agreement had an expectation that we would also assist with negotiations. We weren't set up to do that, so we had to explain regularly that we were there to help with the politics, not textile quotas.

There is also a cultural undercurrent domestically. If your firm has mainly foreign clients, you are sometimes viewed on K Street and elsewhere with a jaundiced eye. There can be a slight stigma—whose side are you on, the United States' or theirs? The very term "foreign agent" does not have the cache of "secret agent." It is more mercenary. To the uninitiated, it might seem that you are working against U.S. interests. That is not the case. FARA registration helps guarantee that, but the stigma can still be there. In fact, we helped a client put controls in place on their exports that were very helpful to the U.S. government. Often, lobbyists representing foreign firms can act as go-betweens with the U.S. government and its foreign counterpart. Such interaction is always informal and never takes the place of real diplomacy, but it can, on the margins, be helpful.

Conclusion

International lobbying, the practice of lobbying on behalf of international interests and issues, has similarities to traditional domestic lobbying. It is different in that it is governed not only by the LDA, but also by FARA, which requires lobbyists to register as foreign agents and face criminal penalties if they do not comply. It is also different in that foreign governments are often involved in the process, sometimes directly as diplomats and sometimes indirectly by hiring lobbyists. Even the smallest of governments have concerns and issues that make them more complicated clients than even the biggest of corporations. They also have direct access to the executive branch of government via the Department of State.

Many of those who lobby on international issues have a unique background. They might be more apolitical, having spent much of their careers ignoring domestic U.S. politics, focusing on U.S. foreign policy and the politics of a particular country or region. Their area of expertise is often not the same of those who lobby on domestic issues. Some of the committees involved are also not the typical committees being lobbied by those who focus on domestic policy.

International lobbying covers three general areas: economics, security, and political issues. And, generally speaking, three groups lobby in the international space: governments; businesses, both domestic and international; and NGOs. While each group and issue has unique characteristics, more often than not in the world of lobbying, they do not stand alone. They connect, form alliances, and work together in support of or in opposition to an issue.

International lobbying is similar to domestic lobbying in that it is about getting the facts to the right policymakers on Capitol Hill or in the executive branch at the right time and in the right context. As is true of domestic lobbying, international lobbying requires developing message-tested arguments and building coalitions with like-minded national interests, think tanks, and citizens. It is likely to also include communications outreach efforts. This is done in all major lobbying campaigns in an attempt to earn supportive or at least fair media coverage. Sometimes it is necessary to ensure precise control of your message. This is commonly accomplished via paid advertising in print, broadcast, and other social media platforms.

As suggested, many of the tools all lobbyists use are also used in working international issues. Even those Russian illegals who may have thought they were international spies found themselves as no more than simple advocates on behalf of their country, subject to the same laws as those who are law abiding and above board, as they advocate for a particular issue or government.

Notes

1. Foreign Agent Registration Act, United States Department of Justice, accessed August 17, 2017, https://www.fara.gov

2. For a discussion of FARA, see *The Lobbying Manual: A Compliance Guide for Lawyer and Lobbyists* (ABA, 2015).

3. "Lobbyist Disclosure Act Guidance," Office of the Clerk, U.S. House of Representatives, http://lobbyingdisclosure.house.gov/amended_lda_guide.html (accessed August 17, 2017).

4. "Turkey Condemns 'Armenian Genocide' Resolution in U.S. Senate," *Reuters*, April 11, 2014, http://www.reuters.com/article/us-turkey-usa-armenia-id USBREA3A10V20140411 (accessed August 17, 2017).

5. See David M. Paul and Rachel Anderson Paul, *Ethnic Lobbies and U.S. Foreign Policy* (Lynne Rienner Publishers, 2009).

6. "Base Erosion and Profit Shifting," OECD, http://www.oecd.org/tax/beps (accessed August 17, 2017).

7. "Andean Trade Preference Act (ATPA)—Expiration of duty-free treatment," U.S. Customs and Border Protection, Department of Homeland Security, https://help.cbp.gov/app/answers/detail/a_id/325/~/andean-trade-preference-act-(atpa) ---expiration-of-duty-free-treatment (accessed August 17, 2017).

8. CAFTA-DR (Dominican Republic-Central America FTA), Office of the United States Trade Representative, https://ustr.gov/trade-agreements/free-trade-agreements/cafta-dr-dominican-republic-central-america-fta (accessed August 17, 2017).

9. Charles Mohr, "Regan Letter to Congress Chiefs Reaffirms Sale of AWACS to Saudis," *New York Times*, August 5, 1981, http://www.nytimes.com/1981/08/06/world/reagan-letter-to-congress-chiefs-reaffirms-sale-of-awacs-to-saudis.html (accessed August 17, 2017).

10. *CQ Almanac*, https://library.cqpress.com/cqalmanac/document.php?id=cqal81-1171966 (accessed August 17, 2017).

11. *Washington Post*, "Don't Make the AWACS Sale a Test of Strength," October 6, 1981, https://www.washingtonpost.com/archive/politics/1981/10/06/dont-make-the-awacs-sale-a-test-of-strength/5d310a2a-1bce-431a-876d-9689b510d679 (accessed August 17, 2017).

12. Charles Mohr, "Reagan Letter to Congress Chiefs Reaffirms Sale of AWACS to Saudis," *New York Times*, August 6, 1981, http://www.nytimes.com/1981/08/06/world/reagan-letter-to-congress-chiefs-reaffirms-sale-of-awacs-to-saudis.html (accessed August 17, 2017).

13. David M. Herszenhorn, "The Iran Nuclear Deal: Congress Has Its Say," *New York Times*, September 7, 2015, http://www.nytimes.com/2015/09/08/us/politics/the-iran-nuclear-deal-congress-has-its-say.html?_r=0 (accessed August 17, 2017).

14. Alisa Chang, "Lobbyists Spending Millions to Sway the Undecided on Iran Deal," National Public Radio, August 6, 2015, http://www.npr.org/sections/itsallpolitics/2015/08/06/429911872/in-iran-deal-fight-lobbyists-are-spending-millions-to-sway-12-senators (accessed August 17, 2017).

15. Peter Baker, "In Congress, Netanyahu Faults 'Bad Deal' on Iran Nuclear Program," *New York Times*, March 3, 2015, http://www.nytimes.com/2015/03/04/

world/middleeast/netanyahu-congress-iran-israel-speech.html (accessed August 17, 2017).

16. Alicia Parlapiano, "Lawmakers Against the Iran Nuclear Deal," *New York Times*, September 19, 2015, http://www.nytimes.com/interactive/2015/09/09/us/politics/lawmakers-against-iran-nuclear-deal.html (accessed August 17, 2017).

17. "The Final Tally: How Congress Voted on Iran," United States Institute of Peace, September 17, 2015, http://iranprimer.usip.org/blog/2015/sep/11/congress-votes-deal (accessed August 17, 2017).

18. "Reagan Announces Caribbean Basin Initiate," History Channel, http://www.history.com/this-day-in-history/reagan-announces-caribbean-basin-initiative (accessed August 17, 2017).

19. Office of the United States Trade Representative, https://ustr.gov/tpp (accessed August 17, 2017).

20. "Foreign Nationals," Fedcral Election Commission, http://www.fec.gov/pages/brochures/foreign.shtml (accessed August 17, 2017).

21. United States Chemical Convention Weapons, Bureau of Industry and Security, http://www.cwc.gov (accessed August 17, 2017).

22. "The Restriction of Political Campaign Intervention of Section 501(c)(3) Tax Exempt Organizations," Internal Revenue Service, https://www.irs.gov/charities-non-profits/charitable-organizations/the-restriction-of-political-campaign-intervention-by-section-501-c-3-tax-exempt-organizations (accessed August 17, 2017).

23. Federal Elections Commission, http://www.fec.gov/info/contriblimits chart1516.pdf (accessed August 17, 2017).

Chapter 4

Jewish-American Foreign Policy Lobbies

Kirk J. Beattie

In this chapter, the focus moves to Jewish-American organizations lobbying Congress on Middle East and North African (MENA) affairs, all of which exhibit special concern for the welfare of Israel. Whether considered in terms of membership or staff sizes, financial assets, or access to members of Congress and congressional clout, one finds a vast array of Jewish-American foreign policy lobbies. And as is widely acknowledged, the preeminent organizations in this category have long served as veritable pioneers and role models for all ethnic lobby shops on how to effectively influence members of Congress.

Before narrowing the focus of this study on Jewish-American foreign policy lobbying organizations, it is essential to note that these groups have worked in a highly propitious environment. A host of factors have created a strong bond between most American political figures and Israel: shared, political democratic values; a range of deeply held Jewish and Christian religious beliefs, fostering great spiritual attachments to Israel; potent, negative reactions to anti-Semitism and the Holocaust; opposition to and cooperation against the former Soviet Union; and longstanding perceptions of Israel as a geo-strategic asset in a critical (oil- and gas-rich) region of the world. Prominent scholars long ago lent support for the United States' "special relationship" with Israel as well. For example, A.F.K. Organski advanced arguments highlighting U.S.-Israeli cooperation in the struggle against communism.[1] In more recent times, many have come to see the countries as partners in the fight against Islamist extremism—that is, as allies in the "clash of civilizations" predicted by Samuel P. Huntington.[2]

For many decades there has been a strong domestic political factor at work in this issue area, with U.S.-based Jewish-American organizations significantly influencing U.S. debate and decision making with regard to Israel. Several individuals from political and scholarly backgrounds have engaged in lengthy research and analysis of those organizations. Major studies have been presented by former Representative Paul Findley (R-IL), *They Dare to Speak Out* (1985), Edward Tivnan, *The Lobby* (1987), Richard H. Curtiss, *Stealth PACs: Lobbying Congress for Control of U.S. Middle East Policy* (1996), J.J. Goldberg, *Jewish Power: Inside the Jewish American Establishment* (1996), John J. Mearsheimer and Stephen M. Walt, *The Israel Lobby* (2007), Dan Fleshler, *Transforming America's Israel Lobby* (2009), Grant F. Smith, *Big Israel: How the Israel Lobby Moves America* (2016) and some of my own work, *Congress and the Shaping of the Middle East* (2015).

In my prior work, I offer insights and arguments for how and why Congress is broken, why the decision-making process is so deeply flawed, and why legislators have behaved the way they do on Middle East matters. I presented eleven different avenues of influence or pressure points utilized by "special interest" groups to influence Congress. For the purpose of this chapter, I believe these eleven points can be consolidated into seven, and that they will provide a useful backbone to analyze how American Jewish lobbies have generated staunch support for Israel among most members of Congress. I will begin, however, with a brief discussion of this chapter's ethnic group, Jewish Americans, as well as the most active lobbying organizations that have emerged from it.

Constituency Size and Breadth, and Relations with the Homeland

The Jewish-American community is small. Best estimates of its size range between 1.7 to 2.1 percent of the total American population, meaning that if one takes the 2016 estimate of 322 million Americans, there are somewhere between 5.5 to 6.8 million Jewish Americans. A 2013 survey estimated the *adult* Jewish-American population at 4.7 million.[3] Like most Americans, members of the Jewish community are much more concerned about the economy, health care, taxes, immigration, and the environment than with Middle East matters and Israel.[4] With regard to U.S. politics, most American Jews have held liberal values and supported the Democratic Party. President Barack Obama won 78 percent of the 2008 Jewish vote, and 69 percent in 2012, at a time when his popularity in Israel was in single digits. In the 2016 presidential election, Hillary Clinton garnered 71 percent of Jewish-American votes, compared to 24 percent for Trump.

According to one report, "only 4–4.5 percent of voting American Jews considered Israel the most important issue for them in 2012. Another report put the figure at 10 percent."[5]

For those Jewish Americans bemoaning the diminution of Jewish identity, as well as any potential, concomitant weakening in a U.S. commitment to Israel, a major nemesis is a sociocultural aspect of America most commonly touted as one of its greatest virtues: the iconic, American "melting pot." A Pew Research Center survey, conducted in the first half of 2013, found that since 2000 some 60 percent of American Jews had married non-Jews; and that the rate of intermarriage had risen to over 80 percent among children of intermarried couples.[6] Disturbed by this change, Elliott Abrams, the well-known neoconservative, observed:

> . . . Pew found that persons of "Jewish background"—mainly, those with only one Jewish parent—express significantly lower levels of support for Israel than do "Jews by religion." Of the former, fully 41 percent report being "not too" or "not at all" emotionally attached to Israel, and only 13 percent have ever traveled there. . . . Intermarriage is of course not the only way to distinguish levels of communal solidarity; religion itself is another. Half of those who identify themselves as Jews by religion say that "caring about Israel" is "essential" to what it means to them to be Jewish, while only 23 percent of those identifying themselves as non-practitioners believe that to be so in their case. And age is another factor: Jews sixty-five and older are far more likely to say caring about Israel is essential than those who are under thirty.[7]

Thus, for many decades, commitment to Israel by U.S. Jews has been steadily declining, and this has occurred despite significant investments in programs like Birthright Israel by U.S. and non-U.S. Jews who share Elliott Abrams's concern. That this decline is strongest among young Jewish Americans is particularly frustrating to staunch supporters of Israel's right-wing governments, like Abrams, because they fear it bodes ill for long-term U.S.-Israel relations. That decline, in turn, has engendered debate over its precise cause(s). As Abrams has opined:

> [Dov] Waxman thinks it is because the young are offended by "the occupation" and the policies of a Likud government, and [Michael] Barnett does not differ very much from that

conclusion. A deeper analysis suggests that we are dealing here with a far broader phenomenon, and one in which sheer indifference may count as much as or more than critical disagreement with Israeli policies or an active desire to disembarrass oneself of association with an "ethnonational" state.[8]

However one explains the causes of the decline, the shift is real, and it does potentially pose serious problems for staunch pro-Israel forces.

Identifying the Jewish-American Foreign Policy Lobbyists and Their Supporters

In contrast with the broader Jewish-American community's sentiments, nearly all leaders and members of Jewish-American foreign policy organizations profess a deep attachment to the state of Israel. For most—but far from all—of these organizations' members, this has meant supporting the Israeli government in power, regardless of its foreign policy orientation and whether any given government is more or less willing to compromise to advance the peace process with the Palestinians and other regional actors.

It is impossible to specify an exact number of Jewish-American lobbies, as organizations appear and disappear, or change names. Fleisch and Sasson counted as many as 774 organizations raising funds in the United States for Israel in 2007, not all of which, but nearly so, would have been predominantly Jewish American in terms of membership.[9] Following a different methodology, Grant F. Smith tracked 336 "Israeli Affinity Organizations" (IAOs) from that same year and beyond, nearly all of which had predominantly Jewish-American leaders and memberships.[10] Smith's population of 336 groups includes the largest organizations reviewed by the [Fleisch and Sasson] Brandeis study, as well as "the advocacy and education organizations left out of the Brandeis study and the federation fundraising IAOs that power much of the Israel lobby 'ecosystem.' "[11] All 336 of these organizations contribute to the mobilization of human and material resources intended, in principle, to support Israel; and only two of them—the International Fellowship of Christians and Jews, and Christians United for Israel—were *not* predominantly Jewish American targeting non-Jewish American audiences to become donors and/or members.[12]

Smith makes it absolutely clear that in limiting his focus to these IAOs, he was setting aside further investigation of three other important parts of the Israel lobby puzzle: (1) unquestioningly pro-Israel (or what Smith labels as "captured") divisions of government agencies; some think tanks; the news media; (2) churches and synagogues actively supporting Israel; and (3) "dark money;" individual and bundled campaign contributions; and PACs.[13] While Smith also notes that "[n]ot all IAOs lobby,"[14] it is clear that most are involved in lobbying efforts. Therefore, all parts of Smith's puzzle included, the number of overwhelmingly Jewish-American organizations contributing to lobbying on behalf of Israel would run into the high hundreds.

In his 2009 book, Dan Fleshler presents an excellent chart in which he classifies seventy-four Jewish-American, Israel-focused lobbying organizations into six ideological camps: six "Far Left or Religious Anti-Zionist" groups, sixteen "Pro-Israel Left" groups, eleven "Center Left" groups, twenty-two "Center" groups, five "Center Right" groups, and fourteen "Far Right" groups (see table 4.1 on page 70).[15] What it means to be "pro-Israel" is in the eyes of individual participants, of course, as shall be discussed. But on balance, the overwhelming majority of Smith's 334 and Fleshler's 74 Jewish-American organizations have continued to assist Israel regardless of changes in the domestic and foreign policy orientations of Israel's leaders over time, thereby helping to sustain an overall positive image and support system for Israeli governments in the American body politic. Fleshler's figure is close to the figure of sixty estimated by Jeffrey Blankfort, a longtime observer of this issue area.[16] As one can readily deduce, all of the aforementioned numbers are impressive in light of the Jewish-American community's small size, and when compared to other ethnic groups' efforts. In addition, as will be shown below, the amount of money raised and expended on congressional lobbying by the Jewish-American organizations by far surpasses that of other ethnic lobbies.

It is important to note that not all of the Smith's 334 groups, or even Fleshler's 74 groups, are identified as powerful players at the national level, and more specifically, in Congress. In my own lengthy study,[17] I adopted an approach according to which I entreated people on Capitol Hill to tell me which lobbying groups were of significance in MENA policymaking. For much of 2005 and 2006, and for roughly two months in the springs of 2011, 2012, and 2013, I conducted over two hundred interviews, most of which were with House and Senate staffers. Interviews on the House side—120 different House staffers—were drawn from a random sample of House members. On the Senate side, I entered every Senate office and despite limited time and resources interviewed over thirty Senate staffers. During my study's time frame, staffers noted twenty-six groups as having some degree of regular participation in deliberations over major MENA issues. Of those twenty-six groups, sixteen were predominantly Jewish-American lobbies. In the spring of 2016, I was able to once again consult

Table 4.1. American Jewish Community Lobby Groups

Far Left or Religious Anti-Zionist	Pro-Israel Left	Center Left	Center	Center Right	Far Right
Israel Committee Against House Demolitions (USA)	Ameinu*	Association of Reform Zionists*	America-Israel Friendship League*	AIPAC*	Agudath Israel
Jewish Voices for Peace	Americans for Peace Now*	Central Conference of American Rabbis*	American Gathering of Jewish Holocaust Survivors and Their Descendants*	AMIT Women*	Americans for a Safe Israel
Jews Against the Occupation	Brit Tzedek v'Shalom	NAAMAT*	American Jewish Committee	Friends of Israel Defense Forces*	American Friends of Likud*
Jews for Justice in Palestine	Israel Policy Forum	Religious Action Center*	American Jewish Congress*	Jewish National Fund*	Committee for Accuracy in Middle East Reporting in America*
Neturei	J Street Project	Union of Reform Judaism*	American Jewish Joint Distribution Committee*	Republican Jewish Coalition	EMUNAH of America*
Satmar Hasidim	Jewish Labor Committee*	Women of Reform Judaism*	American Sephardi Federation*		Jewish Institute for National Security Affairs*

Jewish Peace Lobby	———	American Zionist Movement*	National Council of Synagogue Youth
Jewish Reconstructionist Federation	MERCAZ USA*	Anti-Defamation League*	National Council of Young Israel*
Meretz USA	Rabbinical Assembly*	B'nai B'rith*	One Israel Fund
New Israel Fund	United Synagogue Congress of Conservative Judaism*	B'nai Zion	Rabbinic Alliance of America
Progressive Zionist Alliance	WIZO	Development Corporation for Israel*	Rabbinic Alliance to Save Jerusalem
Rabbis for Human Rights	Women's League for Conservative Judaism*	Hadassah*	Rabbinical Council of America
Shalom Center		Hebrew Immigrant Aid Society*	Union of Orthodox Jew Congregation of America*
Tikkun Movement		Jewish Community Centers Association*	Zionist Organization of America

continued on next page

Table 4.1. Continued.

Far Left or Religious Anti-Zionist	Pro-Israel Left	Center Left	Center	Center Right	Far Right
	Union of Progressive Zionists		Jewish Council for Public Affairs*		
	Workmen's Circle*		Jewish War Veterans*		
			Jewish Women International*		
			National Council of Jewish Women*		
			National Conference on Soviet Jewry*		
			National Jewish Democratic Council		
			ORT America*		
			United Jewish Communities*		

Source: Adapted from Dan Fleshler, Transforming America's Israel Lobby (Washington, DC: Potomac Books, Inc., 2009), 62–63.
Note: The asterisk means the group is a member of the Conference of Presidents of Major American Jewish Organizations, the most well-known and important American Jewish umbrella group. Along with AIPAC, it is one of the twin pillars of the conventional Israel lobby. The Presidents Conference is sui generic, so it is not listed as a separate organization here, and I will discuss it later in the chapter (Fleshler, 2009, 63).

with Hill staffers and Washington, DC *aficionado* on how, if at all, the nature of the game had changed, and if there were any new groups, such as A Jewish Voice for Peace, Inc. (JVP), that had gained traction, and these findings are discussed below.

Among all organizations lobbying on MENA issues, for many decades, one has stood head and shoulders—or perhaps more accurately from the shins up—above all the others. That group is the American Israel Public Affairs Committee, or as it is most commonly called, AIPAC. With an annual operating budget of roughly $70 million, a membership base of over 100,000 nationwide, and well over two hundred Washington, DC, staffers, AIPAC quite simply dwarfs all of its competitors. Other groups noted frequently by congressional staffers in 2005 and 2006 included, in descending order, the left-wing, pro-peace Americans for Peace Now (APN), the harder right-wing Zionist Organization for America (ZOA), the dovish Israel Policy Forum (IPF), the mainstream, staunchly loyal American Jewish Committee (AJC), the strongly pro-peace Brit Tzedek v'Shalom, the somewhat more right-wing than AIPAC, NORPAC, and the AJC-like, mainstream standard bearers, B'nai B'rith, the Anti-Defamation League, and Hadassah.[18] By the early 2000s, another pro–two state solution group, J Street, had made a strong entry into the fray. And by 2016, an even more aggressively pro-peace, heavily grassroots organization, A Jewish Voice for Peace, was making significant strides, albeit more at the state, not national, level. Meanwhile, JVP and its allies were being countered across the country at the local and state levels, primarily by the Jewish Community Relations Councils. JCRCs—there are roughly 125 chapters in the United States—have been in existence for many decades. Some were set up in the 1940s or 1950s. As was true of JVP, not a single staffer or off-the-Hill interviewee spoke of JCRCs, but as noted below, both had entered the Washington, DC, political fray by the mid-2010s.

So what has AIPAC done to earn itself longstanding recognition as the second most powerful lobby in the country, perhaps bested only by the American Association for Retired Persons (AARP)? And how have other noteworthy Jewish-American lobbies exercised their own influence on the Hill?

Pressure Point Number 1: Influencing the Electoral Process

For nearly all members of Congress, survival in office constitutes one of their principal motivational factors.[19] Few lawmakers' behavior is not motivated by such thinking. To become a player in Congress, to get elected and re-elected, nearly all members need money, and lots of it. Indeed, incumbents seeking re-election in the 2014 election cycle raised, on average, over $1.5 million in House races and $12 million in Senate contests.[20]

This need for campaign cash opens the door widely to "special interests." Additionally, party leaders seek to retain or regain majority control; as such, they are often motivated to instruct fellow party members to behave in a manner that maximizes support from major donors. As an example, lawmakers owe dues to their party's campaign arm each electoral cycle. Party leadership sets different targets for different members based on various factors, including seniority, committee assignments, fundraising ability, and re-election needs. Candidates must remain attentive to their constituents' wishes, but they also know that money is a necessary way of life to succeed on Capitol Hill and win re-election. Most resources emanate from a range of special interest groups and individual political donors. On some issues, these special interests are diverse and dissonant, but in others this is not the case, and large doses of campaign funds are largely unmatched by countervailing funding.

Take the example of congressional inaction on gun reform legislation. Campaign contributions alone do not explain this inaction, of course, but they do make a difference. From 1998 to 2016, gun rights advocates, individuals and PACs, averaged slightly more than $2 million in campaign contributions during each election cycle, although never surpassing $4.5 million.[21] Meanwhile, campaign contributions by gun reform advocates were negligible. Similarly, from 1990 to 2016, campaign contributions by individuals and PACs advocating pro-life and pro-choice positions, combined, never exceeded $1.4 million.[22]

These PACs' activity provides some context for those PACs working to advance a "pro-Israel" agenda. During this same time frame, campaign contributions of a "pro-Israel" nature consistently ranked in the middle of the top eighty U.S. "industries" providing campaign finance.[23] In terms of dollars raised and spent, these PACs never raised less than $2 million and reached a high mark of over $15 million in 2012 (see table 4.2). Over time, pro-Israel PACs have come to rely more on contributions from individuals rather than other PACs. In addition, Democratic candidates typically received more of the pro-Israel PAC money over this time period.

Jewish-American groups and individuals play the campaign contribution game in a variety of ways. As both a 501(c)(3) organization and a registered lobbying outfit, AIPAC is barred from financing political campaigns. It circumvents this restriction by holding major events across the country to which incumbent officeholders seeking re-election and their challengers are invited, often to deliver speeches on Middle East matters, with potential donors in attendance. As one House member commented,

Table 4.2. Pro-Israel PAC Activity, 1990–2016

Election Cycle	Total Raised	Contributions from Individuals	Contributions from other PACs	Donations to Democratic Candidates	Donations to Republican Candidates	Percentage of All Donations Going to Democrats	Percentage of All Donations Going to Republicans
1990	$4,268,724	$182,714	$4,086,010	$2,909,120	$1,359,604	68%	32%
1992	$4,946,730	$868,750	$4,048,960	$3,432,768	$1,513,171	69%	31%
1994	$2,664,959	$68,900	$2,386,059	$2,009,447	$654,512	75%	25%
1996	$5,469,229	$3,072,074	$2,386,880	$3,473,380	$1,995,599	64%	36%
1998	$5,629,623	$3,404,542	$2,104,331	$3,650,188	$1,979,435	65%	35%
2000	$6,103,662	$4,153,208	$1,950,454	$3,968,023	$2,132,639	65%	35%
2002	$7,192,477	$4,246,476	$2,946,001	$4,787,701	$2,401,776	67%	33%
2004	$10,987,364	$7,599,926	$3,387,438	$6,928,521	$4,056,343	63%	37%
2006	$11,027,544	$7,851,453	$3,176,091	$5,292,427	$4,450,777	48%	40%
2008	$15,018,871	$11,624,592	$3,394,279	$9,013,251	$6,002,620	60%	40%
2010	$13,300,375	$9,962,395	$3,186,980	$8,304,884	$4,657,076	63%	35%
2012	$15,102,201	$12,107,335	$2,970,989	$8,967,352	$6,056,472	59%	40%
2014	$12,163,155	$9,221,275	$2,941,380	$6,887,423	$5,251,432	57%	43%
2016	$10,834,947	$8,732,153	$2,102,794	$5,921,293	$4,908,654	55%	45%
Total	$124,709,861	$83,095,793	$41,068,646	$75,545,778	$47,420,110	61%	38%

Source: Center for Responsive Politics, "Pro-Israel Long-term Contribution Trends," http://www.opensecrets.org/industries/totals.php?cycle=2016 &ind=Q05 (accessed September 25, 2016).

"This is how AIPAC plays the game." And as many staffer interviewees noted, AIPAC's influence is so powerful in this regard that to ignore it would be "like the kiss of death" to their bosses.

Meanwhile, there is a long list of PACs, long ago identified and labeled "stealth PACs."[24] Spread across the country, bearing names like The Desert Caucus or The Sunshine PAC, these PACs have been responsible for raising millions of dollars in each election cycle over the preceding decades, and it is generally accepted that many of them respond strongly to AIPAC directives.[25]

J Street, by contrast, has created its own JStreetPac, which provides direct campaign contributions to its preferred candidates. J Street entered the fray as an alternative to AIPAC, with a putatively stronger push for a two-state solution to the Israel-Palestine (I-P) conflict. It has made some progress in recruiting a few high-profile senators to its cause, such as Senators Richard Durbin (D-IL) and Dianne Feinstein (D-CA). Many staff interviewed indicate that J Street's appearance was well received by many on the Hill because it afforded members of Congress greater breathing room in their decision making. Of course, not all of JStreetPac's campaign finance recipients have behaved as hoped. As one J Street staffer noted, "Sometimes we have to go remind them that we're not giving them this money for nothing in return."[26]

Finally, single actors can have a huge impact. Sheldon Adelson, who caught nearly everyone's attention by his massive 2012 presidential campaign contributions, also made his mark by donating directly and indirectly to congressional candidates. But Adelson is not alone. To offer just one recent example, in the hard-fought 2016 Maryland Senate Democratic primary, a showdown between Representatives Chris Van Hollen and Donna Edwards (who has been identified as someone more critical of the current Israeli government's policies with respect to the Palestinians), Hollywood mogul Haim Saban—long-time powerful backer of Hillary Clinton—weighed in with a $100,000 donation to Van Hollen's Super PAC to help him win that battle.[27]

Special interests, often representing an extremely small fraction of the overall electorate, heavily affect the electoral process. They make their presence felt early on, vetting candidates through the use of questionnaires and calls for position papers, winnowing out candidates deemed undesirable by providing strong material support for their opponents, and of course threatening to make available or withhold campaign finance donations. The most effective "special interests" also provide opportunities to sensitize prospective and actual candidates to their concerns. They offer free trips to Israel, as noted below, provide informational materials, and mobilize constituents and professional lobbyists to introduce candidates to their point of view.

Pressure Point Number 2: Incumbents' Concerns about Re-election, the Permanent Campaign

Once elected, members of Congress, almost to a person, behave as though the next electoral cycle has begun anew. They spend great chunks of time "dialing for dollars" or meeting possible donors. They have less time to enhance their knowledge of the issues before Congress, and they tend to "fall back on the politics of the issues," as former Representative David R. Obey (D-WI) says.[28] In other words, they are on guard to behave in a manner that will sustain the support or minimize the opposition of powerful special interests in the next election. Members of Congress also know this means paying heed to the special interest–motivated concerns of party leaders, among whom are Super PAC–endowed figures who can offer campaign finance support of their own.

In the area of Middle East policy, the most successful group, AIPAC, keeps very close tabs on congresspersons' behavior. Reluctance to sign on to "Dear Colleague" letters, or support AIPAC-designed resolutions, begets queries by AIPAC-activated constituents to Capitol Hill offices; and votes on critical Middle East issues have come to be explicitly labeled by members of Congress as "AIPAC votes." While not all members are cowed by this scrutiny, most on both sides of the Hill are heavily sensitized and, according to those staffers interviewed, end up feeling it is simply "not worth the risk" to earn AIPAC's displeasure.

Pressure Point Number 3: Orientation Socialization

Newly elected members soon receive visits from lobbyists, replete with new offers of educational trips, professional support, and advice. The most successful lobbyists are seemingly omnipresent, and identifiably powerful lobbyists are ignored at one's peril, as new congresspersons and their staffers learn very quickly. As indicated in many interviews, even staffers who had been on the job for just a few days had already been contacted and/or visited by an AIPAC representative, a degree of "coverage" that is nearly impossible to match by AIPAC's cash-strapped competitors.

High percentages of freshmen members of Congress are entreated to sign up for trips to Israel, often even feeling pressured by more senior party members to accept the invitations, despite the impact this is likely to have on their already demanding schedules. Although numerous organizations now offer such trips, the AIPAC-affiliated American Israel Education Fund (AIEF) has done so on a far grander scale than any other organization. All told, it is not at all off target to speculate that more members of Congress have visited Israel than any other single country, including Canada and Mexico. Firsthand observation of Israel's small size is thought to heighten concerns for its safety by reinforcing visitors' perceptions of it existing in a larger, hostile environment.

Pressure Point Number 4: Time-Constrained Staffers' Dependence on Key Lobbyists' Inputs

Equally if not more importantly, the same heavy time constraints heighten congressional staffers' direct reliance upon off-the-Hill "special interest" groups and lobbyists. Often very young, staffers are placed in charge of large legislative portfolios. It is not uncommon, for instance, for a House staff aide to be responsible for a range of issues, covering foreign policy, defense, intelligence, veterans' affairs, homeland security, immigration, taxes, the environment, health care, and more. Additionally, staffers are deluged with new stacks of mail, and a veritable whiteout of emails from lobbyists and concerned constituents, on a daily basis. Very often, the allure of greater compensation and more regular hours pulls staffers away from the Hill in a very short time. In short, anyone returning to the same House member's office within two years is unlikely to find the same staffer still occupying the position of responsibility for the foreign policy portfolio.

Conditions on the Senate side differ, but only by a degree. The staffers are typically a number of years older than their House counterparts, and on average bring with them greater experience on Capitol Hill and stronger academic credentials, and they usually have only half as many portfolios for which they are responsible. But that said, they too are constantly on the run, extremely hard pressed to complete the tasks assigned them, and also tempted by the "bigger bucks" offered by K Street lobbyists.

In short, for most staffers, especially those on the House side, there is too little time to read, to learn, and to exercise due diligence in processing issues. So, what happens? Although staffers can and do have recourse to other sources of information, "special interest" groups serve the staffers what appear to be excellent talking points on a silver platter. And remember, some "special interest" groups, such as AIPAC, can be ignored only at one's own peril. So many staffers are more than happy to ingest these free offerings, or what Hall and Deardorff have described as lobbyists' "legislative subsidies,"[29] and move on to another task. As a bright House staffer, heavily involved in MENA issues, recalled in the summer of 2013:

Most staffers here, they don't know anything about these issues. It's not their fault. Unless you've gone out of your way to study this, then you take what you've been acculturated to know and you know nothing about the other side. You know little to nothing about the human rights violations, the wrongs and injustices committed against the Palestinians. So if you are an early 20's something person from so many parts of the country, no matter whether you're a liberal, conservative, moderate, whatever, why in the hell are you gonna go out of your way to tell your boss to take a stand that will put him in a real minority position. You'd have to have knowledge, or a Palestinian friend, or to have experienced something to enlighten you. And even then, it would potentially be like shooting yourself in the foot. Why in the hell would you create trouble for yourself? In other words, even if you know what's right, but your boss doesn't, you'd be taking a risk, . . . you don't want to jeopardize your own job. . . . So when you ask me where do staffers get their information from—is it from CRS [Congressional Research Services]? The answer is, for the most part, not even from CRS; it's just what AIPAC wants. That's all that really matters. The staffers know AIPAC is the pro-Israel lobby. They're the safest bet.[30]

Pressure Point Number 5: Staffer Dependence on Key Committee Members

Congressional committees frequently attract memberships that reflect perceptions of their power and value. Membership on the most powerful "A" committees is sought by nearly all members of Congress. Committees of lesser "value" to many members nonetheless attract a smaller subset of legislators because of their personal interest in the issue area, or because of heightened interest in the issue area by their constituents.[31] In consequence, the structure of most committees, the nature of committee member selection, and the system of committee tenure, leave open the possibility for committees' and subcommittees' domination by members motivated by strong personal interests, or in the thrall of constituent interests and/ or special interest groups. Individual members of Congress do not have to recuse themselves in the name of the national interest.

As regards foreign policy, key committees primarily include Senate Foreign Relations, House Foreign Affairs, and Senate and House Appropriations. The committees dealing with foreign affairs *per se* are *not* considered "A" or "exclusive" committees because there is no money for constituents or others involved; the Appropriations committees are seen as "A" or "exclusive" committees precisely because money is in play. As one staffer after the next suggests, "The members on the Appropriations committees and their staffers, they live in rarefied air. Appropriations work, it's where 'the rubber meets the road.'"[32]

Both foreign affairs committees have subcommittees with a regional focus, and the Appropriations Committees have subcommittees dealing with Foreign Operations (or Foreign Ops). Assignment to the full committee or subcommittees' positions of chairperson or ranking member is undertaken by party leadership with the knowledge that key special interests are look-ing on because committee leaders determine committees' agendas and the calling of expert witnesses for briefings and hearings. It bears repeating that members do not have to recuse themselves. Individuals with strong, personal and/or constituent-induced sentiments sit on Appropriations or Foreign Affairs, acquiring additional clout through their lengthy tenure and seniority on those committees, and utilizing these attributes to make the committees' agendas match their own agendas. Besides agenda-setting, they hire committee staff, and solicit testimony for committee briefings and hearings by experts from their preferred think tanks, academics, and others. For example, many staffers interviewed noted that for briefings and hearings, they go to the same Washington, DC–based experts time and again, many of whom are from think tanks such as the AIPAC-affiliated Washington Institute for Near East Policy, or the Jewish Institute for National Security Affairs. In consequence, full and subcommittee mem-bers are more likely to hear the arguments of powerful special interests than be exposed to a broader range of viewpoints. Conducting committee business in a manner designed to create genuine learning opportunities can be completely lost, and briefings and hearings may indoctrinate more than elucidate. Moreover, when members of Congress as a whole, or their staffers, turn to the offices of individuals serving on these committees to request insight on how to vote on Middle East issues, a special interest induced bias is simply being passed along. In essence, other members of Congress are asking the "foxes" who tend the chicken coops what to do, or how to vote.

Pressure Point Number 6: "Special Interest" and Party Leaders as Watchdogs

Lobbyists and special interest groups are constantly watching and scoring lawmakers' behavior, and keeping their concerned memberships informed. If they see members behaving in a manner that meets with their disapproval, they will let the representative or senator and group members know. The threat is clear. In such situations, if "one side" remains largely without serious competition, and possesses superior resources, skills, and efficiency, this makes an enormous difference to staffers and their bosses, and thereby to congressional outcomes. To have lawmakers reminding one another, "It's an AIPAC vote," speaks volumes. For this same reason, the appearance of an organization like J Street, which brought with itself a certain panache and alternative campaign finance resources, created a slightly different environment according to staffers. And this change in the environment has been reinforced by the efforts of APN, IPF, JVP, and other non-Jewish American organizations such as the Friends Committee on National Legislation (FCNL), National Iranian American Council (NIAC), Arab American Institute (AAI), and Churches for Middle East Peace (CMEP).

Party leaders also track their colleagues' behavior, encouraging, and at times "whipping" them to take positions. They are incentivized to do so in order to maximize the continued goodwill of those special interests toward the party. The great majority of congressional members come to this issue area with no dog in any particular MENA congressional fight because their constituents either have no ethno-religious connection to the region or are far too concerned with other matters. As so many staffers indicate, the overwhelming majority of House and Senate members do not know and do not care much about MENA issues.[33] This is not terribly surprising if one considers the litany of other issues they and their constituents are likely to prioritize, such as jobs, the economy, health care, and the environment. An important consequence of this relative lack of knowledge and concern for Middle East issues is that it is all that much easier and even advantageous for members of Congress to sign on to their party's wishes.

Pressure Point Number 7: Concern for Constituents

Constituent voices are very important, especially on the House side.[34] In nearly every single office, all letters or queries received from constituents are answered. For House members, the next election is always just around the corner, just two years away. In the absence of countervailing influence, persistent, like-minded constituent callers, voicing opinions consonant with those of the dominant lobby, can create the impression that the safe bet it to accede to their point of view. At times, this creates the possibility for even a handful of individuals in a particular constituency to influence decisions, potentially to the detriment of the nation as a whole.

Few have done a better job of mobilizing constituents at the national level than AIPAC. In many congressional offices, staffers holding the foreign policy portfolio cite the name of two or three individuals, almost invariably Jewish Americans, with whom they maintain regular contact.[35] But the most visible way in which constituents are mobilized by AIPAC is via its grand annual conference at the Washington Convention Center, a "Hollywood on the Potomac" extravaganza attended by thousands of delegates from across the country. On an AIPAC website posted by staff at AIPAC Colorado before the 2016 annual policy conference, the question was posed, "Who attends the conference?" The answer: "More than 14,000 pro-Israel Americans"; "More than two-thirds of Congress"; "More than 2,300 students from more than 45 campuses"; "260 Student Government presidents from all 50 states"; "More than 275 synagogue delegations"; and "AIPAC members from across the country."[36]

AIPAC's directors use this event as a mechanism to solicit speeches by one major political figure after the next, with each singing the praises of the United States' special relationship with Israel. For some of the staffers interviewed, this is a spectacular, wonderful event that confirms the value of the U.S.-Israel relationship; for others, it is seen as a "grotesque, embarrassing exercise in pandering" and "sickeningly obsequious." The conference is always held in spring, neatly synchronized with the onset of the appropriations cycle. After being energized by the massive conference gathering, AIPAC's legions fan out across Capitol Hill to visit their representatives and senators, usually carrying with them "three asks." Congressional staffers describe the day as one like few others, a day on which many of them have difficulty finding rooms of adequate size to receive their visitors. They also note that while they are most inclined to meet and hear from their constituents, they disapprove of the conscious "planting" of nonconstituent, AIPAC personnel in these groups as a manner for AIPAC to make sure the encounters produce delivery of a clear and consistent message.

AIPAC's rivals, however, are beginning to demonstrate considerable skill in the mobilization of constituents. A Jewish Voice for Peace, with its massive, putative grassroots membership of 300,000, is attempting to make a difference in this regard. By summer 2016, according to many Hill observers, it remained a relatively new and "nowhere to be seen" party in Washington, DC.

The Payoff: Carrying the Legislative Day

On many MENA issues, and particularly those affecting the interests of Israel, skillful use of the aforementioned pressure points has culminated in the ability of an extremely small percentage of American citizens to hold sway over important decision making in Congress. Because Congress holds the "power of the purse," it can and does exercise considerable influence over executive branch decision making as well. Requests by U.S. presidents are ignored or overridden, even by members of Congress sharing those presidents' partisan identity, and legislation is passed that is more in keeping with Israeli government wishes than those of most concerned American citizens.

As regards Congress's policy performance on Middle East affairs and, more specifically, its response to the multidimensional nature of Israel's Middle East (IME) challenges, there are many special interest players. However, few are as richly funded, heavily staffed, highly efficient, and supremely effective as AIPAC. For decades, it has been in a league of its own, largely because it was the sole organization in this issue area that makes its presence felt on every one of the "pressure points." There are other groups that abet AIPAC on most occasions, such as the American Jewish Committee, B'nai B'rith, NORPAC, ADL, and some Christian evangelical groups like CUFI, or which prove useful as an even more hardcore right-wing fringe foil, such as the ZOA No other group, however, successively pressures congresspersons and influences congressional outcomes in this issue area with the same success as does AIPAC.

It is simply not the case that AIPAC is merely echoing the sentiments of the American public. An examination of how Congress responded to the December 2008 to January 2009 Gaza War illustrates AIPAC's influence. While much of the international community criticized Israel's military move against the Gazan population, on January 8, 2009, the Senate supported Israel's actions by unanimous consent. Two days later, the House passed a comparable, nonbinding resolution, with just five members voting against it, and twenty voting "present." But as Glenn Greenwald notes:

> . . . a Rasmussen study in early January—the first to survey American public opinion specifically regarding the Israeli attack on Gaza—found that Americans generally were "closely divided over whether the Jewish state should be taking military action against militants in the Gaza Strip" (41 to 44 percent, with 15 percent undecided), but Democratic voters overwhelmingly opposed the Israeli offensive—by a 24-point margin (31 to 55 percent). Yet those significant divisions were nowhere to be found in the actions of their ostensible representatives.[37]

One must look to the flawed nature of the electoral process, congressional resource shortcomings, and the acquiescence of the major parties' leaderships to discover the factors enabling a special interest like AIPAC and its allies to hold Congress in their grip. With respect to its electoral influence, one need only pose a hypothetical question: What would happen to congresspersons' behavior on the IME conflicts if the bulk of campaign finance assistance shifted, diminishing AIPAC's influence and augmenting that of J Street, APN, or A Jewish Voice for Peace, not to mention non-Jewish lobbies sympathetic to Palestinian interests?

Admittedly, there is great complexity to this issue area and to the big picture. A huge part of the problem is that most Americans, U.S.-elected officials included, remain ignorant of the IME conflicts' histories and hold inaccurate perceptions of their protagonists. Moreover, as both Dan Fleshler and I have independently written, the difference between strong pro–"two state" groups such as APN, IPF, Brit Tzedek V'Shalom, J Street, and A Jewish Voice for Peace, and groups aligned with right-wing Israeli positions such as AIPAC, ZOA, and the Republican Jewish Coalition is deep and real. Again, many of the most active groups on both sides of this divide are overwhelmingly Jewish-American groups.

In discussions about AIPAC's power on the Hill, many Jewish-American staffers, who work for both Democrat and Republican members express dismay, lamentation, and frustration, as well as embarrassment. A clear example came on May 24, 2011, when Israel's Prime Minister Netanyahu spoke to a joint session of Congress.[38] Such invitations to foreign dignitaries are rare privileges, but this was Netanyahu's second speech before Congress, his first having occurred fifteen years earlier. Addressing issues such as the I-P conflict, Netanyahu's statements were lauded by some, emblematic of the special relationship between members of the U.S. Congress and Israel, and received twenty-nine standing ovations. But for individuals with stronger pro-peace perspectives, his remarks were troublesome. As one Jewish-American House staffer, who was present in the chamber stated:

> The first thing that struck me was the reception that this foreign leader got compared to the U.S. President. It highlights the absurdity of what our relationship with this government [of Israel] has become. I've seen State of the Union speeches, the quickness of congresspersons getting to their feet, the low threshold of standing ovations, etc., but again, on this occasion, most of the members didn't know the issues being brought up. They know this guy [Netanyahu] doesn't like the President, and what he's saying fits their hawkish views, and that there's no cost to it. . . . What also fed into this atmosphere was that the gallery was filled with AIPAC people. [The enormous, annual

AIPAC conference, was underway in Washington, DC, and many congresspersons had given their gallery tickets to big AIPAC donors.] Just about all the people in the seats were 50- [to] 70-year-old AIPAC Jews who were leaping to their feet even before the members of Congress were.[39]

From the vantage point of another progressive House member's staffer, bipartisan support for Netanyahu was readily apparent: "I was there. It was clear that applause was coming from both sides [Republicans and Democrats] even on statements by Netanyahu that were against President Obama's stated policy positions." And both staffers agreed that many House Democrats were taking cues from Democratic Party Whip Debbie Wasserman-Schultz (D-FL), herself a Jewish American, regarding when to stand and applaud Prime Minister Netanyahu.

Four years later, Prime Minister Netanyahu stood before Congress to warn lawmakers about supporting the Iran nuclear deal. This time, however, the mood on Capitol Hill was markedly different. The House Republicans' invitation to Netanyahu was undertaken without prior notification to the White House, a move interpreted by most Democrats as an affront to the president. Indeed, Netanyahu's speech was boycotted by eight senators and fifty House members. Of the boycotting senators three were Jewish Americans: Al Franken (D-MN), Bernard "Bernie" Sanders (I-VT), and Brian Schatz (D-HI). Among the fifty House members, fully one half were liberal members of the Congressional Black Caucus or Congressional Hispanic Caucus. They were joined by a long list of liberal Democrats well known for their greater propensity to question right-wing Israeli policy, as well as Jewish-American Representatives Janice D. "Jan" Schakowsky of Illinois, Steve Cohen of Tennessee, and John A. Yarmuth of Kentucky. Representative Cohen wrote:

> While Americans and members of Congress may disagree on anything, even foreign policy, providing a forum of such immense prestige and power to the leader of another country who is opposing our nation's foreign policy is beyond the pale. It endangers the negotiations, insults the good faith of the other nations involved in the negotiations and emboldens Iran who may well view this schism in our government as an opportunity for advantage. While we can disagree with our President, we as a nation should be as one on our foreign policy and any disagreements should be presented in a respectful, appropriate and time-honored manner.[70]

In some ways even more striking was condemnation of Netanyahu's speech by others who attended the speech, including long-time supporters of Israel such as Democratic Minority Leader Nancy Pelosi of California, as well as Jewish-American Senator Barbara Boxer (D-CA), a generally stalwart supporter of Israel on the Senate Foreign Relations Committee. Both were incensed by Speaker of the House, Republican John Boehner's politicization of U.S.-Israel relations in Congress. Over the ensuing months, this event created a rare opportunity for AIPAC opponents to unite and register a major victory in defense of President Obama's support for the Iran nuclear deal. By mid-September 2015, forty-two senators had announced their support for the deal, or eight more senators than needed to sustain a presidential veto. On September 10, 15, and 17, Democrats successfully thwarted three efforts by the House Republican leadership to derail the nuclear accord with Iran.

How did AIPAC's opponents succeed? AIPAC and its allies invested over $40 million to scuttle the deal, a five-to-one ratio according to Hill cognoscenti, and Israeli government officials and others called heavily upon JCRCs to activate their memberships in an unprecedented fashion. But "pro-deal" Jewish-American groups APN and J Street combined with the FCNL and others to recruit nuclear arms experts to explain just how tightly the bill had been negotiated, thereby convincing many lawmakers to adopt their recommendations. The groups above were major components of an amazingly broad coalition involving faith-based organizations (the FCNL, U.S. Conference of Catholic Bishops, Pax Christi USA, the Presbyterian Church), other ethnic lobbies (National Iranian American Council), peace activist groups (MoveOn.Org, CREDO Mobile, Women's Action for New Directions), and labor unions (e.g., the U.S. Steelworkers). Their success was broadly hailed as one of the most stunning victories Washington, DC had witnessed, and did underscore AIPAC's inability to claim victory on all occasions.

But to conclude this chapter, one must also ask: Why *do* Republican lawmakers repeatedly vote in large numbers against Republican presidents (e.g., both Bush presidencies), and why *do* Democrats vote in large numbers against Democratic presidents (e.g., Clinton and Obama) on issues about which they collectively, according to their own principal aides, know and care so little? Why defy presidents from their own party, acutely embarrassing them and complicating their foreign policymaking efforts? And what are the consequences of legislative and executive branch clashes for efforts to bring a peaceful end to the Israel-Palestine conflict? What are the ramifications of failure to resolve that conflict for U.S. relations with

Arab, Iranian, and/or predominantly Muslim peoples and states, and in turn, for the security of American citizens?

Based on interviews with congressional staff, the vast majority of members of Congress are swayed not by matters of principle and righteousness, but by fear of bucking powerful special interests, concern for the most vocal of their constituents, and a desire to acquiesce to the calls of party leaders. And despite the impressive 2015 "win" registered by AIPAC's opponents, it is essential for all concerned citizens to take a giant step back to take in the larger historical picture. That picture reveals that support by Congress to Israel, already unprecedented in its size and scope compared to that offered to any other single country in our nation's history, is now slated to increase from just over $3 billion to at least $3.8 billion per annum in Foreign Military Financing over the next ten years, in keeping with the Memorandum of Understanding (MOU) set to begin in 2018. While this MOU was being negotiated, many in Congress sought to supply an additional $600 million for missile defense, some $450 million more than requested by the Obama administration.[40] Indeed, nothing more poignantly depicts the power of pro-Israel supporters in Congress, most of which are Jewish-American groups, than the propensity for members of Congress to rebuff the wishes of presidents, including presidents from their own party. It remains to be seen whether APN, J Street, JVP, and others will succeed in rocking the conscience of American citizens and their representatives and senators in a new direction, or if Israel's right-wing supporters will continue to prevail. Donald Trump's presidential victory, and the Republicans' sweep of Congress, did not bode well. According to Hill *cognoscenti* interviewed in early summer 2017, even AIPAC's leadership was having to deal with the newfound clout of its far-right-wing rivals, such as the ZOA.

Notes

1. A.F.K. Organski, *Israel: The $36 Billion Bargain* (New York: Columbia University Press, 1990).

2. Samuel P. Huntington, "The Clash of Civilizations?" *Foreign Affairs* 72(3) (Summer, 1993).

3. Grant F. Smith, *Big Israel: How Israel's Lobby Moves America*, Washington, DC: Institute for Research on Middle East Policy, 2016, p. Xx.

4. Beattie, *Congress and the Shaping of the Middle East* (New York: Seven Stories Press, 2015), 39.

5. Ibid. The first of these reports was "AJC 2012 Survey of American Jewish Opinion," American Jewish Committee, http://www.ajc.org/site/apps/nlet/content3. aspx?c=70JILSPwFfJSG&b=847955&ct=12477481. The second report is by Akiva Eldar, "American Jews Giving Up on Israel," *Ha'aretz,* Nov. 12, 2012.

6. See the Pew Research Center Survey of U.S. Jews: A Portrait of Jewish Americans; http://www.jewishdatabank.org/studies/details.cfm?StudyID=715 (accessed July 18, 2016).

7. Elliott Abrams, "If American Jews and Israel are Drifting Apart, What's the Reason," *Mosaic,* April 4, 2016, http://mosaicmagazine.com/essay/2016/04/ if-american-jews-and-israel-are-drifting-apart-whats-the-reason

8. Ibid.

9. Eric Fleisch and Theodore Sasson, *The New Philanthropy: American Jewish Giving to Israeli Organizations,* Brandeis University, April 2012, https:// www.brandeis.edu/cmjs/pdfs/The NewPhilantropy.pdf

10. Grant F. Smith, *Big Israel: How Israel's Lobby* Moves *America* (Washington, DC: Institute for Research on Middle East Policy, Inc., 2016), 12. To qualify as one of Smith's IAOs, any organization had to fulfill four criteria: (1) to be an IRS recognized tax-exempt 501(c)(3) or 501(c)(4) organization; (2) actively and unconditionally support Israel as a major function; (3) raise the majority of its funding in the United States; and (4) be headquartered in the United States. As Smith states, nearly all of his IAO groups are predominantly Jewish American in leadership and membership.

11. Ibid., 12–13.

12. Information provided by Grant F. Smith, July 25, 2016.

13. Smith, 15.

14. Ibid., 10.

15. Dan Fleshler, *Transforming America's Israel Lobby* (Washington, DC: Potomac Books, Inc., 2009), 62–63.

16. Author's interview with Jeffrey Blankfort, August 10, 2016.

17. Beattie, *Congress.*

18. Beattie, *Congress,* 20. For lengthier descriptions of these groups, see pages 118–126.

19. Fenno, Richard F. Jr. *Home Style: House Members in Their Districts* (Boston: Little Brown, 1978).

20. http://www.opensecrets.org/overview/incumbs.php (accessed September 12, 2016).

21. http://www.opensecrets.org/industries/indus.php?ind=Q13++ (accessed July 18, 2016).

22. http://www.opensecrets.org/industries/indus.php?ind=Q14 (accessed July 18, 2016).

23. Peruse the data at opensecrets.org.

24. Richard H. Curtiss, *Stealth PACs: Lobbying Congress for Control of U.S. Middle East Policy* (American Educational Trust, 1996).

25. See the discussion in Beattie, *Congress,* 49–56.

26. Author's interview with J Street staffer, awarded anonymity.

27. Zaid Jilali, "Pro-Israel Billionaire Haim Saban Drops $100,000 Against Donna Edwards in Maryland Senate Race," The Intercept, https://theintercept.com/2016/04/25/pro-israel-billionaire-haim-saban-drops-100000-against-donna-edwards-in-maryland-senate-race (accessed September 14, 2016).

28. Author's interview.

29. Richard L. Hall and Alan V. Deardorff, "Lobbying as Legislative Subsidy," *American Political Science Review* 100(1) (Feb., 2006): 69–84.

30. Beattie, *Congress*, 403–404; in addition to quote made from Beattie's personal interview notes.

31. David R. Mayhew, *Congress: The Electoral Connection*, 2nd ed. (New Haven, CT: Yale University Press, 2004).

32. Beattie, *Congress*, 349.

33. See Beattie, *Congress*, 201–251, for detailed analysis of this dimension.

34. See Beattie, *Congress*, for additional detail.

35. Beattie, *Congress*, 349.

36. http://www.jewishcolorado.org/event/aipac-2016-policy-conference-in-washingto/. Note that the emphasis on student or youth attendance is designed by AIPAC in an effort to win younger hearts and minds.

37. Glenn Greenwald, "Unanimous Consent," *The American Conservative*, January 26, 2009. See http://www.theamericanconservative.com/articles-unanimous-consent

38. See Beattie, *Congress*, 407.

39. Ibid.

40. Dan Williams, Patricia Zengerle, and Matt Spetalnick, "Exclusive: Differences over missile defence, fine print snag U.S.-Israel aid deal, *Reuters,* May 5, 2016. http://www.reuters.com/article/us-usa-israel-defence-exclusive-idUSKCN0XU1UQ (accessed July 21, 2016).

Chapter 5

Uphill on the Hill

Pro-Arab Lobbying after the Arab Winter

KHALIL MOUSA MARRAR

As the dictatorships of the Middle East and North Africa met protests with violence during the Arab Spring, Americans of ancestry in that region experienced a new level of civic maturity while trying to shape Washington, DC's response. Those identifying as Arab or Muslim exhibited some of the greatest advances as well as setbacks in conveying their policy preferences while improving the perception of themselves and the nations from which they descended among fellow citizens. In these respects, pro-Arab ethnic lobbying on Capitol Hill played a role.[1] This chapter will illustrate how the pro-Arab leadership fared in shaping policymaking through public opinion on the uprisings and the Islamist Pandora's box opened by the regime backlash in what came to be known as the "Arab Winter."[2] The multifarious and multifaceted linkages between these developments to lobbying Congress will have special import in the pages to come.

The stated positions and ultimate conducts of the following organizations inform the analysis below: American-Arab Anti-Discrimination Committee (ADC), Arab American Institute (AAI), American Task Force on Palestine (ATFP), Council on American-Islamic Relations (CAIR), and National Network of Arab American Communities (NNAAC). These organizations are important for a couple of reasons. First, they sit at the nexus of domestic politics and foreign policy, devoting themselves to lobbying in both arenas at any given time. Second, each had a vocal stance on the Arab revolts, issuing public and policymaker guidance in memoranda, talking points, briefs, expert testimony, and news interviews.

Irrespective of whether or not these tools commanded a satisfactory scale of influence to sway the media, the majority of Americans, and either side of the rotunda in the Capitol, each helps tell a story about *where* pro-Arab activism was heading, *what* objectives it sought, and *how* they might have been accomplished.

The Arab and Muslim Lobby

Despite Arabs' and Muslims' growing numbers as well as their socio-economic and political visibility in the United States, lobbying on their behalf has been either dismissed as "weak to non-existent" or hyped as the "invisible alliance that undermines America's interests in the Middle East."[3] A major reason for such an extreme polarization in the prevailing literature revolves around fundamental misunderstandings of the two communities, their political (in)efficacy, the interests of the subgroups within each of them, and whether the lobbying they are associated with is done by foreign governments or domestic agents.[4] Moreover, in the heated politics of the Arab-Israeli conflict, there has been plenty of willful ignorance serving one side or another. And since, obviously, the two opposing scholarly positions cannot both be true at the same time, there is dire need for accurately capturing the extent of influence on the policymaking arena and the complex linkages to ethnic lobbying, be it Arab/Muslim-American, as examined here, or Israeli/Jewish-American, or Cuban/Latino-American subjects of other chapters in this book.[5]

As noted in the opening chapter, a number of scholars have examined the composition and effectiveness of ethnic lobbies in the United States.[6] The analysis here tackles comparable themes but approaches lobbyists and policymakers as exogenous to the outcome of any policy they might have initiated, sponsored, promoted, or drafted. The pro-Arab organizations under examination are worthwhile because of their interactions with policies concerning what is perhaps the most dramatic geopolitical development in generations: revolt and mayhem in the cradle of civilization. Yet the proliferation of activism in the United States furthering the welfare of Arabs and Muslims before, during, and after the uprisings has engendered only a handful of works explicitly referring to that activity as "lobbying." Shying away from the term corresponds to limitations in Congress stemming from the pro-Arab constituency's lack of unity, and especially in the vast shadow of the more unified, better-funded pro-Israel lobbies, whose political action committees (PACs) have outspent their Arab-Muslim opponents by 1,000 percent.[7]

Dania Koleilat Khatib's *The Arab Lobby and the U.S.: Factors for Success and Failure* is a recent exception.[8] The book's contributors looked intently at the "Arab Gulf states" and their activities across time for influencing the U.S. government at every level. However, they had less to say about the homegrown components of pro-Arab lobbying, as well as the diverse ethnic coalitions it brings together in the United States based on a shared political culture and mutually beneficial policy goals. There was virtually no mention of how foreign interests were hostile to domestic ones, whereby lobbyists hired by Arab capitals tried to crush any activism in the United States supporting the revolts against them, as I detail below. Nevertheless, Khatib provides a welcome collection highlighting the multidimensionality of a formidable lobbying unit.

Taking off from her premise that international and domestic factors[9] complement one another in the determination of American policy, I examine the adaptation of pro-Arab lobbying to events on the ground in the Middle East and North Africa. My overarching objective is to identify the importance of the Arab Spring and Winter in laying the parameters for what was politically possible at home *and* how lobbyists calibrated their policy expectations accordingly. In the case of Washington, DC's difficult-to-pinpoint reaction to the uprisings and their generally nightmarish aftereffects, all kinds of developments were game-changers for pro-Arab interest articulation and the greater pluralist experiment of "Democracy in America."[10]

Separating Foreign Outcomes from Domestic Inputs

First, the weakening or outright collapse of several Arab regimes and the subsequent lawlessness, bloodshed, and the rise of the Islamic State in Iraq and Syria (ISIS) carved out a space for different approaches to the region than the status quo ante endorsed in Congress by the American Israel Public Affairs Committee (AIPAC) and Saudi oil money (e.g., ARAMCO).[11] The results, from a long-term regional policy standpoint, have been unprecedented. The Obama administration reproached the Islamic Republic and floated the prospect for future normalization that would rely on Iranian-Shiite power for checking obstacles to U.S. hegemony from Sunni actors such as ISIS, Egypt's now-deposed Muslim Brotherhood, or the Justice and Development Party, the ruling Islamist faction taking Turkey, a founding NATO member, into Russia's orbit.[12]

Second, the majority of Americans showed sympathy for the protesters at the outset of the Arab Spring and an eagerness for Washington, DC to help any nation wanting democracy on a humanitarian basis, even if "this resulted in the country being more likely to oppose U.S. policies."[13] This sentiment, highest among the Arab and Muslim segments of American society, urged elected officials to revisit the posture of cozying up to dictators as the foundation for order. Compared to the executive branch and the Senate, the House of Representatives was particularly sensitive to unease about that strategy within every demographic. An explanation for the difference is the two-year election cycle, making representatives heed public pressure or risk losing their seats if they did not.[14]

The third factor was the increasing diversity of the American body politic. Lawmakers from districts with larger Arab or Muslim populations, such as those encompassing the Bridgeview neighborhood in Chicago, or Dearborn, a Detroit suburb, had the most at stake in steering legislation in directions consistent with the passionate demands permeating their electorates down to the grassroots.[15] This motivation held regardless of the Congress member's party affiliation. However, the most outspoken and principled support came from Democrats led by Keith Ellison (D-MN), the first Muslim elected to Congress and a runner-up to head the Democratic National Committee. Representing Minnesota's fifth congressional district, the congressman, who is African American, a prime figure of the Congressional Black Caucus (CBC), and a champion of human rights, was instrumental in encouraging a more pro-Arab legislative agenda. Ellison not only helped constituents navigate through the federal government's procedural maze, he gave political substance and crossover to some of their highest foreign and domestic policy priorities. He did so by connecting the plight of those suffering injustice in the Arab World to their counterparts in the United States who were battling police brutality, wrongful incarceration, inner-city/rural poverty, urban food deserts, and civil rights or liberties infractions, among the many, *many* other issues having mass appeal.

Fourth, and related to that last development, the effort Ellison and his colleagues on Capitol Hill typified took on a life of its own, amplifying pro-Arab lobbying in ways once unimaginable without a broad, multiculturalist spectrum of constituencies. And in this regard alone, the coalition was earthshattering. Representative Ellison brought together a never-before-seen mishmash of black, brown, and white, male and female, rich and poor, gay, straight, and transgendered, Buddhist, Christian, Hindu, Jew, and Muslim, native-born and immigrant—documented or undocumented. Leveraging the power of these identities and their often-overlapping interests from the bottom up, Ellison and his allies worked to change the tenor in Congress on a whole host of policies, including "Don't Ask Don't Tell," gun control, "Dodd-Frank," the Iran nuclear deal, "reproductive rights," protecting religious minorities, fighting Islamist terrorism, and so forth.[16]

Growing Foreign Policy Momentum in Congress?

The impact of the four converging developments above was that Washington, DC had to balance reinforcing old alliances while courting new ones with the rights demanded in the Arab Spring and echoed by pro-Arab organizations and collaborators sharing their interests. Such a balancing act had many intricacies. For the purposes here, the most relevant were how events abroad were narrated back in the United States, by whom, and for what political ends. Several pro-Arab groups participated on every count, capitalizing on Washington, DC's confusion about the upheavals, and proposing distinct path(s) forward to policymakers. The primary message was for the United States to pivot away from its singular *security* focus and toward an emphasis on individual *dignity*, the Arab Spring's defining precept and the first casualty of the Arab Winter.

Pro-Arab lobbying for that objective utilized techniques classifiable into three categories. The first was alerting constituents about Congress's forthcoming legislation, its imminent implementation by the executive branch, and urging the communication of a desirable course of action to both branches.[17] Second, lobbyists offered expertise to the media for educating the public, trying to gain its support in opinion polls (which can send a strong message to a member of Congress who is up for re-election, or will be soon). The third was providing data and context for guiding policy or, at the very least, extending political cover to sympathetic officials against detractors.[18] Employing each technique for overlapping—though not always harmonious—goals, the pro-Arab lobbies sought unity among disparate constituencies under a common set of interests. Field activists synchronized multiple agendas and tailored proposals for addressing what policymakers and the public perceived as serving the national interest. Yet bridging the distance between all participants—be they influence peddlers on the East Coast, farmers in the Midwest, or screenwriters on the West Coast—became a daunting—if not impossible—task as the Arab Spring turned to Winter.[19] Since public opinion provides the limits and discursive space for every type of interest articulation,[20] pro-Arab tacticians aimed at manipulating the congressional policy narrative by courting the predilections of the voter.

The Political Home Front Encounters Policies
on the Regional Frontlines

While pro-Arab organizations collectively encouraged American support of the aspirations underlying the Arab Spring in some fashion, their efforts individually varied across different battles, particularly as policy evolved according to an unforeseen necessity rather than deliberate strategy. The subsequent calamity exemplified by ISIS seizing swaths of Iraq, then Syria, and metastasizing elsewhere signaled the need for better planning from all corners of the Washington, DC establishment. Here, and given their exceptional concern about the destiny of that troubled region, Arab and Muslim Americans had a momentous window of opportunity to offer their positions on the turmoil at influential policy circles. Taking advantage of that access, activists coordinated substantive approaches and strategies on many occasions. There was unanimity on the perils of direct U.S. military intervention in any Arab state and a necessity for exploiting "domestic mass dissent to overthrow an incompetent and brutal regime and replace it with a more legitimate elected leadership," as Rami Khoury put it.[21] The idea was never far out of step with attitudes in the United States post–Arab Winter, despite public opinion's sometimes wild fluctuations.[22]

As conditions throughout the region deteriorated in the Arab Winter, however, lawmakers were not as receptive to the uprisings. Public compassion for protesters had declined to all-time lows.[23] The percentage of Americans supporting the revolts varied during the Libyan crisis, but those favoring intervention never again reached a majority. It was not difficult to see why, as violent anti-Americanism gripped the region. In that atmosphere, lawmakers paid less attention to ethnic lobbying and more to strategists from the Pentagon.[24] The reason was fairly straightforward: the regional order was falling apart and security challenges from ISIS and others grew exponentially. The belief in Congress was that such military problems required military solutions.[25] In short, the once bourgeoning solidarity with the Arab masses—in allied states particularly—died down in the United States, starting on Capitol Hill, leaving one pro-Arab lobbyist feeling "disgusted, disheartened, [and] defeated!"[26]

Yet, the flurry of pro-Arab activism continued on the airwaves and in the public discourse. The goal was interpreting and acknowledging the *security* implications of regional events for the United States without sacrificing why the revolts started in the first place: *liberty*.[27] Pundits fluent in the affairs of the region along with its cultures, languages, and religions added depth to an anxious national dialogue about the latest threats to the homeland. The commentary ranged from how extremists had weaponized the "implements-of-the-every-day," such as using pressure cookers as improvised explosive devices, to why Americans were susceptible to radicalization.[28] News reporting throughout the United States featured explanations for terrorism that previously were marginalized because of assumed bias attributed to the ethnicity of those proffering them.

Pushing Perception to Pull Policy

The pro-Arab agenda, however, did not stop at trying to get the public on its side. Activists proposed humane regional policies out of Washington, DC. The AAI led the way. Dr. James Zogby noted, "it is advisable for policy makers to dismiss the critics and proceed, as they have, with carefully calibrated messages that affirm both principles and interests."[29] This statement and others similar in substance and symbolism often worked in conjunction with behind-the-scenes meetings between lobbyists and those deciding on matters of national and international significance. And privately, many pro-Arab insiders lodged complaints to receptive officials that the revolts were being dubbed "anti-American" not just in Congress or the White House, but also by the U.S.-allied regimes arduously trying to maintain power.[30] Thus, just as Zogby argued weighing the nation's interests against its values, his pro-Arab associates tried dispelling the largely negative popular and policymaker mindset on their constituencies. Reflecting on the matter, former ATFP Senior Fellow Hussein Ibish, argued:

> Any serious, honest appraisal of what is spreading throughout the Arab world refutes every aspect of [Orientalist] mythology. Certainly, the size, scope, and bravery of the demonstrations for democracy, good governance, and accountability mean that no one can continue flogging the Orientalist shibboleth that Arabs are inherently resistant to change—at least not with a straight face.[31]

Countering such ingrained assumptions has been a staple of pro-Arab advocacy's success in recalibrating Washington, DC's priorities in the Mid-East and North Africa.

To that end, Ibish's position—characteristic of his life's work—offers an understanding of the revolts that fits with America's liberal heritage. His hope, like Zogby's, is for the world's only remaining superpower to act both according to realist and idealist pursuits which, according to him, were never mutually exclusive.[32] Many activists besides Zogby and

Ibish used that logic for various policy outcomes. But there are plenty of material, political, military, and even moral limits when specifying prescriptions.[33] Hence, Ibish's open call for "regime change in Damascus" as "a goal of U.S. Policy," like Obama's "redline" against Assad's deployment of chemical weapons, never materialized—and that was despite the growing hawkishness about Syria in Congress.[34]

Spontaneity and Incremental Change

Adding another voice to the national discourse was CAIR, which typically documents the hardships confronting American Muslims to policymakers—similar to what the Southern Poverty Law Center does for poor blacks and whites[35]—and works for an attitudinal shift about Islamic countries as the crux of carrying out that mission in the United States.[36] Through its Chicago chapter, CAIR promoted wider awareness of Islamophobia as a disease crossing all borders, motivating the crackdowns on the Muslim masses' desire for democracy as it did the wrongful belief among Christian Americans, who make up the vast majority of the population in the United States, that they were more likely to be targeted by ISIS than innocents over in the Middle East or North Africa.[37] The generally unacknowledged degree to which Sunnis are indeed victimized by militants clinging to the same faith has made it so that Congress only pays attention to Islamist atrocities when they involve the region's religious minorities—the Yazidi massacre in Iraq on Mount Sinjar being one example and attacking Egypt's Copts as another.[38]

Armed with such information, CAIR consistently availed its staff to media outlets reporting on the local angle of stories unfolding internationally, trying to change the narrative one precinct at a time in order for the same to happen at the top. In addition to CAIR's work on Iraq, during the disturbances in Egypt, Executive Director and longtime Chicago resident Ahmed Rehab spoke to news stations back home about the Mubarak regime, the aims of the uprising against it, and the jovial mood on the picket lines in Tahrir. An Egyptian by ethnicity, Rehab set a hard-to-imitate tone in the coverage of his ancestral homeland after using personal resources to hop a plane from Chicago to Cairo on a whim. The trip allowed him to convey the news to fellow Americans as it happened while making the uprising in Egypt easily digestible to the average U.S. citizen.[39]

This spur-of-the-moment lobbying aimed at influencing public opinion personified a break with perceptions of American Muslims as politically docile while simultaneously negating the iconography, particularly among some congressmen, of Rehab's Egyptian-Muslim coreligionists as violently intolerant.[40] Although the extent of his impact was not measured, CAIR-Chicago earned a sort of free advertising to showcase its domestic activities through a major world development. The organization, which has its offices across the street from Chicago's other religious, academic, and cultural institutions, also arranged for rallies locally to coincide with the ones taking place in Cairo and other Arab cities. CAIR used the spotlight for urging constituents to contact their elected representatives (i.e., grassroots lobbying) for the advancement of Muslim-American civil liberties as well as the human rights of demonstrators in Egypt, one of the largest Muslim nations on earth.[41]

Tweaking Differences

Along with CAIR's activities, pro-Arab lobbying employed a variety of other tactics for influencing public and policymaker opinions, including forums for the leading authorities on the revolts to discuss them in their historical and political contexts. As an example, an informational panel entitled "Arab Uprisings: Our Community's Role," moderated by ADC Legal Director Abed Ayoub, included the former Arab League ambassador to the United States, the late Clovis Maksoud,[42] Bassam Haddad, and Adel Iskandar, all distinguished intellectuals, debating American foreign policy. While the panelists disagreed on what to expect down the road from Washington, DC, they were unanimous on its policies' decisive position in the region. They also agreed on the challenges Arab and Muslim Americans still face while seeking influence, whether in Congress or the White House. As usual, the biggest challenge was finding common principles because "the community" is divided by class, national origin, ideology, and sect. Each division uniquely hampers the coordination of pro-Arab efforts to shape foreign policy.[43] The revolts' blood-curdling aftermaths and subsequent dangers to the United States added further complication for unifying constituents and brought them under increased suspicion based on their backgrounds.[44] On the flipside, domestic problems like racial profiling at airports made that unity easier.[45]

At the leadership level, the largest impediments to lobbying from a united position were brought into focus when a pro-opposition artist was disinvited from the annual ADC convention at the peak of the then largely peaceful anti-Assad protests in Syria. The apparent silencing measure sparked "a rising chorus of Arab-American activists" that had "denounced the American-Arab Anti-Discrimination Committee for canceling the performance of a musician over the pro-freedom song he was due to perform."[46] And just as in the past, elite cleavages reflecting diversity from below were highlighted by a spirited exchange between the ATFP and ADC. Critical of the latter, where he was communications director for a decade before joining the former, Ibish remarked that revoking the invitation was "exceptionally disturbing," adding "the explanation that [the] ADC appears to be offering to various people," was "totally unconvincing."[47]

Piling on to the heap of displeasure, one-time ADC Executive Director Kareem Shora condemned his former employer's act as "politically suicidal."[48] And, although the ADC's record on fighting for members' liberty remains firm, its hesitation to take a stand on Assad's widely purported atrocities, as implied by the convention snafu, undermined the group's credibility, which could impact their lobbying success later. Above all else, some accused ADC officers of being two-faced for not caring about innocent Syrians. Or so this was the idea forwarded by the other pro-Arab organizations. As with any not-for-profit inter-organizational setting, the impetus for attacking the ADC may have been the stiff competition for lobbyists, donors, and memberships as it might have been the musician's *prima facie* right to self-expression.

Missed Opportunities, Realized Potential, and Lessons (Un)Learned

Because the constituency can sometimes conflate what is a domestic and foreign policy issue (e.g., civil liberties in the United States versus those of the Arab-Muslim masses abroad), pro-Arab activists have to garner congressional support for one set of interests without sacrificing the other. Assuming differently has hurt both in the past. A way to overcome the challenge of juggling between causes and/or issue spaces was to start with topics everyone could agree to. The human rights agenda has been the hottest in that regard, especially considering the diversity among the pro-Arab base, wherein 80 percent of Arab Americans are Christian and descend from twenty-two to twenty-three nation-states, whereas Muslim citizens come from as many nations as there are on earth. This diversity makes it so that agreeing on foreign policy is difficult, especially when the problem under consideration involves—for a few examples—Turkey's continuing occupation of Iraq, Islamists murdering and enslaving Assyrian Christians, or Alawites ethnically cleansing Sunni Muslims. Yet, starting from the point of what is presumed "unalienable" by most Americans—

to use the Jeffersonian parlance—has been a more effective, less divisive strategy for influencing policies at every tier. Thus, consistent with their twin dedication to universal rights, the ADC, CAIR, and NAAC shielded political dissidents from harm without discriminating whether they were operating in the Arab/Muslim world or in the United States. Each organization has also opposed the murderous religious intolerance of terror networks abroad with the same gusto as calling out the unfair treatment of Muslim laborers in the American workplace, when it was based on their belief.[49]

Comparably, the ATFP, which is committed to a peaceful resolution of the Israeli-Palestinian conflict, frequently connected the misery of those living under illegitimate Arab governments to Israel's occupation of the Palestinians.[50] Meanwhile, the AAI informed constituents as well as fellow Americans about the magnitudes of political and economic disenchantment in the Arab-Muslim nations. Zogby emphasized the need for a rational strategic orientation to win a secure, prosperous future there and at home as the Arab Spring became Winter. To effectively lobby on these and all other matters, every pro-Arab organization has some kind verbiage in its mission that sounds a lot like the ATFP's: "our primary target audience is the policy-making and discourse-shaping establishment in our nation's capital."[51]

Stretching to reshape a souring mood in the United States reflecting the ugliness of regional events, lobbyists exhorted Congress to carefully consider where the public temperament might be heading after undertaking corrective policy moves like nation-building or strengthening civil society in the Arab states. This thinking became more pronounced as the Arab Winter wore on and the United States returned to acting out of exigency, as happened at the outset of the Tunisian Revolution. Except today, the stakes are much higher with ISIS on its heels in the region militarily but still gaining ground in recruits worldwide. The pro-Arab effort to look to the next policy showdown instead of how Muslims are perceived because of ISIS or its syndicates, trail blazed by a select cadre of pro-Arab lobbyists, was meant to, as one of them put it,

> maximize bang for buck—Gallup charges a huge load for its products—by hitting where politicians might be heading, effectively towing the popularity pageant behind, instead of sticking our heads in the quicksand of milliseconds ticking by, like we've been freaking doing ever since some[one] in law enforcement down the road in Langley got a hold of *Dabiq* [the propaganda magazine for ISIS].[52]

Passionate though she or he might have been, the person uttering those admittedly cryptic fragments hit the proverbial nail on the head. Lobbying from a position of weakness needs a good dose of sensibility. And anticipating the direction of public opinion nationally *is not* as efficacious as looking to the commitments of the individual policymaker, starting from the district level.

Whereas congressional and public sympathies may have converged at the beginning of the Arab spring, the threats posed to civilians running for their lives in distant places under siege around the region and subsequent concerns about national security have destroyed any consensus in the United States on what ought to be done. In the same vein, Arab–Muslim American unity in the public square and the show of solidarity with friends and relatives halfway across the world has all but disappeared.[53] This retreat has placed the community's elites in a glum position, since to support freedom or even reform abroad meant that they would have to denounce regimes that have been integral stabilizers regionally for some time, long before ISIS's IT specialists uploaded their first piece of propaganda to recruit new soldiers.[54]

Despite the shellshock of the Arab Winter, most of the pro-Arab advocacy organizations continued expressing themselves to policymakers and the public alike. The AAI, for example, still works to highlight the mood in Arab countries relative to U.S. foreign policy.[55] A more hopeful sign from a pro-Arab perspective has been the consistency of issues linked to an American and global sense of social justice. Thus, whereas before the beginning of the Tunisian disturbances, people in the broader region primarily concerned themselves with "bread and butter issues of: expanding employment opportunities, improving the health care system, and improving the educational system," in the midst of the Arab Winter, "issues like political reform, advancing democracy, and protecting personal and civil rights have broken into the top tier of concerns in almost every country."[56] Such opinions left an impression on policymakers who attempted to address the worsening regional climate for democracy by "honoring the Tunisian people for their democratic transition" in House Resolution 277, which

> [c]ommends the people of Tunisia for their commitment to democracy, the rule of law, and free and fair elections. Commends the government of Tunisia for holding successful legislative elections and the peaceful and fair completion of the presidential election. Recognizes Tunisia's legislative and presidential elections as an example of a peaceful, democratic

transition of power for other nations throughout the region to follow. Encourages all political parties in Tunisia to work together to realize the standards of transparency, inclusiveness, and equality established in the Tunisian Constitution. Affirms the U.S. commitment to strengthening our bilateral relationship with Tunisia. Calls on the President to advance the U.S.-Tunisia relationship by engaging in a Strategic Partnership.[57]

And while frustration with the other American-backed Arab regimes had festered for decades, once protesters took to the streets, information on their demands was available for anyone interested in turning down the temperature on the simmering insurrections, which started out neither loving nor hating far-off powers such as the Washington, DC policy establishment.

Instead, the immediate concerns were primarily with bad governance and inequality in "the Arab state."[58] Of course, U.S. action or inaction has been a crucial piece of an otherwise puzzling trajectory the region has taken. Congress had consented to the persistence of absolute monarchies in most of the Persian Gulf States under heavy pressure from the foreign Arab lobby. And despite their lack of popularity all over the world, autocracy still rules most of the Arab nations from the Pacific Ocean to the Arabian Sea. The entrenchment coincides with the wishes of the Persian Gulf's royal families who, along with the other Arab states, spend billions on American weapons and elections.[59] Members of Congress look the other way given the immense federal budget and trade deficits and the cost of winning re-election.

There have been exceptions or disruptions abroad in Libya, Egypt, and Tunisia—though not in that order chronologically—as well as the specifics of governance or lawlessness in place throughout the Arab World. Enjoying some congressional support, the U.S.-led Libya mission was, in addition to protecting civilians, about toppling a murderous dictatorship over the petroleum-rich North African country as its leader promised to rid "Benghazi of 'rats and cockroaches,'" referring to unarmed protesters, whom he accused of being drugged-up on "pills provided to them from abroad."[60] These horrifying comments did not go unnoticed by policymakers. In fact, under Saudi pressure, the Senate passed a resolution "strongly condemning the gross and systematic violations of human rights in Libya." The administration used the statement to launch the NATO assault on Tripoli.[61]

Similarly, deposing Mubarak, while the opposite of U.S. strategic intentions, was an important step to clearing Egyptian cities of their massive protests and eventually allowing the Muslim Brotherhood to fail at governing the people, who again took to the streets briefly for over-throwing Mohamed Morsi, one of the most reviled foreign statesmen in Congress.[62] This is not to say that there is nothing wrong with the now-jailed leader. However, one must question the extent to which the regime change had more to do with Riyadh's hatred of Morsi's party, viewed as an ideological threat to the Wahabbis for political legitimacy in the mostly Muslim region going on decades now. Putting it bluntly, Saudi lobbying in Congress helped by AIPAC, which believed the Muslim Brotherhood government next door to Israel threatened its survival, might have played a role in the Egyptian military's return to power.[63] Abdel Fattah el-Sisi's regime may be among the worst in the country's modern history, but the achievements made by the masses have not been lost entirely. An instance of the generational progress is the judiciary in Cairo standing up to the president on cases previously considered a matter of executive fiat.[64]

And while the United States has been indecisive on Syria because Assad may be "too big to fail,"[65] especially as ISIS feeds on the spoils of what was formerly a secular republic, Tunisia has welcomed its first demo-cratic parliament and presidency, thanks in part to American indifference toward the country's uprising and eventual support of the transition in Tunis, as detailed earlier. Continued congressional support for democracy is crucial in forcing the White House to honor the U.S. commitment to it in the Arab World, irrespective of the objectives at the National Security and Central Intelligence Agencies. Nevertheless, while the carnage of bad or no rule has thrown a wrench into the mechanics of pro-Arab lobbying toward American backing of better governance, that gain is a significant step for its future potential.

Rediscovering Unifying Objectives and the Basics of Pluralism

Opposed by the stronger lobbies representing Israel and the Persian Gulf states, pro-Arab groups have humbled their lobbying goals, refocusing energy nearby rather than waging a losing fight by seeking influence dur-ing an unsettled context halfway across the world. The hot-button issue of looking out for asylum-seekers from Muslim countries as a result of trouble there has been very popular among some Americans, even as they, on the whole, continue to be evenly split in the wake of terror attacks internationally, fearing the same thing can happen at home.[66]

Advocacy on such matters has been instructive about the workings of pro-Arab organizations in a variety of ways germane to the United States' pluralist-representational model. Hence, the ADC and AAI have persisted legislatively and in the courts at the federal, state, and local layers, to protect the rights and liberties of their constituents from infringement.[67] Long before Trump declared he would ban Muslims (he then shifted his language to saying he would employ "extreme vetting" of Muslims) coming to America if elected president,[68] both organizations reached out to the sitting administration for protecting targeted populations from abuses they would surely face if they were denied Temporary Protected Status. TPS designation allowed Syrian refugees in particular, most of whom are Sunni Muslim—some quite radicalized—to have asylum until the cessation of the civil war in their country. As Assad intensified the crackdown on his opponents, the AAI reported in press release that it, the ADC,

> and representatives from a number of Arab American and Syrian American organizations met with officials from the Department of Homeland Security (DHS) to discuss the implementation of government protections for Syrian nationals currently residing in the United States.[69]

In opposing repatriation or deportation at the executive branch, such action placed the advocacy in a key position to parlay its work into Congress, crafting more suitable legislation on the matter, and for the judiciary to weigh in if called upon in the case of any suit challenging the constitutional limits of the DHS directive in place. At every level, there was considerable solidarity from non-Arab, non-Muslim lobbying titans, including the American Civil Liberties Union (ACLU), National Association for the Advancement of Colored Persons (NAACP), La Raza (a pro-immigrant Mexican American organization), and Anti-Defamation League (ADL).[70]

The pro-Arab lobbying under examination, its emergent alliances, and dealings with the array of entities making, framing, reviewing, or implementing policies have had a synergistic effect on all other political activities, especially those concerning the shaping of foreign policy in the future. Summing up the ethnic agenda as the Arab uprisings still raged on, CAIR posited:

> It is significant for the president of the United States to support the massive popular demonstrations for freedom and self-determination in the region, particularly since our country has supported some of the dictators who have been and are oppressing their people. The president made the important point that all people deserve human dignity and self-determination, and we support his intention to defend those universal rights.[71]

And while the statement was made during more optimistic times and under a previous White House, it applies for all time and has a spectacular weight in the destiny of all Americans, beginning with Arabs and Muslims, who will uniquely have to bear the consequences of good or evil policies in the Middle East and North Africa. With that understanding, pro-Arab lobbying in Congress has called for a supportive posture on regional liberalization and reform. For one example of how lobbyists took up both issues, they presented members of the Senate's Foreign Relations Committee with opinion polling in "six Arab countries, Iran, and Turkey" showing:

> That people are more likely to blame "corrupt, repressive, and unrepresentative governments" and "religious figures and groups promoting extremist ideas and/or incorrect religious interpretations" for the rise of violent groups like al-Qaeda and the Islamic State than they are to blame "anger at the United States.[72]

And given deepening U.S. involvement to fight terrorism, the quest for building transparent governance across the region has become more necessary—though far from easier—to translate into policy on Capitol Hill. In light of public and elite weariness about protracted entanglements abroad, especially those that are costly in lives and treasure, such lobbying pressure has become indispensable. This point has quite a bit of evidence given the dire consequences of the military intervention in Libya to unfasten Qaddafi's tight grip on power after forty-two years. Despite the leader's petro-alliance with the United States, France, and the United Kingdom, the fact that he could be toppled by his people with America "leading from behind" gives any lobbyist interested in Arab and Muslim preferences an opportune moment to chart an affirmative path for Washington, DC instead of simply accepting the limitations of the "pro-Arab lobby" in Congress.[73]

Conclusion

Aside from offering pro-Arab constituencies a rarefied chance for successfully lobbying policy, the Arab Spring and its fallout have forced congressmen to envisage the region as a more humanized environment, with struggles, failings, and ambitions common to all civilizations. On many occasions, it was assumed that Middle Easterners and North Africans were not capable of progressive thinking, let alone transitioning to democracy. The people rallying for political rights and liberty along with economic transparency, freedom, and prosperity have changed all of that. Despite today's ongoing turmoil, the not-too-far-in-time exuberance of nascent revolution gave pro-Arab proponents in the United States ample opportunity to inform a sympathetic public and, therefore, policymakers more receptive to the cries for *karama*, the Arabic word for dignity. The Arab Spring—even as it turned Winter—also allowed American ethnic-coalition-based lobbying on behalf of millions worldwide to earn unprecedented access to a once unreachable media as outlets searched for answers in a time that may have looked like Armageddon. And although humanity has survived, the scars remain in the Muslim World. In Syria and Iraq, for example, Christian communities speaking the Aramaic said to have been the language of Jesus are now nearly extinct. Meanwhile, both war-torn countries have turned into sectarian cauldrons where Sunnis kill Shiites, Shiites kill Sunnis, and both kill non-Muslims. And just as the White House's ambition for a comprehensive Arab-Israeli peace[74] was frustrated by intransigence on all sides, the winds of change sweeping throughout the region, beginning with Iran's 2009 Green Revolution and culminating in Egypt and Libya after Tunisia's Jasmine Revolution of 2011–2012, have placed plenty of thrust in pro-Arab lobbying.

As Arab and Muslim organizations re-embark to influence congressional policy in a direction favorable to their future interests, they must look to that era, which has laid the foundation for a post-ethnic, post-religious lobbying agenda, or one that's not purely based on blood or identity, but rather on issues that bring people of all religions and backgrounds together. In a telling case, pro-Arab lobbying against military intervention often lines up with the mission of the American Association of Retired Persons (AARP) to avoid "cost-shifting to seniors in Medicare and Medicaid" because of the exponentially growing national debt caused in part by so much spending on Middle East wars.[75] The (re)alignment of interests places pro-Arab activism in good company since the AARP is one of the most preeminent lobbies in Congress.[76]

Such an unlikely friendship is also quite revealing of what is generally happening to lobbying and what it means to lobby Congress. Call it postmodern, but the activity is quickly evolving as the electronic marketplace of ideas makes it so that the weakest constituency could defeat the strongest, using nothing more than someone sitting in a room with internet skills, a little motivation, and a whole lot of public support or shared interests with powerful constituencies. No, lobbying is not an activity to be taken lightly, and it never will be so long as the American political system endures. However, as Thomas Hobbes once put it, "the weakest has strength enough to kill the strongest, either by secret machination or by confederacy with others that are in the same danger with himself."[77] And while pluralism in the United States is far from being a Hobbesian "state of nature," literally, a state of "civil war," it is nevertheless a very competitive space where policies matter just as much as ethnic lobbying and both have to adapt to what happens in the international, anarchic, condition of world politics or the tremendous competition for economic and political resources domestically. As the momentum for change reaches a geostrategic crescendo abroad, it is also heralding a landslide in pluralism, wherein, all lobbying, while still significant to policy decisions, has become more "outmoded," perhaps "passé," to paraphrase Khalil Jahshan, a celebrated Arab-American leader.[78]

Notes

1. Henceforth interchangeable with "pro-Arab lobby." Khalil Marrar, *The Arab Lobby and U.S. Foreign Policy: The Two-State Solution* (New York: Routledge, 2010). The community covers every element of multiculturalism. Check out Engy Abdelkader, "Muslim. Black. Women." *Huffington Post*, September 16, 2016; http://www.huffingtonpost.com/entry/57dc212ae4b0d5920b5b2a58?timestamp=1474047356613 (accessed October 3, 2016).

2. Ishaan Tharoor, "An Arab Winter?" *Time*, December 4, 2012; http://world.time.com/2012/12/04/top-10-international-news-lists/slide/an-arab-winter (accessed September 29, 2016).

3. John Mearsheimer and Stephen Walt, *The Israel Lobby and U.S. Foreign Policy* (New York: Farrar, Straus and Giroux, 2007), 141–142, and Mitchel Bard, *The Arab Lobby: The Invisible Alliance That Undermines America's Interests in The Middle East* (New York: Harper Collins, 2010), respectively.

4. Both communities run the gamut of multiculturalism in the U.S. Engy Abdelkader, "Muslim. Black. Women." *Huffington Post*, September 16, 2016; http://www.huffingtonpost.com/entry/57dc212ae4b0d5920b5b2a58?timestamp=1474047356613 (accessed October 3, 2016).

5. One of the best examples of how ethnic lobbying has become an unavoidable tributary of mainstream foreign policy analysis is a book by Donald M. Snow and Patrick J. Haney, *American Foreign Policy in a New Era* (New York: Pearson, 2013).

6. For a few of seminal examples, see Patrick J. Haney and Walt Vanderbrush, *The Cuban Embargo: The Domestic Politics of an American Foreign Policy* (Pittsburgh, PA: University of Pittsburgh Press, 2005), David M. Paul and Rachel A. Paul, *Ethnic Lobbies and U.S. Foreign Policy*, (Boulder, CO: Lynne Reinner Publishers, 2009), Mohammed E. Ahrari (ed.), *Ethnic Groups and U.S. Foreign Policy* (New York: Greenwood Press, 1985), and Alexander DeConde, *Ethnicity, Race, and American Foreign Policy* (Boston: Northeastern University Press, 1992).

7. As of last count in 2006, according to Open Secrets, a public advocacy group tracking money in politics. The figure applies to foreign and domestic lobbying dollars combined. If there's one silver lining for Arab and Muslim Americans, it's that lobbying in favor of Israel has recently adopted policies that they hold dear. For instance, the sole purpose of J Street, a Jewish-American 501(c) 4, is the two-state solution to the Israeli-Palestinian conflict, which has overwhelming support among Arabs and Muslims in America and everywhere else. During the last election cycle, J Street led the pack in political contributions to congressional candidates. See Open Secrets, "Top Pro-Israel Contributors, 2015–2016" at https://www.opensecrets.org/industries/indus.php?ind=Q05++ (accessed October 2, 2016). Nevertheless, and as I've discussed in *The Arab Lobby and U.S. Foreign Policy*, the ethnic constituencies represented by pro-Arab lobbying remain divided by nationality and religion. Both divisions led Joseph Baroody, an Arab-American lobbying giant in the 1970s and 1980s, to lament, "we can't represent the Arabs the way the Jewish lobby can represent Israel. The Israeli government has one policy to state, whereas we couldn't represent the 'the Arabs' if we wanted to. They're as different as the Libyans and Saudis are different, or as divided as the Christian and Moslem Lebanese." Originally Quoted in Steven L. Spiegel, *The Other Arab-Israeli Conflict: Making America's Middle East Policy, from Truman to Reagan* (Chicago: University of Chicago Press, 1985), 8.

8. Dania Koleilat Khatib (ed.), *The Arab Lobby and the U.S.: Factors for Success and Failure* (New York: Routledge, 2016).

9. The term "factors" covers a whole host of topics from infighting between the three branches of government to the perception of arms control by bureaucrats. Colton C. Campbell, Nicol C. Rae, and John F. Stack, *Congress and the Politics of Foreign Policy* (Upper Saddle River, NJ: Prentice Hall, 2003).

10. Alexis de Tocqueville, *Democracy in America and Two Essays on America* (New York: Penguin, 2003), ch. 10.

11. Robert Parry, "Did Money Seal Israeli-Saudi Alliance?" *Consortium News*, April 15, 2015; https://consortiumnews.com/2015/04/15/did-money-seal-israeli-saudi-alliance (accessed September 4, 2016). For another understanding of the warming relationship and the American foreign policy connection, see *Al Jazeera*, "Why Saudi Arabia and Israel Oppose Iran Nuclear Deal," April 14, 2015, at http://www.aljazeera.com/news/2015/04/saudi-arabia-israel-oppose-iran-nuclear-deal-150401061906177.html (accessed September 28, 2016).

12. Those include Hamas, ostensibly a Muslim Brotherhood proxy in Gaza and a recurring headache for Israeli Arabs and Jews alike as well as the region beyond. See Khalil Marrar, "Allies in Flux: American Policy after the Arab Spring," *Air and Space Power Journal, African and Francophonie* 6(4) (Winter, 2015): 21–35. On the Russo-Turkish rapprochement and its implications for the United States, see Neil MacFarquhar, "Russia and Turkey Vow to Repair Ties as West Watches Nervously," *The New York Times*, August 9, 2016; http://www.nytimes.com/2016/08/10/world/europe/putin-erdogan-russia-turkey.html?_r=0 (accessed October 12, 2016).

13. Shibley Telhami, "Americans on the Middle East: A Study of American Public Opinion," October 8, 2012, *Brookings Institution Report*; https://www.brookings.edu/research/americans-on-the-middle-east-a-study-of-american-public-opinion (accessed September 4, 2016).

14. Or, if they're contending for office, never getting elected in the first place. James A. Thurber, "An Introduction to Presidential-Congressional Rivalry," James A. Thurber (ed.), *Rivals for Power: Presidential-Congressional Relations*, 5th ed. (Lanham, MD: Rowman & Littlefield Publishers, 2013). Putting it differently, the policy preferences of the constituents sending representatives to Capitol Hill have made or broken careers since 1789. The same idea applies on a longer-term basis to all elected officials in every branch of government and at every level: local, state, and national.

15. *Arab American Institute*, "Demographics"; www.aaiusa.org/demographics (accessed September 29, 2016). On the relationship between candidates for congressional office and the politics of foreign policy at the district level, see Peter F. Trumbore and David A. Dulio, "Running on Foreign Policy? Examining the Role of Foreign Policy Issues in the 2000, 2002, and 2004 Congressional Campaigns," *Foreign Policy Analysis* 9(3): 267–286.

16. For a full list, see Congressman Keith Ellison's website at https://ellison.house.gov/media-center *and* https://ellison.house.gov/about/keiths-biography (accessed October 2, 2016).

17. NNAAC, "Advocacy and Civic Engagement"; http://www.nnaac.org/advocacy_and_civic_engagement (accessed October 12, 2016).

18. *AAI Opinion Polls*; http://www.aaiusa.org/opinion-polls (accessed October 12, 2016).

19. For opposition to pro-Arab activism borders on Islamophobia, see Robert Spencer, *Arab Winter Comes to America: The Truth About the War We're In* (Washington, DC: Regnery, 2014).

20. See Marrar, *The Arab Lobby and U.S. Foreign Policy*, ch. 2; Benjamin I. Page and Robert Y. Shapiro, "Effects of Public Opinion on Policy," *The American Political Science Review* 77(1) (March, 1983): 175–190.

21. Rami Khoury, "Arab Regime Change Is Best Left to Arabs," *The Guardian*, January 25, 2012; https://www.theguardian.com/commentisfree/2012/jan/25/arab-regime-change-egypt-syria-iraq?0p19G=c (accessed September 30, 2016).

22. Ross Logan, "Syrian Women Celebrate Freedom from ISIS Tyranny by Burning Their Burkas in the Street," *Mirror*, August 4, 2016; http://www.mirror.co.uk/news/world-news/syrian-women-celebrate-freedom-isis-8561268 (accessed September 30, 2016); Justin McCarthy, "Americans' Approval of Obama on Foreign Affairs," *Gallup*, August 15, 2016; http://www.gallup.com/poll/194624/americans-approval-obama-foreign-affairs-rises.aspx (accessed September 14, 2016).

23. Bruce Drake, "Americans Put Low Priority on Promoting Democracy Abroad," *Pew Research Center Fact Tank*, December 4, 2013; http://www.pewresearch.org/fact-tank/2013/12/04/americans-put-low-priority-on-promoting-democracy-abroad (accessed September 21, 2016).

24. That's not to say the personnel at the Defense Department are free from identity-based interests. See John Hudson, "For Muslims at the Pentagon, a Tough Election Year," *Foreign Policy*, September 17, 2016; http://www.arabamerica.com/for-muslims-at-the-pentagon-a-tough-election-year (accessed September 28, 2016).

25. And the military is far more popular among the public than Congress in the United States. James Fallows, "The Tragedy of the American Military," *The Atlantic*, January/February 2015; http://www.theatlantic.com/magazine/archive/2015/01/the-tragedy-of-the-american-military/383516 (accessed October 14, 2016).

26. Anonymous 501(c) 4 registrant, interview by the author, Washington, DC, March 11, 2016.

27. There's a critical perspective on the misuse of the liberty-security tradeoff. One example brings Ben Franklin's eighteenth-century quote into the twenty-first. Gregory Ferenstein, "How the World Butchered Benjamin Franklin's Quote on Liberty Vs. Security," February 14, 2014; https://techcrunch.com/2014/02/14/how-the-world-butchered-benjamin-franklins-quote-on-liberty-vs-security (accessed September 20, 2016).

28. Marissa Bailey, "New Video: NY Bombing Suspect," *CBS 2*, September 19, 2016; https://www.cbsnews.com/news/new-york-city-explosion-search-for-suspect-motive-five-questioned (accessed September 20, 2017).

29. James Zogby, Limited Options in the Face of Turmoil," *Washington Watch*, January 31, 2011, http://www.aaiusa.org/dr-zogby/entry/limited-options-in-the-face-of-turmoil (accessed January 31, 2011).

30. Arshin Adib-Moghaddam, *On the Arab Revolts and the Iranian Revolution: Power and Resistance Today* (New York: Bloomsbury, 2013), 24–30.

31. Hussein Ibish, "Under Western Lies," in *Bookforum*, April/May 2011, http://www.bookforum.com/inprint/018_01/7265 (accessed March 18, 2012).

32. Ibid.

33. This argument could go either way, that is, in favor or opposition of military intervention. Shadi Hamid, "Islamism, the Arab Spring, and the Failure of America's Do-Nothing Policy in the Middle East," *The Atlantic*, October 9, 2015; http://www.theatlantic.com/international/archive/2015/10/middle-east-egypt-us-policy/409537 (accessed September 17, 2016).

34. Hussein Ibish, "Yes, America Can Act in Syria!" *Now Lebanon*, March 13, 2012; http://www.nowlebanon.com/NewsArticleDetails.aspx?ID=375483 (accessed March 13, 2012); Deirdre Walsh and Leigh Ann Caldwell, "Most Positive Reaction to Syria Airstrikes Comes from Obama's Critics," *CNN*, September 23, 2014; http://www.cnn.com/2014/09/23/politics/syria-airstrikes-congress-reaction (accessed October 13, 2016).

35. SPLC, https://www.splcenter.org (accessed September 17, 2016).

36. Ahmed Rehab, conversation with the author, March 21, 2011.

37. Washington's Blog, "Muslims Are the VICTIMS of 'Between 82 and 97% of Terrorism-Related Fatalities:' U.S. Government," March 25, 2016; http://www.

globalresearch.ca/muslims-are-the-victims-of-between-82-and-97-of-terrorism-related-fatalities-us-government/5516565 (accessed October 2, 2016).

38. Jose R. Gonzalez, "Congress Considering Safe Zone for Persecuted Christian Yazidis in Iraq," February 9, 2016; http://www.cnsnews.com/news/article/jose-r-gonzalez/congress-will-push-safe-zone-persecuted-christians-yazidis-iraq (accessed October 14, 2016).

39. Ahmed Rehab, conversation with the author, March 21, 2011.

40. "Senator Kirk Holds Hearing on ISIS Terror Threat in Chicago," ABC 7, October 27, 2014; http://abc7chicago.com/news/sen-kirk-holds-hearing-on-isis-terror-threat-in-chicago/368548/ (accessed October 13, 2016).

41. For example, see CAIR-Chicago, "CAIR-Chicago Executive Director Ahmed Rehab Speaks to Students at Chicago-Kent College of Law," April 12, 2012, http://www.cairchicago.org/2012/04/12/cair-chicago-executive-director-ahmed-rehab-speaks-to-students-at-chicago-kent-college-of-law (accessed March 17, 2013); Ahmed Rehab, "Chicago Now: Chicago's Muslim Community Stands with the People of Syria," *Chicago Now*, March 1, 2012, http://www.chicagonow.com/people-power/2012/02/chicagos-muslim-community-stands-with-the-people-of-syria/ (accessed March 20, 2012).

42. The legacy of Clovis Maksoud has an entire volume of the *Arab Studies Quarterly* devoted to it. See *Arab Studies Quarterly* 39(3) (Summer 2017).

43. American-Arab Anti-Discrimination Committee, "Recap: Panel Discussion on Arab Uprisings and Our Community's Role," October 12, 2011, http://www.adc.org/media/press-releases/2011/october-2011/recap-panel-discussion-on-arab-uprisings-and-our-communitys-role (accessed March 20, 2012).

44. Bill Chambers, "NSA & FBI Spying on Muslims: Old Story, New Target," *Chicago Monitor*, July 14, 2014; http://chicagomonitor.com/2014/07/nsa-fbi-spying-on-muslims-old-story-new-target (accessed October 2, 2016).

45. This was something that would eventually prove essential in the fight against the Trump administration's so-called "Muslim ban." Shayan Modarres, "The Fight Over Trump's Muslim Ban Is a Fight Over America's Identity," *Huffington Post*, May 9, 2017; https://www.huffingtonpost.com/entry/the-fight-over-trumps-muslim-ban-is-a-fight-identity-americas-identity_us_5911ef2ae4b050bdca5fd398 (accessed May 29, 2017).

46. Ben Smith, "Concerns Rise about ADC Move, but Justice Department Will Attend," *Politico*, June 9, 2011, http://www.politico.com/blogs/bensmith/0611/Concerns_rise_about_ADC_move_but_Justice_Department_will_attend.html# (accessed June 9, 2011).

47. Ibid.

48. Ibid.

49. See ADC activities at http://www.adc.org/countering-violent-extremism-cve/ (accessed September 27, 2016) and CAIR's at https://www.cair.com/about-us/vision-mission-core-principles.html (accessed September 27, 2016).

50. See Aaron David Miller, "For America, an Arab Winter," *Woodrow Wilson International Center for Scholars*, July 7, 2011; http://www.americantaskforce.org/daily_news_article/2011/07/07/1310011200_11 (accessed September 13, 2016),

Hussein Ibish, "The Great Debate: Middle East Peace," November 16, 2011, http://www.americantaskforce.org/in_media/mm/hussein_ibish/2011/11/16/1321419600 (accessed March 22, 2012).

51. ATFP, "Raison d'être of the American Task Force on Palestine," http://www.americantaskforce.org/raison_d%C3%AAtre_american_task_force_palestine_2 (accessed October 14, 2016).

52. Author's interview.

53. Stephen Reader, "In Show of Solidarity with Egyptians, Hundreds Converge on Times Square," *WYNC News Blog*, February 4, 2011, http://www.wnyc.org/blogs/wnyc-news-blog/2011/feb/04/show-solidarity-egyptians-protesters-converge-times-sq (accessed March 22, 2012). Solidarity assemblies took place in major cities worldwide.

54. For an example, see Smith, "Concerns Rise about ADC Move, but Justice Department Will Attend."

55. Some of the fruits of their labor are above.

56. James Zogby, "The Arab Spring Effect," December 19, 2011, http://www.aaiusa.org/dr-zogby/entry/the-arab-spring-effect (accessed March 21, 2012).

57. For the full text and proposed actions, see United States House of Representatives, "H. Res. 277," May 19, 2015; https://www.congress.gov/bill/114th-congress/house-resolution/277 (accessed September 7, 2016).

58. For how those concerns came about, see Ghassan Salame (ed.), *The Foundations of the Arab State* (New York: Routledge, 2002).

59. For instance, see Helene Cooper, "Senate Narrowly Backs Trump Weapons Sale to Saudi Arabia," *The New York Times*, June 13, 2017; https://www.nytimes.com/2017/06/13/world/middleeast/trump-weapons-saudi-arabia.html (accessed August 3, 2017).

60. Quote is the author's translation of Qaddafi's speech in Arabic. For more, see John-Paul Ford Rojas, "Muammar Gaddafi in his Own Words," *The Telegraph*, October 20, 2011; http://www.telegraph.co.uk/news/worldnews/africaandindianocean/libya/8838644/Muammar-Gaddafi-in-his-own-words.html (accessed September 27, 2016).

61. U.S. Senate, Resolution 85, March 1, 2011; https://www.congress.gov/bill/112th-congress/senate-resolution/85/text (accessed October 17, 2016). Saudi Arabia also played an essential role at the UN. AFP, "UN Votes to Condemn Syria over Rights Violations," *Middle East Eye*, November 20, 2015; http://www.middleeasteye.net/news/un-votes-condemn-syria-over-rights-violations-173302367 (accessed October 17, 2016).

62. Marvin Heir and Abraham Cooper, "Recognize Muslim Brotherhood for the Hate Group It Is," *The Hill*, August 5, 2013; http://thehill.com/blogs/congress-blog/foreign-policy/315363-time-to-recognize-the-muslim-brotherhood-for-what-it-is-a-hate-group (accessed October 14, 2016).

63. Hussein Ibish, "Saudi Arabia's New Sunni Alliance," *The New York Times*, July 31, 2015; https://www.nytimes.com/2015/08/01/opinion/hussein-ibish-saudi-arabias-new-sunni-alliance.html?_r=0 (accessed May 30, 2017).

64. Rami G. Khouri, "A Court Case in Egypt Worth Watching," *The Jordan Times*, June 23, 2016; http://www.jordantimes.com/opinion/rami-g-khouri/court-

case-egypt-worth-watching (accessed September 14, 2016). This is not to say that Egyptian courts are places where justice is served. For a dreadful example, see Robert Trafford, Mays Ramadhani "Egypt's Year of Youth: How 'Generation Protest' became 'Generation Jail,'" September 13, 2016; http://www.independent.co.uk/news/world/africa/so-much-for-egypts-year-of-youth-how-generation-protest-became-generation-jail-a7234256.html (accessed September 14, 2016).

65. Aaron David Miller, "Too Big to Fail?" *Foreign Policy Magazine*, May 12, 2011.

66. Elizabeth McElvein, "What do Americans Really Think About Syrian Refugees?" *Brookings*, March 4, 2016; https://www.brookings.edu/blog/markaz/2016/03/04/what-do-americans-really-think-about-syrian-refugees/ (accessed September 27, 2016). Polling showed "53% of Americans said . . . that the United States should stop accepting refugees altogether."

67. See Colton C. Campbell and John F. Stack, *Congress Confronts the Court: The Struggle for Legitimacy and Authority in Lawmaking* (Lanham, MD: Rowman & Littlefield Publishers, 2001).

68. There's unfortunately nothing new about this. David Reimers, *Unwelcome Strangers: American Identity and the Turn Against Immigration. The New Nativism* (New York: Columbia University Press, 1998).

69. Omar Tewfik, "Media Advisory," February 24, 2012; http://www.aaiusa.org/blog/entry/adc-aai-joint-statement-regarding-temporary-protected-status (accessed February 24, 2012).

70. *Anti-Defamation League*, "A Wave of Ugly Rhetoric Targeting Muslim Immigrants," March 23, 2015; http://www.adl.org/civil-rights/immigration/c/a-wave-of-ugly-rhetoric.html#.V-srdSgrKhc (accessed September 27, 2016). A web search will reveal the activities of the other organizations helping the pro-Arab effort.

71. Council on American-Islamic Relations, "CAIR: Obama's 'Arab Spring' Address Sets the Right Tone," May 19, 2011, http://www.facebook.com/note.php?note_id=10150195895039442 (accessed March 22, 2012).

72. The Zogby Research Service report of those findings, put out by a polling firm headed by the AAI president's brother, John Zogby, was picked up by major news networks and prominently featured on foreign policy blogs all over the internet. My source for the quote on this page is Derek Davison, "New Poll Highlights Need for Reform in the Middle East," IPS News, December 14, 2015; http://www.ipsnews.net/2015/12/new-poll-highlights-need-for-reform-in-the-middle-east (accessed October 13, 2016).

73. Marrar, *The Arab Lobby*, 116–118.

74. Philip Weiss, "Palestinians are Finally Welcome in Washington," *Modoweiss*, October 17, 2008, http://mondoweiss.net/2008/10/mj-rosenberg-whos-a-lot-closer-to-the-ground-than-i-am-says-that-this-is-the-year-that-every-thing-has-changed.html (accessed October 19, 2008).

75. Allyson Funk, "AARP Opposes Cost-Shifting to Seniors in Medicare and Medicaid," *AARP Press Center*, November 20, 2016; http://www.aarp.org/about-aarp/press-center/info-11-2012/AARP-Opposes-Cost-Shifting-to-Seniors-in-Medicare-and-Medicaid.html (accessed October 3, 2016).

76. John J. Coleman, Kenneth M. Goldstein, William G. Howell, *Understanding American Politics and Government, National/State/Local Edition*, 3rd ed. (New York: Pearson, 2014), ch. 12. Full disclosure: this is a book to which I contributed a solicited endorsement.

77. Thomas Hobbes, *The Leviathan* (Cambridge, MA: Hacket, 1994), ch. 13.

78. Khalil Jahshan, former president of the National Association of Arab Americans and Representative of Association of Arab American University Graduates and Palestine Research and Educational Center, interview by the author, Arlington, VA, March 14, 2006. Originally quoted in Marrar, *The Arab Lobby*, p. 118.

Chapter 6

The Armenian and Turkish Lobbying, and the (Non-) Recognition of the Armenian Genocide by the United States

Julien Zarifian

The year 2015 marked the centennial of the Armenian genocide. Observed all across the world, many ceremonies and remembrances took place allowing world leaders an opportunity to publicly affirm or re-affirm that what happened to the Ottoman Armenians between 1915 and 1917 was genocide. These observations occurred, of course, despite the vocal opposition of the Republic of Turkey, which denies the genocide and opposes its international recognition. Many of these world leaders, including heads of state, parliament speakers, foreign ministers, and religious leaders, came to Yerevan on April 24 for Genocide Remembrance Day and to commemorate the genocide in Armenia. Others, such as German President Joachim Gauck and Pope Francis, chose this special year to use the word "genocide" publicly for the first time in reference to Armenia. The United States, however, decided not to send any major representative to Yerevan. Rather, the United States decided to maintain a political line established decades ago designed not to irritate Turkey. Then-President Barack Obama, who had formally and repeatedly promised to recognize the genocide while a presidential candidate, made a statement commemorating the genocide that circumvented the use of the word "genocide." He also decided not to visit Yerevan for the ceremonies on April 24, to which he sent "only" Secretary of the Treasury Jacob Lew, accompanied by four members of Congress.

In doing so, President Obama, like other American presidents before him, strongly disappointed his compatriots of Armenian background, and their friends and supporters, most having been enthusiastic supporters of Obama as a candidate for president in 2008. Politically speaking, the one to two million Armenian Americans have made genocide recognition by the United States their main lobbying goal, and they have spent significant amounts of time, energy, and money to reach that goal. The core of their efforts has concerned Congress and specifically centered on passing a bill recognizing the Armenian genocide, but despite a dynamic and often remarkable activism, they have not been successful. Indeed, many countries of the world have recognized the genocide, but the United States has yet to do so. This is mainly because the Armenian lobby is not the only lobby concerned with the issue. Congress has felt substantial pressure from the Republic of Turkey, which refuses to admit that its Ottoman predecessor committed genocide against its Armenian subjects. In addition, Congress has been lobbied by the executive branch (be it a Democratic or Republican administration), which has been concerned with maintaining good relations with Turkey, an important and strategic Middle-Eastern and NATO ally.

My goal in this chapter is to examine the political struggle for U.S. (non-)recognition of the Armenian genocide by looking at the Armenian and Turkish lobbies and analyzing their internal complexities, organizations, and strategies, as well as their successes and failures over the past few decades. To do so, in the first part of the chapter I will focus on the state of the Armenian genocide recognition in the United States by discussing which U.S. institutions and political figures have recognized the Armenian genocide and which have not. In the chapter's second and third sections I will discuss the U.S.-Armenian lobby and its lobbying methods. In the last three sections I will examine the group's successes and failures as well as how Turkish Americans and Turkey interact with and lobby Congress and the executive branch to ensure legislation recognizing the Armenian genocide is not passed.

The United States and the
Question of the Armenian Genocide

Although the Armenian genocide has not been a central element of American political and public life, as has the Jewish Holocaust,[1] it has still played a part in it, from its perpetration in 1915–1916 until today. This role has been mostly political, as the Armenian massacres and then their recognition as genocide soon became of political and geopolitical importance to the United States. But the question of the Armenian genocide has also affected American society, the intellectual sphere, and the media.

During the genocide and in its aftermath—and even before, during the Hamidian massacres of 1894–1896[2]—the American public and
its elected leaders were particularly concerned, providing considerable
humanitarian support to the Armenians, and also some political support.
But then, as the Turkish Republic and the former Soviet Union imposed
themselves in the international arena, sweeping away the very idea of an
independent Armenia, and as the genocide survivors started a new—and
often extremely difficult—life in the many countries of the diaspora, the
question was somewhat forgotten. It was only after World War II and
the Holocaust that the Armenian genocide became an issue again in the
United States. For many Armenians it became clear that what happened
to the Ottoman Armenians in 1915–1916 was genocide, and they thus
renewed and intensified their claims for justice. These claims intensified
again in the 1960s and 1970s, when the children and grandchildren of
the survivors started to take on the question, and started to face an active
and elaborate denial from the Turkish authorities, for which it proved to
be a highly sensitive issue.

The question became, progressively, very sensitive for the United
States, too. On the one hand, Armenian Americans asserted openly that
what happened in 1915–1916 was genocide, and many of them asked for
a formal recognition of it by Turkey and the international community,
including the United States. On the other hand, Turkey, a NATO member
since 1952, and a major ally in the Middle East and in the fight against
communism, firmly refused any type of recognition and opposed any
official recognition by the United States. Turkish authorities regularly and
vehemently opposed those among the U.S. media or civil society who
recognized the Armenian genocide or even used the "G word." To cope
with this uncomfortable situation, the U.S. executive branch opted for a
rather ambiguous position. With notable exceptions,[3] it has chosen not to
use the "G word" to characterize the massacres of 1915–1917. However, it
has never directly denied the Armenian genocide and, particularly through
the voice of the president, mentioned and even commemorated the massacres on a regular basis. While the executive branch over the years has
maintained this ambiguous position, many American people, organizations,
and media representatives[4] formally recognized the genocide, especially
in the 1980s and 1990s.

At the local and state level, an impressive number of elected authorities began taking a firm position on the question. Many municipalities
now recognize the genocide, including large cities such as New York,
Boston, San Francisco, Philadelphia, and Los Angeles, as well as smaller
communities, especially the greater Los Angeles area and central valley in

California, which is home to a sizeable Armenian-American community.[5] Many monuments and other commemoratives have also been constructed in these areas, giving a more concrete and visible form to these communities' policies of recognition. In the meantime, no fewer than forty-eight states in the United States have recognized the Armenian genocide,[6] either through a vote by their state legislature or a proclamation by their executive branch, or both.[7] In some cases this recognition has been accompanied by an affirmation of a State Remembrance Day. California, which is, with Rhode Island, Pennsylvania, and New York, the state whose positions on this issue have been the firmest and most repeated, established a Week of Remembrance of the Armenian genocide between 2007 and 2010.[8]

At the federal level, although no binding legislation has been passed by Congress, the House of Representatives has twice voted in favor of a measure recognizing the Armenian genocide (1975 and 1985).[9] In 1996 and 2004, the House also added amendments to the Foreign Operations Appropriations bill mentioning the Armenian genocide.[10] The Senate has never passed a measure recognizing the genocide, but was close to doing so in the 101st Congress, when former Senator Robert J. "Bob" Dole, a long-time friend of the Armenians,[11] introduced legislation declaring April 24, 1990, a "National Day of Remembrance of the 75th Anniversary of the Armenian Genocide of 1915–1923." Although the measure was defeated by a small margin, it was co-sponsored by forty-three senators.[12] In 2014, the Senate Committee on Foreign Relations favored recognition legislation,[13] as did its House counterpart, the Committee on Foreign Affairs. Most, if not all, of this congressional activity was the direct result of the Armenian-American lobby, whose role, as pointed out by Representative Frank Pallone (D-NJ), a close friend of the Armenians for several decades, has been instrumental "for calling for recognition of the Armenian genocide."[14]

The Armenian-American Lobby

While the Armenian-American community is relatively small in number (estimates place it between one and two million people),[15] this community is well integrated—socially, economically, and politically—in densely populated areas such as Boston, Los Angeles, Fresno, New York, Detroit, Chicago, San Francisco, and Miami. A diverse group themselves, many Armenian Americans tend to unify around a major unifying theme: the Armenian genocide. The genocide is considered one of the major identity and political "cements" of the community, and its recognition by the United States has become a major collective claim of Armenian Americans. This claim, along with a few others, mostly related to the security and prosperity of the Republic of Armenia, has been politically carried mainly by two lobbying groups: the Armenian National Committee of America (ANCA) and the Armenian Assembly of America (AAA).[16]

The ANCA is affiliated with a major Armenian political party, the Armenian Revolutionary Federation (ARF or "Dashnaktsutyun" in Armenian), created in 1890, and is of socialist inspiration. It is therefore close to the numerous ARF-affiliated or "sister" organizations and media in the United States, but also in Armenia and in the diaspora. It is the eldest of the two groups and finds its origin in the American Committee for the Independence of Armenia created at the beginning of the twentieth century.[17] The group proudly presents itself as "the largest and most influential Armenian-American grassroots political organization" and relies on thousands of supporters and a network of more than fifty chapters and offices across the United States, organized around two main branches, the ANCA-WR (i.e., Western Region), headquartered in Glendale, near Los Angeles, home of roughly 80,000 Armenians, and the ANCA-ER, with headquarters in Watertown, Massachusetts, an historic town of Armenian settlement.

The AAA, on the other hand, was founded in the early 1970s by prominent Armenian Americans not affiliated with the ARF. While the AAA has experienced serious financial difficulties over the past few years—and therefore has seen its activities slow down[18]—it is often considered less "radical" than the ANCA. It is also often perceived as more "elitist" in the sense that its ties with the Armenian community seem less numerous than the ANCA, and because it tends to rely more on the activism of a few influential people than on grassroots lobbying efforts—despite its "grassroots" affiliation, the Armenian American Action Committee (ARAMAC). As with the ANCA, the AAA's lobbying activities are led by a long-time emblematic executive director. In addition to ARAMAC, the AAA counts a few affiliated or "sister" structures. One is the Armenian National Institute, a "non-profit organization dedicated to the study, research, and affirmation of the Armenian genocide."[19] In addition, there is the Armenian Trees Project, "a non-profit program [that] conducts vitally important environmental projects in Armenia's cities and villages and seeks support in advancing its reforestation mission"[20]; since 1999, it has also maintained representation at the United Nations.

Lobbying by Armenian-American Groups

In terms of legal status, of the two aforementioned organizations, only the ANCA operates under a 501(c)(4) status, which allows it to make lobbying its main activity. The AAA is a 501(c)(3) organization and therefore is limited in its lobbying and political activities.[21] For example, the Assembly cannot directly or officially support candidates in election campaigns. In terms of objectives and methods, the two organizations are quite different, too, but have proven to be—fortuitously for their cause—quite complementary of one another.

The ANCA's main goals are "[t]o foster public awareness in support of a free, united and independent Armenia; to influence and guide U.S. policy on matters of interest to the Armenian-American community; to represent the collective Armenian-American viewpoint on matters of public policy, while serving as liaison between the community and their elected officials."[22] The objectives of the AAA seem less "aggressive" than those of the ANCA, whose reference to "a free, united and independent Armenia" explicitly refers to the unification of historical Armenian territories, which are today part of other countries (namely, the eastern regions of Turkey and the region of Javakhetia in Georgia)—and therefore to the territorial dismemberment of two allies of the United States. The AAA affirms being more focused on the Armenian community and its role in U.S. political life, and the improvement of "U.S.-Armenia and U.S.-Karabakh relationships based upon a common vision of democracy, the rule of law, open markets, regional security and unfettered commerce."[23] For a long time, the AAA has practiced a "personal" lobbying effort, aimed primarily at specific members of Congress, but also at officials of the executive branch. Conversely, the ANCA tended to practice traditional grassroots lobbying, which has been efficient at influencing members of Congress but less so the executive branch. This is no longer the case, however, as both organizations have diversified their lobbying practices, accentuating and complementing each other's efforts.

The Armenian-American lobby has been able to practice all the types of lobbying identified by David Paul and Rachel Anderson Paul in their important book of 2009 on the influence of ethnic lobbies on U.S. foreign policy:[24] direct lobbying (i.e., establishing a direct contact with decision makers to influence them), grassroots lobbying (i.e., mobilizing supporters to impress and influence decision makers and/or public opinion), coalition building (i.e., allying with other groups or people to be more influential), and monitoring the policymaking process (i.e., being able not only to influence the decisions, but also to define the process and impose the agenda).[25]

As far as direct lobbying is concerned, both the ANCA and the AAA[26] frequently meet with sympathetic members of Congress, as well as with executive branch officials. For example, in July 2015, an ANCA delegation met with then-Secretary of Treasury Jacob Lew to thank him for having led the U.S. official delegation to the international ceremony of the Armenian genocide centennial in Yerevan, Armenia. In the meantime, reports surfaced that they "also [. . .] discuss[ed] the Treasury Department's role in the further growth of the U.S.-Armenia economic relationship. During the meeting, the ANCA raised a number of policy priorities, including the mutual benefits of a new U.S.-Armenia Tax Treaty."[27] The Armenian lobby has also practiced grassroots lobbying considerably often, organizing, for example, demonstrations and marches. The ANCA also regularly leads email writing, letter writing, and phone call campaigns with the goal of having Armenian Americans pressure lawmakers to recognize the Armenian genocide.

For instance, in 2015, it launched the March to Justice, "a robust interactive global online platform for the growth of sustained grassroots engagement in support of justice for the Armenian genocide and durable security for the Armenian nation."[28] Through this initiative it invited people to, among other things, "[s]end letters to elected officials and international leaders (automatically addressed based on the country of the sender) demanding justice for the Armenian genocide." It continued by explaining: "America-based advocates will have the opportunity to share their views with UN Secretary General Ban Ki-Moon, President Barack Obama and Vice-President Joe Biden, and Senate and House members with just a few clicks."[29]

Although it has probably not been its strongest point, the Armenian lobby has also been able to ally with other groups and to build coalitions. Their main allies have traditionally been other ethnic lobbies that oppose Turkey, including Greek and Kurdish groups, as well as human rights groups[30] (in the 2000s, these groups included Genocide Intervention Network, the Center for American Progress, Enough!, and Save Darfur[31]). In the 1990s and 2000s, the Armenian lobby has often had to face the opposition of Jewish and Pro-Israeli groups, which were generally advised by Israel to counter lobbying against its long-time ally Turkey.[32] It is even very likely, as clearly implied in Thomas Ambrosio's appropriately titled study, "Entangling Alliances: The Turkish-Israeli Lobbying Partnership and Its Unintended Consequences," that U.S. and possibly Turkish authorities sometimes also directly ask Jewish-Americans leaders to oppose the Armenian genocide resolutions.[33]

Finally, the Armenian lobby has also proved to be capable of monitoring the policymaking process, especially thanks to the tight contacts it has built with many lawmakers, notably through the Congressional Caucus on Armenian Issues. Created in 1995, the Caucus had 97 representatives in 2016,[34] but has at times been as large as 150 members. It is co-chaired by two or more members (often one or two Democrats and one or two

Republicans, and often representing different regions of the United States) who are particularly active in promoting and defending Armenian interests. Members of the Caucus routinely propose and co-sponsor "pro-Armenian" legislation, as well as publicly advocate for and defend causes important to the Armenian-American community. Moreover, the Congressional Caucus on Armenian Issues is closely linked to the Armenian-American lobby and its leaders, with whom it meets on a regular basis.

Over the past several Congresses, membership of the Caucus has routinely included influential representatives, including former and current House Speakers Nancy Pelosi (D-CA) and Paul D. Ryan (R-WI), former Deans of the House Representatives John Dingell, Jr. (D-MI) and John Conyers (D-MI), former House Minority Whip and Majority Leader Eric Cantor (R-VA), as well as members from key committees, such as the House Foreign Affairs Committee. Some of the more active Caucus members are lawmakers of Armenian descent, such as Representatives Anna G. Eshoo and Jackie Speier, both Democrats from California.[35] The Caucus also counts on the firm support of several senators, often with large Armenian populations in their states, such as Robert Menendez (D-NJ) and Majority Leader Mitch McConnell (R-KY) or, in the past, Robert "Bob" Dole (R-KS), Joseph R. Biden (D-DE), John F. Kerry (D-MA), and Barack Obama (D-IL).[36]

Both the ANCA and AAA have also created their own political action committees (PACs) to make their presence felt through campaign contributions. The ARMENPAC is officially independent of the AAA, but its founders and key members are closely linked with the group, while the ANC-PAC is officially linked with the ANCA.[37] Although the ARMENPAC and the ANC-PAC have not been as active at the federal level in recent years as they were in the 1990s and early 2000s, they have helped finance the campaigns of dozens of representatives and senators, both Democrats and Republicans. In 2004, for example, the ARMENPAC contributed more than $100,000 to congressional campaigns. It supported 136 candidates to the House (donating amounts ranging from $500 to $5,297 to each one) and eleven candidates to the Senate (these candidates received between $500 and $2,000).[38] While the ANC-PAC has not contributed as much to congressional campaigns, it has regularly spent between $30,000 and $50,000 per electoral cycle, often giving significant amounts of money to a few candidates (including, for example, the maximum allowable contribution to Senator Menendez in 2008[39]). Contrarily, the ARMENPAC tends to contribute to a larger number of candidates but with smaller amounts. In the end, although all lawmakers who received financial support from the Armenian-American lobby are not always proactive in promoting

Armenian interests, the most emblematic "pro-Armenian" ones, such as Senator Menendez, former Senator Mark Kirk (R-IL), and former Representative Joe Knollenberg (R-MI), the two latter having been co-chairs of the Armenian Caucus, are those who received the most frequently significant amounts of money from the Armenian lobby.

While the AAA cannot officially pronounce itself in favor of or in opposition to a candidate because of its 501(c)(3) status, the ARMENPAC can. The ANCA can do it also, and it is an important part of its political activism. It supports candidates—both for congressional and presidential elections.[40] Moreover, the ANCA gives grades (from A+ to F), much like other interest groups, such as the National Rifle Association and Planned Parenthood, to members of Congress, based on their records on questions of interest to Armenian Americans. As in all their political efforts, the ANCA is trying to influence sympathizers' vote choices on issues they care most about.

The Successes (and Failures) of the Armenian-American Lobby

The multifaceted and often complementary lobbying effort led by the ANCA and the AAA has permitted them to gain influence in Washington, DC, especially on Capitol Hill. Although the precise influence of ethnic lobbies on U.S. foreign policy, and the "scientific" way to evaluate it, are difficult to establish,[41] the Armenian-American lobby is often presented as a very efficient and influential lobby. Zbigniew Brzezinski ranked it among the three most effective ethnic lobbies in Washington, DC, in 2006 (along with Jewish Americans and Cuban Americans),[42] as do David Paul and Rachel Anderson Paul.[43] This influence has often been perceived as excessive and has been criticized, even by some in the media.[44]

The Armenian-American lobby has obtained a few positive results, especially in relation to U.S.-South Caucasian policy, but it has also experienced failures and/or mixed results. Indeed, the two most famous instances of efficient lobbying by the Armenian-American lobby relate to U.S. policies toward the Republic of Armenia and the Nagorno-Karabakh conflict,[45] and U.S. policies toward Azerbaijan. In the first case, the Armenian-American lobby and its friends on Capitol Hill succeeded in granting Armenia a considerable annual financial assistance, approved every year in a congressional appropriations bill and distributed mostly through the United States Agency for International Development (USAID).[46] Since 1992, Armenia has received more than $2 billion in U.S. financial assistance, making Armenia one of the most important recipient countries of U.S. *per capita* foreign direct financial aid. In the second case, the U.S.-Armenian lobby and its supporters in Congress have succeeded in excluding Azerbaijan from receiving similar foreign assistance. Insisting on the fact that Azerbaijan was imposing a blockade on Armenia, the Armenian-American lobby succeeded in convincing lawmakers that Azerbaijan was the aggressor in the Karabakh conflict, and thus passed Section 907 of the Freedom Support Act that banned Azerbaijan from U.S. foreign aid.[47]

As for the question of the Armenian genocide recognition, as well as other strategic questions, such as the (non-)integration of Armenia into Caspian energy transportation routes, because of Azerbaijan's opposition, the results of the Armenian-American lobby are much more mixed. A negative, although not inexact, way to assess these results is to consider them as totally unconvincing, as despite several decades of considerable efforts, the Armenian-American lobby has been not successful with the biggest issue on its agenda—full U.S. recognition of the Armenian genocide. Others look at the lobby's efforts as a qualified success, however. Indeed, another way to consider the Armenian-American lobby's efforts to obtain this recognition and its results is first to recognize that without these efforts the issue would not be on the radar of Congress. As political analyst Fraser Cameron explains, "[d]espite the relatively small size of the Armenian-American community and its limited resources, both the ANCA and the Assembly have registered considerable success, not the least in placing the Armenian genocide as a permanent item in the U.S. legislative and foreign policy agendas."[48] Indeed, although the ultimate goal has not been reached, the political recognition of the genocide has evolved from an unknown and neglected theme until the 1970s to a significant domestic and foreign policy question, especially in the 1990s and onward. As noted earlier, a great majority of states and many local authorities have recognized the Armenian genocide, and even at the federal level, the House of Representatives has voted in favor of recognition. It is obvious that all these results are the direct fruit of the activism of the Armenian-American lobby, which regularly prides itself on what it—along with other players, including its Turkish opponents—tends to present as successes.

Lobbying by Turkish Americans

The mixed results that the Armenian-American lobby has obtained on the genocide recognition issue are not directly and/or only due to mistakes or weaknesses on its part. The fact that the United States has yet to fully recognize the Armenian genocide is also largely due to Turkish activism. Contrary to the government of the Republic of Armenia, which rarely interferes on this question, the Turkish government is often on the frontline of lobbying against recognition. Turkish governments—regardless of their political affiliation—have always firmly opposed the recognition of the Armenian genocide by the United States. They actively support the lobbying of the relatively small, but active, Turkish-American community and, more significantly, initiate direct and indirect lobby in Washington, DC.[49]

The main Turkish-American lobbying organization is the Turkish Coalition of America (TCA).[50] Fairly new to the lobbying scene (2007), it engages in educational, cultural, and social, as well as political activities.[51] With headquarters in Washington, DC, as well as offices in Boston and Istanbul, it, according to information available on its website, does not receive funding from the Turkish government and is financially supported only by Turkish Americans in the United States.[52] The Turkish-American community is not as large as the Armenian-American population—estimates place it between 350,000 and 500,000—nor is it as geographically distributed across the country, or as politically active. However, some of its members are strongly opposed to recognizing the Armenian genocide and support the TCA, which clearly is a denialist organization, asserting, for example, that "[t]he Armenian Diaspora claim of genocide is a one-sided assessment of the inter-communal war between Ottoman Armenians and Ottoman Muslims in 1915."[53] Although it does not focus only on the question of the Armenian genocide, it has been particularly active in opposing its recognition in and by the United States. It has notably produced documents and lobbied members of Congress to oppose resolutions recognizing the Armenian genocide.

Indeed, while the TCA is a 501(c)(3) organization, limited in its lobbying and political activities, it is closely aligned to the Congressional Caucus on Turkey and Turkish Americans. Founded in 2001, this congressional member organization (CMO) currently has a membership of 156 members, the large majority of whom (98) are Republicans.[54] The Turkish-American lobby can also count on several affiliated PACs, the most important being the TCA-USA PAC, which since its creation in 2008 has contributed more than $100,000 to every congressional campaign.[55] Although contributing to congressional campaigns through PACs is a relatively new practice for Turkish Americans, it is nonetheless developing fast. According to the TCA-USA PAC, over two hundred contributors donated approximately $314,000 to the Turkish PACs in 2015, representing an increase of 60 percent comparing to 2014. It uses these donations to support some strategic candidates in specific districts to underline the Turkish-American role and power. For example, in Maryland's 2016 U.S. Senate Democratic primary, Turkish Americans contributed $26,000 to Representative Donna F. Edwards, a member of the Congressional Caucus on Turkey and Turkish Americans, rather than to Senator Chris Van Hollen (D-MD), a strong supporter of Armenian and Greek issues.[56]

Lobbying by Turkey

In addition, to counter lobbying efforts by Turkish Americans, a long-time anti–Armenian genocide recognition strategy has also been directly led by the Turkish government, for decades. Concretely, Ankara has used several different techniques to prevent the United States from fully recognizing the genocide. First, it has frequently used direct pressure on the executive branch and Congress, sometimes threatening with diplomatic and geopolitical consequences in case of recognition. As early as 1975, there are records of the Turkish ambassador in Washington, DC meeting directly with then-House Majority Leader Thomas P. "Tip" O'Neil (D-MA), who supported a resolution recognizing the genocide, to try to influence him.[57] More recently, in 2007 and 2009, in reaction to congressional committee votes in favor of recognition, Turkey recalled its ambassador in Washington, DC for consultations several times. The Turkish government has also threatened the United States with a severe cooling of its bilateral relations. In 2010, for instance, then-Prime Minister Recep Tayyip Erdogan issued an explicit warning that a congressional vote recognizing the genocide would harm U.S.-Turkish relations,[58] whereas President Abdullah Gul explained: "Turkey will not be responsible for the negative results that this event may lead to."[59]

This diplomatic pressure, sometimes accompanied by phone calls or working visits of Turkish diplomats, tends to be directed first toward the executive branch, which has then applied pressure on Congress when necessary. Former Secretary of State Condoleezza Rice explains in her memoirs that since she began her diplomatic career in 1991, every president and secretary of state has fought to prevent Congress from recognizing the genocide. In 1991, while she was President George H.W. Bush's special assistant for European affairs, she was asked "to mobilize an effort to defeat [a] resolution [branding the Ottoman Empire's mass killings of Armenians as genocide] in the House of Representatives." She insists on the fact that "[t]he Turks, who had been essential in the first Gulf War effort, were outraged at the prospect of being branded for an event that had taken place almost a century before," and then explained that she "had succeeded in [her] assigned task" being very clear on the fact that if the House did not pass the resolution it was because of presidential direct pressure. In 2007, while serving as secretary of state, after the House Foreign Affairs Committee had voted in favor of a similar resolution, and while the resolution was about to be voted on by full House, Rice went as far as "begging" Speaker Nancy Pelosi "to do something to prevent a vote" and also explained that "[w]e managed to convince the Turks that we would do everything possible to prevent a vote in the full House, which we eventually did."[60] More recently, the Obama administration also strongly opposed passage of genocide recognition resolutions. In 2010, for example, then-Secretary of State Hillary Clinton, who recognized the genocide before taking office, publicly said, after the passage of such a resolution in the House Foreign Affairs Committee: "We'll work very hard to make sure it does not go to the House floor."[61] It never did.

Turkey has also spent huge amounts of money to influence U.S. elected officials. According to one source of the late 1980s, "Turkey ha[d] long had a $1 million-a-year PR [public relations] contract with [famous lobbying firm] Hill & Knowlton."[62] And then, in 1989, Turkey had an annual lobbying budget in the United States of more than $2 million, putting it in a league with South Africa and South Korea.[63] Although most lobbying at that time was directed toward a strong partnership between the United States and Turkey in the areas of defense, other issues of importance to Turkey were also lobbied. Then, "[i]n 1990, Turkey hired McAuliffe, Kelly, Rafaelli, and Siemens for $800,000 to supplement its lobbying efforts. After Democrat Bill Clinton's victory in the 1992 presidential election, the services of these companies were terminated. Six new firms with closer contacts with the Democrats were hired at an annual cost of more than $3 million. Fleishman-Hillard and Capitoline/MS & Lee received the largest of these contracts."[64] In all these cases, it is difficult to determine the exact importance of the genocide recognition question in the lobbying efforts generated by these firms, but it seems obvious that they play an indirect and/or direct role in preventing recognition resolutions from being passed in Congress.

More recently, Turkey hired other lobbying firms, such as the Livingston Group, Dickstein Shapiro LLP, DLA Pipers, and the Gephardt Group, to help prevent Congress from enacting legislation recognizing the Armenian genocide—lobbying firms with such famous members as former Representative Robert L. Livingston (R-LA), former House Minority and Majority Leader Richard A. "Dick" Gephardt (D-MO), former Speaker Dennis J. Hastert (R-IL), and former member of the House and CIA Director, Porter Goss (R-FL).[65] While with DLA, Gephardt, who co-sponsored a recognition resolution when he was in Congress, earned $1.2 million from his year-long contract with Turkey in 2005 to 2006.[66] More recently, his company, the Gephardt Group, working for Turkey since 2008, signed a contract of $1.7 with the Turkish government, a contract that subcontracts with six other firms.[67] Turkey is also currently under contract with the lobbying firm Mercury LLC, and although prevention of the Armenian genocide recognition has not apparently been on its agenda yet, one of its targets is the Republic of Armenia and, more specifically, to denounce its ties with Russia.[68] In the end, according to an article of *The Nation* of 2013, "the Turkish government [. . .] since 2007, has retained at least six lobbying firms to shape public opinion and court elected officials."[69] And, as stated by the *Washington Post* in 2010, "[t]he Turkish government has spent millions on Washington lobbying over the past decade, much of it focused on the Armenian genocide issue."[70] These lobbying activities did not slow down after the election of Donald Trump. On the contrary, the Turkish government signed a contract of $1.5 million from May 15, 2017, to May 14, 2018, with Ballard Partners—whose director, Brian Ballard, is a long-time lobbyist for President Trump—and the Turkish Embassy in Washington, DC did the same with Burson-Marsteller, for $1.1 million from May 1, 2017, to December 31, 2017.[71] Meanwhile, it was reported in late 2016 that Trump's former National Security Adviser, Michael Flynn, lobbied, through his consulting firm Flynn Intel Group, for Inovo BV, a Dutch consulting firm with ties to Turkish President Erdogan.[72]

Turkey has also focused on influencing the media and university circles. It helped create and finance research centers, such as Princeton's Institute of Turkish Studies,[73] and has sometimes tried to directly and personally influence journalists to incite them not to recognize the genocide.[74] One lobbying firm, Finn Partners, Inc., under contract in 2014 with the New York Turkish Culture and Tourism Office, which is affiliated with the Turkish government, worked to "arrange trips for journalists."[75] In a different vein, Turkish organizations, including the Turkish embassy in Washington, DC,[76] have routinely bought advertising pages in different newspapers, including the *New York Times* and *Washington Post*, to present anti–Armenian genocide recognition propaganda and to persuade lawmakers not to vote in favor of recognition bills.

In the end, it is also important to note that the Turkish lobby can also count on a steady alliance with the Azerbaijani lobby. The two countries are close allies, and significant parts of their political agenda is close or common. In particular, they are both firmly opposed to any recognition of the Armenian genocide. Azerbaijani President Ilham Aliyev has repeatedly stated that the Armenian lobby was "Azerbaijan's main enemy."[77]

and has spent significant amounts of money on lobbying in Washington, DC. As of mid-2017, the Azeri government was under contract with PR and lobbying firms The Podesta Group (for $45,000 per month), BGR Government Affairs (for $50,000 per month), and the Tool Shed Group.[78]

Conclusion

It is often asserted that if the United States has not fully and officially recognized the Armenian genocide yet, it is because the executive branch wants to spare Turkey, for geopolitical and strategic reasons. This assertion is true but does not shed light on an essential aspect of this issue: for decades Turkey has led an active and multifaceted lobbying effort to prevent such recognition. In other words, the U.S. nonrecognition of the Armenian genocide is not only about Middle East and Eurasia geopolitics, but also relates to decisions in Washington, DC, and therefore to power struggles between different factions and interest groups engaged on Capitol Hill. It seems obvious that the United States, which humanitarianly and officially supported the Armenians during the massacres and in the 1920s, would naturally be inclined to recognize the Armenian genocide. Symbolically, it would make perfect sense for the United States to do so, and that would strengthen the image of the human rights champion the country tries to convey. It would also make sense because a sizeable number of Armenian Americans want the United States to fully acknowledge the historical episode that changed the fate of their families. Through educational awareness and lobbying by the Armenian-American community, well organized mostly around the ANCA and the AAA, a significant amount of headway has occurred. But then, the intense, repeated, and diverse pressures of Turkey appear to be too strong in forcing administrations to pressure Congress to ensure it does not legislate on the matter.

Notes

1. Peter Novick, *The Holocaust in American Life* (Boston: Houghton Mifflin, Boston, 1999).

2. See Ann Marie Wilson, "In the Name of God, Civilization, and Humanity: The United States and the Armenian Massacres of the 1890s," *Le Mouvement Social* 227(2) (2009).

3. Over the past three or four decades, whereas most presidents, vice-presidents, and secretaries of state recognized the genocide before they took office, one president, Ronald Reagan once used the "G word" while in office. He did

so in a proclamation for the sixty-sixth anniversary of the genocide in 1981—a proclamation written by his chief speechwriter Ken Khachigian, of Armenian background, who received a Lifetime Achievement Award by the Armenian lobby. One U.S. ambassador to Armenia did the same, despite the opposition of his hierarchy, in 2005 (and was then forced to leave his position). Moreover, Professor William Schabas (president, since 2009, of the International Association of Genocide Scholars) found a Department of State document from 1951 addressed to the U.N. International Court of Justice, recognizing the genocide.

4. See Julien Zarifian, "The U.S. and the (Non-)Recognition of the Armenian Genocide," *Études Arméniennes Contemporaines* 1 (Sept., 2013): 75–95; and Julien Zarifian, "Les médias américains et la (non-) reconnaissance du génocide des Arméniens aux États-Unis," *Revue française d'études américaines* 142 (2015): 55–72.

5. Chad Garland, "Why Armenia Genocide Recognition Remains a Tough Sell," *Los Angeles Times*, April 26, 2015.

6. "Indiana Becomes 48th State to Recognize the Armenian Genocide," *Armenian Weekly*, November 6, 2017.

7. "Genocide Recognition by U.S. States," ANCA website, http://www.anca.org/genocide/states_map.php (n.d.; copyrighted in 2009).

8. April 24, 1915, being commonly considered the starting point of the Armenian genocide, when Ottoman authorities arrested and then deported about 250 Armenian leaders in Constantinople. It has become the commemoration day of the Armenian genocide.

9. House Joint Resolution 148 designated April 24, 1975, as National Day of Remembrance of Man's Inhumanity to Man, 94th Congress (1975–1977), *Congress.gov*, https://www.congress.gov/bill/94th-congress/house-joint-resolution/148/committees; "Congressional Bill Tracker," *www.realclearpolitics.com*, http://dyn.realclearpolitics.com/congressional_bill_tracker/bill/98/hjres247

10. Harut Sassounian, "Sassounian: All 3 Branches of U.S. Government Recognize Armenian Genocide," *Armenian Weekly*, June 5, 2012.

11. Senator Dole's close association and kindliness to the Armenians dated back to World War II, when an Armenian-American surgeon, Dr. Hampar Kelikian, saved the use of his right arm, which he was close to losing from wartime injuries.

12. Senate Joint Resolution 212, a joint resolution designating April 24, 1990, as "National Day of Remembrance of the Seventy-Fifth Anniversary of the Armenian Genocide of 1915–1923." 101st Congress (1989–1990), *Congress.gov*, https://www.congress.gov/bill/101st-congress/senate-joint-resolution/212/all-actions

13. "Senate Foreign Relations Committee Adopts Armenian Genocide Resolution," *Asbarez*, April 10, 2014.

14. *Congressional Record*, Proceedings and Debates of the 105th Congress, 2nd session, House of Representatives 144(45) (April 22, 1998): H2205.

15. The 2010 census counts 447,580 citizens who identify themselves as Armenians. Data available at http://factfinder2.census.gov/faces/tableservices/jsf/pages/productview.xhtml?pid=ACS_10_SF4_B01003&prodType=table

16. It is important to note that a few other organizations exist or have existed, such as the USAPAC (U.S.-Armenian Public Affairs Committee) or the

Armenian Council of America, and that some individuals can also, occasionally, play a role in trying influence political leaders. However, it appears that, at least since the 1980s, most of the lobbying activities of the Armenian community has been taken in charge by the ANCA and the AAA.

17. Garo Adanalian, "Pursing the Armenian Cause in the 21st Century: An Interview with Sharistan Ardhaldjian," *Armenian Weekly Online* (May, 2001).

18. Whereas the lobbying expenditure of the Armenian Assembly of America exceeded $150 million per year between 1998 and 2011 (with a peak at $320 million in 2009) it has decreased to about $30 million per year since 2012. In the early 2000s, up to eight lobbyists worked for it compared to only one, Bryan Ardouny, also its executive director. Data and information available on the OpenSecrets.org website (http://www.opensecrets.org/lobby/clientsum.php?id=D000047289&year=2012, and http://www.opensecrets.org/lobby/clientlbs.php?id=D000047289&year=2015).

19. As stated on the website of the Armenian National Institute: http://www.armenian-genocide.org/mission.html

20. As stated on the website of the Armenian National Institute: https://www.armeniatree.org/en/intro.asp

21. Many lobbying organizations operate under the 501(c)(3) status—primarily dedicated to charitable organizations—because it is fiscally more attractive than 501(c)(4) status. This allows them to lobby, but theoretically prevents them from making lobbying their main activity.

22. "About the ANCA," ANCA website: https://anca.org/about-anca/profile

23. "Vision and Mission," AAA website: http://www.aaainc.org/index.php?id=86

24. For a critical review of Paul and Paul's book, see Julien Zarifian, "Commentaire: *Ethnic Lobbies and U.S. Foreign Policy*," *Politique américaine* 16 (2010): 121–131.

25. David Paul and Rachel Anderson Paul, *Ethnic Lobbies and U.S. Foreign Policy* (Boulder, CO: Lynne Rienner Publishers, 2009), 59.

26. In its prosperous years, the AAA has counted up to eight lobbyists, the ANCA up to four. Data available on the OpenSecrets.org website.

27. "ANCA Makes Case for U.S.-Armenia Tax Treaty in Meeting with U.S. Treasury Secretary," *Armenian Weekly*, August 5, 2015.

28. "ANCA Launches 'March to Justice' Online Advocacy Campaign," *Armenian Weekly*, March 27, 2015.

29. Ibid.

30. Suhnaz Yilmaz, "Impact of Lobbies on Turkish-American Relations," in Mustafa Aydin and Cagri Erhan, *Turkish-American Relations: Past, Present and Future* (New York: Routledge, 2004), 191.

31. "ANCA Welcomes Darfur Movement's Call on Obama to Oppose Al-Bashir's Visit to Turkey," *Asbarez*, November 5, 2009.

32. Alexander Murinson, *Turkey's Entente with Israel and Azerbaijan: State Identity and Security in the Middle East and the Caucasus* (New York: Routledge, 2009), 76.

33. Thomas Ambrosio, "Entangling Alliances. The Turkish-Israeli Lobbying Partnership and Its Unintended Consequences," in Thomas Ambrosio (Ed.), *Ethnic Identity Groups and U.S. Foreign Policy* (Westport, CT: Praeger, 2002), 158.

34. "Armenian Caucus. 114th Congress Membership List," ANCA website, https://anca.org/armenian-caucus/.

35. A few other members of Congress of Armenian descent who belonged to the Caucus include Representative Charles "Chip" Pashayan (R-CA), who served between 1979 and 1990, and who introduced two resolutions recognizing the Armenian genocide in 1983 and 1984.

36. John Cheves, "Foreign Aid Wins friends; Senator's Generosity Rewarded," *Lexington Herald Leader*, October 18, 2006.

37. Note that other "Armenian" PACs, such as the Armenian-American PAC, the California Armenian American Democrats, Carmen's List, the National Organization of Republican Armenians, U.S.-Armenia PAC, and Southern California Armenian Democrats, exist or have existed, but their financial impact is/was less significant, and they often do/did not play a role at the federal level.

38. Data available at OpenSecrets.org website: http://www.opensecrets.org/pacs/pacgot.php?cmte=C00352054&cycle=2004

39. Data available at OpenSecrets.org website: http://www.opensecrets.org/pacs/pacgot.php?cmte=C00146969&cycle=2008

40. In the 2008 presidential elections, the ANCA supported Barack Obama in the primaries of the Democratic Party and the general elections, whereas the ARMENPAC supported Hillary Clinton in the primaries and then Barack Obama in the general elections. In 2012 and 2016, the Armenian organizations decided not to support a presidential candidate because they were extremely disappointed and discouraged by the nonrespect of their word by the previous presidents, including Barack Obama who had vehemently promised to recognize the genocide when he was a candidate and did not do so when elected.

41. On the debates on the influence of ethnic lobbies and on how precisely to evaluate it, see Julien Zarifian, "Les lobbies ethniques aux États-Unis et la question de leur influence sur la politique étrangère américaine," in François Pernot and Julien Zarifian, *Dans les allées du pouvoir. Lobbies et réseaux d'influence* (Paris: Éditions de l'Amandier, 2015).

42. Zbigniew Brzezinski, "A Dangerous Exemption. Why Should the Israel Lobby be Immune from Criticism?" *Foreign Policy* (July, 2006): 63–64.

43. Paul and Paul, *Ethnic Lobbies*.

44. For example, among newspaper articles presenting the influence of the Armenian lobby as disproportionate, we can mention the following ones: Marc Lacey, "Oil, Politics and a Blacklist," *New York Times*, March 2, 2000; John Brady Kiesling, "Reining in the Ethnic Lobbies," *Huffington Post*, December 20, 2007; Fred Hiatt, "When Special Interests Block National Interest," *Washington Post*, December 19, 2011.

45. The Nagorno-Karabakh region, composed of a large majority of ethnic Armenians, was placed during the Soviet period in the Soviet Republic of Azerbaijan. At the very end of the USSR, a process of separation from Azerbaijan

was initiated, which turned into a full war between Azerbaijan and Karabakh Armenians supported by Armenia in 1991. This war ended in 1994 with the *de facto* independence of Nagorno-Karabakh (although not recognized by Azerbaijan and internationally) and caused several thousand deaths and about one million refugees (about 700,000 Azeris and 300,000 Armenians). Since that time, the conflict has been considered frozen—although soldiers are quite frequently shot along the front line, and although a four-day war took place between both parties in April 2016—and the United States has been co-president, with Russia and France, of the OSCE Minsk Group, in charge of the peace negotiations.

46. As an example, Armenia received $89.7 million in U.S. foreign assistance in 2003, which corresponded to 21.3 percent of its annual budget. For detailed analysis on this topic, see Julien Zarifian, "L'aide financière américaine à l'Arménie: tenants, aboutissants, signification," *Revue arménienne des questions contemporaines* 5 (Sept., 2006): 6–17.

47. Section 907 has always been criticized by the administration, which considered that it complicated relations with oil- and gas-rich Azerbaijan. In October 2001, invoking the potential role Azerbaijan could play in the war against terrorism, President Bush waivered Section 907. He and his successors have done so every year since 2001.

48. Fraser Cameron, *United States Foreign Policy after the Cold War. Global Hegemon or Reluctant Sheriff?* (New York: Routledge, 2002), 91.

49. See, for example, Dietrich Jung, Wolfango Piccoli, *Turkey at the Crossroads: Ottoman Legacies and a Greater Middle East* (London and New York: Zed Books, 2001), 169.

50. Note that other organizations exist or have existed, such as the Turkish Heritage Organization, the Turkish Institute for Progress, and U.S. Turkish Business Counsel, but their lobbying activities seem more marginal and/or sporadic.

51. James M. McCormick, "Ethnic Interest Groups in American Foreign Policy," in Allan Cigler and Burdett Loomis (eds.), *Interest Group Politics*, 8th ed. (Washington, DC: CQ Press, 2012), 330.

52. Turkish Coalition of America, "About Us," http://www.tc-america.org/about.htm

53. Turkish Coalition of America, "Armenian Issue," http://www.tc-america.org/issues-information/armenian-issue-31.htm

54. Information available on the website of the TCA at http://www.tc-america.org/in-congress/caucus.htm

55. Data available at the OpenSecrets.org website: http://www.opensecrets.org/pacs/lookup2.php?strID=C00432526&cycle=2008

56. Ragip Soylu, "Turkish Lobby in U.S. Hits Record High in Campaign Donations," *Daily Sabah*, December 24, 2015.

57. Michael Bobelian, *Children of Armenia: A Forgotten Genocide and the Century-Long Struggle for Justice* (New York: Simon & Schuster, 2009), 169–170.

58. "Turkish Anger at U.S. Armenian 'Genocide' Vote," BBC.com, March 5, 2010.

59. Desmond Butler, "Armenian Genocide Resolution Passes House Committee, Straining U.S.-Turkey Ties," *cnsnews.com*, March 5, 2010.

60. Condoleezza Rice, *No Higher Honor. A Memoir of my Years in Washington* (New York: Broadway Paperbacks, 2011), 598–599.

61. "Obama Administration 'Strongly Opposes' Genocide Resolution, Will Work to Prevent Its Passage," *Armenian Weekly*, March 6, 2010.

62. Note that the chairman and only member of the advisory board was the influential political advisor and lobbyist Richard Perle. John J. Fialka, "Former Defense Official Creates Firm to Lobby in Washington for Turkey," *Wall Street Journal*, February 16, 1989.

63. Joe Stork, "Talking Up Turkey," *Middle East Report*, 160(19) (Sept./Oct., 1989).

64. Suhnaz Yilmaz, "Impact of Lobbies on Turkish-American Relations," in Mustafa Aydin and Cagri Erhan, *Turkish-American Relations: Past, Present and Future* (New York: Routledge, 2004), 196–197.

65. "Turkish Government Hires Former CIA Director for Lobbying," *Today's Zaman*, May 9, 2015.

66. Marilyn W. Thompson, "An Ex-Leader in Congress Is Now Turkey's Man in the Lobbies of Capitol Hill," *New York Times*, October 17, 2007.

67. Julian Pecquet, "Turkey Deploys Lobbyist Army to Shut Down Gulen," *Al Monitor*, August 16, 2016.

68. Akbar Shahid Ahmed and Nick Baumann, "Turkey's Lobbyists Seek U.S. Help by Calling Tiny Armenia a Big Threat," *Huffington Post*, April 1, 2016.

69. Lee Fang, "Demonstrations Test Turkey's Lobbying Clout in Washington," *The Nation*, June 5, 2013.

70. Dan Eggen, "Armenia-Turkey Dispute over Genocide Label Sets Off Lobbying Frenzy," *Washington Post*, March 4, 2010.

71. Harout Sassounian, "Turkey Spends $2.6 Million to Hire Two New Lobbying and PR Firms," *California Courier*, June 20, 2017.

72. Theodoric Meyer, "Flynn Lobbied for Turkish-Linked Firm after Election, Documents Show," *Politico*, March 8, 2017.

73. See, for example, David Holthouse, "State of Denial. Turkey Spends Millions to Cover Up Armenian Genocide," *Intelligence Report* 130 (Summer, 2008); and William Honan, "Princeton Is Accused of Fronting For the Turkish Government," *New York Times*, May 22, 1996.

74. For a detailed study on this topic, see Julien Zarifian, "Les médias américains et la (non-)reconnaissance du génocide des Arméniens aux États-Unis," *Revue française d'études américaines* 142 (2015): 55–71. See also Roger Smith, Eric Markusen, Robert Jay Lifton, "Professional Ethics and the Denial of the Armenian Genocide," *Holocaust and Genocide Studies* 9(1) (1995): 3.

75. Document entitled "Exhibit A to Registration Statement Pursuant to the Foreign Agents Registration Act of 1938, as amended," "Registration 6212," available at the Foreign Agent Registration Act (FARA) website: http://www.fara.gov/docs/6212-Exhibit-AB-20140310-3.pdf

76. Michael Crowley, "Armenian Genocide Update," *New Republic*, October 7, 2007.

77. See, for example, "Aliyev Tells Azeri Ambassadors to Be Active Fighters against 'Armenian lobby,'" *Interfax*, September 22, 2012; and "Aliyev: Azerbaijan's Main Enemy is the Armenian Lobby," *Horizon Weekly*, July 23, 2015.

78. Harout Sassounian, "Azerbaijan Employs Four Lobbying and PR firms," *California Courier*, June 27, 2017.

Chapter 7

Opportunistic Partners

Mexican and Mexican-American Interests in Congressional Lobbying

WALTER CLARK WILSON AND WILLIAM CURTIS ELLIS

The fates of Mexico and the United States have long been intertwined. But the relationship between these countries, like the diaspora that links them culturally and economically, has taken on more significance in the twenty-first century than ever before. Neither the United States nor Mexico has shared such a mutually dependent relationship with any other country since the nineteenth century. This makes the intersection of Mexican and Mexican-American interests uniquely important in contemporary American politics and society, and a critical case for understanding both domestic policy and foreign policy in an increasingly globalized world.

Diaspora politics frequently prioritize the interests of mother countries in American foreign policy. For example, the members of the American-Jewish community acting through organizations such as the American Israeli Public Affairs Committee (AIPAC), and Cuban Americans acting through organizations such as the Cuban American National Foundation (CANF), have had outsized effects on American foreign policy toward Israel and Cuba, respectively. The sheer size of the Mexican-American diaspora (more than thirty-five million according to the Pew Hispanic Center), not to mention the increasingly dispersed nature of the population, would appear to position Mexican Americans to exercise substantial political influence on U.S. policy toward Mexico. Indeed, this possibility has been the source of substantial intrigue and some concern in recent scholarship.[1]

Interestingly, there is little evidence that the interests of Mexican Americans align with those of Mexico in ways that substantially affect

U.S. foreign policy.[2] Instead, the limited dimensions of alignment that exist between these interests appear primarily with regard to the domestic priorities of Mexican Americans. A portion of this alignment is confined to the interests of Mexican-American elites who seek business and investment opportunities. But Mexico also appears tentatively aligned with Mexican-American interests on issues related to immigrant civil rights and discrimination. Mexican support for Mexican-American agendas is tied most clearly to the country's economic interests in cultivating both investment in and remittances to Mexico.[3] Although open advocacy by Mexico on behalf of Mexican-American interests has spiked recently, partly in response to anti-immigrant rhetoric voiced by Republican presidential candidate Donald Trump, such forceful displays are abnormal. Instead, Mexico has tended to pursue limited and relatively low-profile policies designed to develop and maintain cultural ties and to strengthen economic bonds between the country and its diaspora.

In this chapter we explore the lobbying objectives and strategies of Mexican and Mexican-American interests in U.S. politics, with particular focus on their activities since the turn of the century. We begin with a brief historical review of Mexican and Mexican-American interests. We then consider contemporary lobbying by Mexican and Mexican-American interests, respectively. Our analysis relies on Mexican lobbying data submitted in accordance with the Foreign Agents Registration Act, data on Mexican-American lobbying collected by the Center for Responsive Politics, and interviews conducted with several former Mexican-American members of Congress and current and former officials with the Mexican government and Mexican-American advocacy groups.

Mexico's limited efforts to cultivate a transnational Mexican community based in the United States appears to be the outgrowth of several key events: the liberalization of the Mexican economy and implementation of the North American Free Trade Agreement (NAFTA), the growth of a new Mexican-American business class, and rising anti-immigrant xenophobia, particularly following the terrorist attacks of September 11, 2001. These developments have gradually increased the incentives for Mexico to take an interest in the agendas of its Mexican-American diaspora. However, as our analysis reveals, the evolving alignment between the economic interests of Mexico and the political and economic aspirations of Mexican Americans has not fostered substantial direct cooperation when it comes to lobbying. The focus of Mexican Americans on domestic policy issues and their relative ambivalence toward Mexican politics, combined with the limited ability of Mexican foreign interests to effectively participate in American domestic policymaking, suggests that the alignment between Mexican and Mexican-American policy objectives will remain more opportunistic than strategic.

Historical Overview

Since the mid–nineteenth century, the relationship between the interests of the United States, Mexico, and Mexican Americans has evolved more in response to historical developments than it has facilitated them, changing in nature and scope along with Mexican regimes, world events, and political expediency. At the end of the Mexican American War in 1848, between 75,000 and 100,000 Mexicans residing in newly annexed territories opted to become U.S. citizens instead of moving south.[4] In the decades that followed, the political and economic climate of the United States, combined with the domestic economic strategies pursued by Mexico, prompted substantial Mexican emigration to the United States. Under President Porfirio Diaz (1876–1911) Mexico's economic development efforts modernized urban centers, but did little for rural areas.[5] As revolutionary violence in Mexico spread between 1910 and 1920, and the U.S. economy boomed, Mexican migration to the United States surged.[6]

The Great Depression instigated an era of mass deportation and anti-immigrant sentiment in the United States.[7] From 1929 into the late 1930s, the Mexican-American population in the United States decreased by 41 percent. As many as 500,000 Mexicans were deported,[8] forcing Mexico to establish official repatriation programs.[9] This pattern of circular migration based on consumer-driven demand in the United States for cheap labor marks the beginning of an enduring linkage between Mexican and Mexican-American interests.[10] Periods of high labor demand in the United States, such as those coinciding with the world wars, are characterized by policies that encourage Mexican immigration. They have been followed by periods of excess labor supply, such as during the Great Depression, and later, due to agricultural mechanization. In such times, U.S. immigration policies were reversed to emphasize domestic labor protection.

The depression era also witnessed the rise of early Mexican-American advocacy organizations. The most prominent, and still the largest Mexican-American advocacy organization by membership, was the League of United Latin American Citizens (LULAC), founded in 1929. LULAC's founding membership was comprised only of U.S. citizens, mostly from the relatively small, urban Mexican-American middle class in southern Texas.[11] The organization actively promoted assimilation as a civil rights strategy, encouraging Mexican Americans to adopt the broader "cultural patterns and attitudes" of American society in order to achieve "social equality and upward mobility."[12]

As agricultural labor needs in the Southwest became acute due to deepening U.S. involvement in World War II, demand for Mexican labor increased.[13] Despite concerns about the treatment of Mexicans, particularly in Texas, and lingering resentment over the depression-era expulsion of Mexican laborers, Mexico bowed to its economic interests and a desire to contribute to the war effort.[14] The 1942 Bracero agreement sent temporary Mexican migrants from impoverished rural areas to the United States in hopes that they would return with resources and skills for modernization. The program identified the U.S. government as the official employer, required adequate housing and sanitary conditions for workers, guaranteed a prevailing wage (not less than 30 cents an hour) and work for 75 percent of the duration of the contract, and stipulated that 10 percent of wages earned be withheld until Braceros returned to Mexico, where such resources might be used to enhance local agricultural operations.[15] The initial agreement also forbade Bracero contracts in Texas over concerns about discrimination and abuse.[16] Although frequently abrogated, these terms illustrate Mexico's interests in maintaining circular migration by a specific Mexican demographic, and in the protection of its nationals abroad.

LULAC opposed the Bracero program in part because Mexican migrants might compromise the organization's assimilation strategy.[17] Migrant labor arguably added to confusion over the status of Mexican Americans as citizens, and perpetuated the civil rights concerns LULAC considered solvable by assimilation. During World War II, opposition to the Bracero program by Mexican Americans was also justified in defense of frequently mistreated migrant workers.[18]

The Bracero Program was extended in 1951 over protests from Mexican-American advocacy groups and amid growing undocumented immigration from Mexico by workers pejoratively termed "wetbacks."[19] In 1954, U.S. Attorney General Herbert Brownell, Jr. determined Mexican black market labor to be a serious immigration, labor, and law enforcement problem. He initiated "Operation Wetback," deporting approximately 1.3 million mostly undocumented Mexican migrants by the end of 1955.[20] Both LULAC and the G.I. Forum supported the operation, although LULAC later shifted its focus to reducing demand for illegal labor rather than deporting the laborers themselves.[21] The number of Braceros contracted rose during the period from fewer than 200,000 in 1951 to more than 400,000 in 1960. But as American agriculture became increasingly mechanized, demand for contract labor from Mexico dissipated, and the Bracero program was allowed to expire in 1964.[22]

Throughout the Bracero period, Mexico increasingly embraced an economic model based on import substitution by emphasizing domestic production as a substitute for foreign imports. The strategy facilitated substantial industrialization and urban growth, but did little to stimulate rural economies, helping to explain Mexico's interest in the Bracero program. By the 1970s, Mexico's economy began to stagnate, and the country began a slow shift away from import substitution.[23] The Mexican pivot toward neoliberal economic policies coincided with increasing pressure for democratization in Mexico and the return of relatively permissive U.S. immigration enforcement. Mexico's economic and political liberalization also coincided with new efforts to foster relationships with the Mexican-American diaspora, particularly with organizations such as La Raza Unida, a political party that grew out of the 1960s Chicano movement. These new leftist and social movement organizations challenged more traditional organizations such as LULAC for leadership in the community, and clashed with assimilationist strategies by openly challenging the political system through protest and an embrace of Chicano nationalism. La Raza Unida Party met with the Mexican government under Luis Echeverria Alvarez in 1970, and later Carlos Salinas de Gortari.[24] Outreach to Mexican Americans also came from Mexican opposition parties, including the Party of the Democratic Revolution (PRD) and the National Action Party (PAN).[25] But increasing political competition in Mexico, and for leadership in the Mexican-American community, did not foster lasting or widespread political ties between Mexico and its diaspora. Indeed, by the late 1990s, Mexican immigrants living in the United States generally expressed far greater affinity for the United States than for their mother country, and harbored skepticism of the Mexican government.[26]

In the 1980s, Presidents Madrid and Salinas initiated efforts that led to further economic liberalization, and ultimately to NAFTA. Many Mexican-American organizations also lobbied in favor of NAFTA, forming a significant cross-border coalition.[27] Although, NAFTA did not fundamentally change the overall nature of the Mexico-U.S. relationship, it substantially deepened economic ties.[28] Following NAFTA, undocumented immigration to the United States surged, and a growing Mexican-American business class incentivized Mexico to deepen economic ties with the Mexican-American community.[29] Their outreach appeared limited in both scope and effectiveness, especially to potential investors in the Mexican-American business class. One former diplomat we spoke with viewed Mexico's lack of substantial economic linkages with its diaspora as a "missed opportunity" for the country.[30] Now an official with the interest group Mexicans and Americans Thinking Together (MATT), he indicated that "Mexico has largely assumed that promoting cultural links are enough [to encourage investment], but there has not been much strategic outreach to build relationships with major Mexican-American business interests."

NAFTA's failure to address immigration policy fostered a growing coalescence of Mexican-American interests around immigrant rights and issues associated with discrimination, and gradually drew Mexico into a tentative political alignment. The September 11, 2001, terrorist attacks accelerated this process, as did massive 2006 protests that followed the passage of a border-protection bill by the U.S. House. Indeed, the latter appeared both to racialize Latinos as a political group and to promote pan-Latino, in addition to Mexican-American, solidarity on the issue of immigration.[31] Donald Trump's 2016 presidential candidacy, which began with promises to "build a great wall [along the U.S.-Mexico border]" and to "have Mexico pay for that wall"[32] for the purpose of keeping Mexican "rapists" and drug dealers out of the United States brought Mexican officials into the American political fray. Former President Fox stated that Mexico is "not paying for that [expletive] wall."[33] Sitting Mexican President Enrique Peña Nieto said "[t]here is no scenario" in which Mexico would pay for a wall.[34] Former Mexican Foreign Minister Jorge Castañeda actively opposed Trump's rhetoric.[35] The Trump campaign also criticized NAFTA as bad for the U.S. economy. In the Mexican-American community, LULAC released a resolution denouncing Trump in July of 2015. The Hispanic Chamber of Commerce endorsed the Democratic nominee, Hillary Clinton, during the Republican National Convention.[36] Post-election analysis suggests that at least 66 percent of Latinos (and probably a much larger percentage), voted for Clinton.[37] In sum, the Trump campaign's immigrant and trade rhetoric may have deepened links between the political interests of Mexico and Mexican Americans on these issues.

The gradual convergence of Mexican and Mexican-American interests on immigration and trade has become significant, but appears more coincidental than strategic.[38] Mexican efforts to promote relationships with emigrants and Mexican Americans by offering dual citizenship and opportunities to some Mexican Americans to vote in Mexican elections, and to encourage remittances and other forms of investment, have not enticed Mexican Americans to significantly involve themselves in shaping U.S. policy toward Mexico or Mexican politics.[39] Instead, Mexican Americans appear to have continued to prioritize domestic policy concerns.[40] As examined in further detail below, these conclusions are supported by a relative lack of collaboration between Mexican-American and Mexican lobbies. To the extent that these lobbying efforts align, it is most commonly on issues prioritized by Mexican-American groups, and driven by Mexico's recognition that assisting those efforts may indirectly serve Mexico's economic interests.

The Mexico Lobby

Mexico has long negotiated with the United States on immigration and trade, but the country's contemporary lobbying strategy is relatively new. Eisenstadt argues that Mexico "completely restructured" its political strategy in U.S. politics during the 1980s and 1990s.[41] The opening of Mexico's economy during that period came with an increasing need to participate effectively in trade politics. Accordingly, expenditures by Mexican registered foreign agents in the United States increased from $12.8 million in 1980 to nearly $34 million in 1991.[42] Stimulated primarily by the effort to forge NAFTA with the United States and Canada, the Mexican government adopted an aggressive lobbying campaign. From 1991 to 1993, Mexican interests spent nearly $38 million on direct lobbying,[43] a threefold increase from years prior.[44] A collection of private and public interests were involved, with the majority of lobbying expenditures made by the Mexican Secretariat of Commerce and Industrial Development (SECOFI), now known as the Secretary of the Economy.

In addition to its direct lobbying operation on NAFTA, SECOFI pursued an indirect lobbying strategy aimed largely at pressuring Washington, DC by winning the support of the Mexican-American community. They dispatched representatives and hired regional ambassadors to win the support of journalists, Mexican-American business leaders, and major Mexican-American advocacy organizations, including NCLR, MALDEF, and LULAC. These efforts included organization visits to Mexico for various U.S. delegations as well as advertising campaigns in the United States.[45]

The eleven Mexican-American members of the 103rd Congress, most of whom ultimately supported NAFTA over the objections of labor leaders, were among those targeted by the Mexican lobbying effort. However, the support of Mexican-American representatives, not to mention the passage of NAFTA, may be attributed as much to deal-making with the Clinton administration as to Mexican lobbying efforts. Four liberal Mexican-American members of Congress,[46] for example, collectively received $1 billion in infrastructure spending for their districts in exchange for their NAFTA support.[47]

The general support for NAFTA and other free trade policies among Mexican-American members of Congress reflects a common attitude among elites in both major American political parties that is supportive of globalization and connectivity. The former Mexican-American representatives we spoke with all expressed varying degrees of support for NAFTA and free trade, typically with the caveat that the agreement addressed the movement of products without effectively addressing the movement of people. "Puede pasar los tomates pero no puede pasar la gente," quipped one—"the tomatoes can pass, but not the people [who pick them]."[48] This statement is not inconsistent with Mexico's desire for greater linkages between Mexicans on both sides of the border, and also rebuts the "closed border" preferences of some U.S. conservatives. But the alignment of Mexican and Mexican-American interests here appears more coincidental than strategic, as this member's concerns focused primarily on the families residing along the border rather than macroeconomics.

The NAFTA case illustrates that the relationship between Mexico and Mexican-American members of Congress can be mutually beneficial, but is not particularly close. It was generally agreed on by former members we spoke with that Mexican officials preferred to operate with a low profile and to avoid embarrassment to American legislators that could be caused by the impression of improper foreign influence. One former congressman, for example, indicated that "it was assumed" that the doors of Mexican-American members of Congress are open to Mexican officials based on cultural ties, but that open doors did not translate into automatic policy support.[49] Former Mexican officials agreed that while dialogue between Mexican interests and Mexican-American representatives was open, there was no special deference given to Mexican interests. These observations would appear to echo the Mexican experience with NAFTA, during which Mexican interests lobbied Mexican-American representatives but were not instrumental in shaping their decisions.

Since the passage of NAFTA, the Mexican lobby has sustained a strong focus on trade issues, but given little attention to immigration, drugs, or crime. "Mexico simply doesn't advance much of an agenda [in Washington] beyond trade," one former diplomat indicated.[50] Frequently, private Mexican interests work alongside government initiatives to focus attention on relatively narrow trade issues. Mexican interests also continue to pursue a strategy that emphasizes both direct lobbying of representatives and government officials and indirect lobbying through public relations efforts. Table 7.1 displays recent spending by Mexican interests in the United States between 2001 and 2014 as reported to Congress under the Foreign Agents Registration Act.[51] As the data illustrate, direct lobbying made up only about 22 percent of the overall expenditures by private and public Mexican interests (about 10 percent of expenditures by private interests and 30 percent of expenditures by Mexican government agents).

Private lobbying by Mexican interests was dominated by one organization: Grupo Televisa. Grupo Televisa is a major Spanish language mass media company that owns much of the programming aired by Univision

Table 7.1. Spending by Mexican Interests Registered as Foreign Agents, 2001–2014 (in Millions of Dollars)

Non-Governmental Spending Only

	2001	2002	2003	2004	2005	2006	2007	2008	2009	2010	2011	2012	2013	2014	Total
Advertising	–	–	–	–	1.63	–	–	–	–	–	–	–	–	–	1.63
Legal/lobbying	1.35	1.86	1.45	0.96	0.97	1.01	1.08	–	–	–	–	–	–	–	8.68
PR/media	2.97	2.33	2.59	22.45	4.94	–	0.04	0.14	0.29	0.34	0.29	4.86	0.12	0.54	41.87
Tourism promotion	0.84	0.78	0.67	21.83	6.02	1.14	0.63	–	0.71	0.71	–	–	0.06	0.05	33.43
Investment	0.01	0.01	–	–	–	–	–	–	–	–	–	–	–	–	0.02
Total	5.17	4.97	4.71	45.24	13.55	2.15	1.76	0.14	1.00	1.05	0.29	4.86	0.18	0.58	85.63

Governmental Spending Only

	2001	2002	2003	2004	2005	2006	2007	2008	2009	2010	2011	2012	2013	2014	Total
Legal/lobbying	2.13	3.73	3.38	2.30	1.47	0.96	1.30	1.52	2.15	4.28	5.01	6.14	4.48	3.20	42.05
PR/media	0.36	0.43	0.89	0.45	0.96	0.72	0.07	0.03	0.79	2.46	2.01	0.93	0.04	–	10.13
Consulting	0.20	0.28	–	–	0.02	0.59	0.33	–	0.16	0.19	0.18	0.12	0.03	0.05	2.15
Tourism promotion	1.45	1.72	1.22	1.19	1.51	0.72	0.39	0.95	1.02	0.38	26.70	30.80	4.26	–	72.37
Trade promotion	–	0.04	–	–	–	1.44	1.30	0.91	1.04	2.35	2.91	1.70	1.47	1.36	14.54
Total	4.13	6.21	5.49	3.94	3.97	4.43	3.40	3.40	5.15	9.65	36.82	39.68	10.27	4.61	141.24

All Non/Governmental Spending

	2001	2002	2003	2004	2005	2006	2007	2008	2009	2010	2011	2012	2013	2014	Total
Total	9.30	11.18	10.19	49.18	17.52	6.58	5.16	3.54	6.16	10.70	37.12	44.54	10.46	5.19	226.87

*Calculated by the authors using data from the U.S. Justice Department in accordance with the Foreign Agents Registration Act.

in the United States.[52] The bulk of their lobbying was focused on communications regulations and copyright and trademark law associated with their investments in U.S. broadcasting.

Lobbying by Mexican government interests was more diversified, but focused primarily on issues related to trade. The government and president's office, the Mexican Embassy, the secretary of the economy, secretary of agriculture, the state-owned petroleum producer PEMEX, the Mexican Senate, and the states of Chihuahua and Hidalgo all hired registered lobbyists between 2001 and 2014. The most consistent and sustained lobbying effort throughout the period was conducted by the secretary of the economy, which annually spent an average of nearly $890,000 during the period. The firms they hired met with officials in Congress and in multiple state governments to discuss immigration and a wide range of trade-related issues, including avocado exportation, trade in textiles, and cross-border trucking. The Mexican Senate spent $1.5 million between 2001 and 2010 lobbying Congress on immigration reform, and to establish and enhance relations between the legislatures. In the early 2000s, the Secretary of Agriculture hired lobbyists to represent Mexican interests related to food safety, the U.S. Farm bill, and other agricultural trade issues.

Some of the biggest lobbying expenditures by the Mexican government—over $10 million between 2010 and 2012—dealt not with trade but rather with protecting the rights of Mexican nationals in the United States and of Mexico as a sovereign government. In 2004, the International Court of Justice (ICJ) issued an opinion in *Mexico v. The United States of America* that Texas and other states had breached U.S. obligations under the Vienna Convention on Consular Relations of 1963 by failing to inform detained Mexican nationals of their rights to contact the Mexican Consul, and by failing to inform the Mexican Consulate about the detentions.[53] Texas, represented by then-Solicitor General Ted Cruz, challenged the ICJ decision against Bush administration objections. The state won a 2007 Supreme Court decision that international agreements could not be imposed by the federal government upon U.S. states in ways that forced states to change their criminal proceedings.[54] Texas subsequently executed a Mexican national, Jose Ernesto Medellin Rojas, for rape and murder after denying him access to the Mexican Consul.[55] The move opened the door to a number of other executions. Mexico responded with an aggressive lobbying campaign, and continues to issue warnings that noncompliance with the 2004 ruling will hurt bilateral relations between the United States and Mexico in other areas.[56]

In spite of unresolved issues over rights to consular access, lobbying by the Mexican government has continued in recent years. Mexico consistently hired Public Strategies Washington, Inc., between 2001 and 2014 to conduct ongoing lobbying related to NAFTA and free trade, spending nearly $3.8 million on the effort. Meanwhile, petroleum giant PEMEX spent over $7 million between 2011 and 2014, mostly to fight a major international arbitration judgment against the company.[57]

The direct lobbying efforts by Mexican interests in the United States accompany significant indirect lobbying. Tourism promotion, in particular, on which private interests spent more than $33 million and public interests spent more than $72 million between 2001 and 2014, constitutes the plurality of spending by Mexican agents. Mexico appeals directly to tourists in the United States and elsewhere in an effort not just to sell travel to its destinations, but to enhance the country's international image. Mexico's $14 billion tourism industry is a pillar of the national economy, and a major source of foreign investment in the country.[58]

Public and private interests also invest heavily in public and media relations. For example, the Mexican government conducted a public relations campaign in conjunction with its lobbying efforts related to the ICJ dispute over access of Mexican nationals to the Mexican Consul. The expenditure demonstrates a relatively sophisticated effort to influence the issue not only in the American courts, but also in the court of American public opinion. In 2004 and 2005, the state of Michoacán coordinated a multi-million-dollar advertising campaign with the Mexican Tourism Board and several financial institutions, including Banco Internacional, Bancomer, and BBVA Bancomer. During the Fox administration, PAN spent $115,000 to conduct a public relations campaign targeting officials in the legislative and executive branches. The states of Hidalgo and Tamaulipas also conducted PR campaigns targeting elected leaders designed to facilitate working relationships with state and federal officials.

The importance of Mexico's public relations and media outreach extends beyond its impacts on American public opinion and indirect effects it might have on U.S. policymaking. It is also an important part of Mexico's global initiative to spur tourism and investment. As one former diplomat explained, "[t]he U.S. is also the center of the global media. The rest of the world monitors American media closely. Therefore, Mexico attempts to shape its global image by investing in public relations and media in the United States."[59]

Several governmental interests also invested sporadically in policy consulting. The Mexican Embassy, the secretary of foreign relations, and the state of Sonora all hired policy consultants in at least one year between 2001 and 2014 on issues including the civil rights of Mexican nationals, possible amendments to the Foreign Operations Appropriations Bill (in

2011), immigration and border policy developments, counter-narcotics policy, and visa backlogs.

Finally, Mexican government interests engaged in the promotion of investment and trade. The Secretary of Agriculture was the leader in this area, spending $14.5 million on trade promotion between 2006 and 2014. Documents in FARA reports to Congress reveal that a substantial portion of the activity associated with "trade promotion" was in fact comprised of monitoring the activities of government and multinational organizations such as the World Trade Organization, providing council on issues that might damage U.S.-Mexico trade relations, and public relations outreach to congressional staffers on trade issues.

Mexico's lobbying focus, interestingly, bears little relationship to the high-profile statements of its leaders on issues such as immigration, drugs, and crime. Anti-immigrant rhetoric has received push-back from Mexican officials in the past, but rarely with the force used to respond to statements made by then-Republican presidential candidate Donald Trump. Mexican opposition to anti-immigrant rhetoric is geared at least as much to Mexico's global public relations efforts as it is strategically aligned with the objectives of most Mexican Americans in immigrant civil rights. "Think of the damage Donald Trump has done to Mexico's international image," one former diplomat suggested. "Mexico has to counter his statements aggressively in the U.S. media in order to prevent them from becoming an accepted international narrative about Mexicans."[60]

Mexico appears relatively ambivalent with regard to the ultimate objective of most Mexican-American immigration reform advocates—a pathway to citizenship for undocumented immigrants. One former diplomat did argue that Mexico's interests were served by larger numbers of Mexican Americans becoming U.S. citizens to the extent that those new citizens become politically influential.[61] New policies allowing Mexican Americans to maintain dual citizenship if they are naturalized in the United States provide some evidence that promoting U.S. citizenship has become part of Mexico's diaspora strategy. But the slow development of Mexican-American influence in American politics led one Mexican-American business group official to argue that Mexico's economic interests remained at least as much in promoting cyclical migration.[62] The country has established programs for repatriation, and according to one Mexican-American advocacy organization official we interviewed, there is limited cooperation between Mexico and Mexican-American organizations when it comes to offering services to detained immigrants.[63] The mix of Mexican policies on Mexican emigration thus provides little evidence of a coherent agenda, nor do they align closely with any specific Mexican-American agenda on the issue.

Mexican statements on drug control policy are similarly disconnected both from the country's lobbying priorities and from Mexican-American interests. Mexico generally places responsibility for the drug wars on American demand for illegal substances.[64] Presumably, liberalized drug laws in the United States would diminish demand for illegal drugs, and alleviate much of the ongoing incentive for smuggling throughout Mexico and into the United States. Furthermore, U.S. gun policies have led to the illegal importation of massive cartel arsenals that hinder the Mexican government's efforts to maintain peace and order.[65] Mexico thus has great interest in changes to U.S. gun policies. The United States has addressed these concerns primarily with rhetoric.[66] Still, U.S.-Mexico cooperation in fighting drug crime is substantial. In particular, the United States has invested heavily in assisting Mexican security officials in battling cartel violence in Mexico.[67]

While it is difficult to evaluate the effectiveness of Mexican lobbying in Congress and other U.S. government institutions, it seems clear that lobbying—both in direct and indirect forms—is an "important and permanent tool" for advancing Mexican interests in American public policy.[68] Overall, direct and indirect lobbying by Mexican interests in the United States cannot be characterized as coordinated with Mexican-American lobbying efforts. Furthermore, the high profile rhetorical positions taken by Mexican officials on U.S. policy appear to be directed toward a broader global audience, and more closely related to the indirect lobbying Mexico pursues through public relations and media campaigns rather than to their formal direct lobbying efforts. The next section reveals that Mexican-American interests largely lobby on issues of only peripheral concern to Mexico. At times, such as on immigration, those interests coincide, primarily by offering opportunities for Mexico to establish and deepen linkages with its diaspora. More often, these lobbies act independently, and with relative ambivalence toward one another's goals. Thus, in spite of the large Mexican diaspora in the United States, Mexican lobbying shares many of the characteristics of foreign lobbying conducted by other states that do not have such significant diaspora populations in the United States.

The Mexican-American Lobby

We identify four major types of groups within the Mexican-American lobby. The largest and best-known type includes public interest groups such as the League of United Latin American Citizens (LULAC), the Mexican American Legal Defense and Education Fund (MALDEF), National Council of La Raza (NCLR), Southwest Voter Research and Education

Project (SVREP), American G.I. Forum, and others. These organizations are structured in a variety of ways—as membership organizations, grant-funded organizations, and interest group coalitions. They also pursue a wide variety of issue agendas that range from very focused to very broad. The American G.I. Forum, for example, focuses on veteran's issues in the Latino community. Meanwhile LULAC and NCLR are involved in literally dozens of issue agendas and policy debates. In spite of their differences, these public interest groups share the characteristic of representing the civil rights concerns of the vast majority of working-class Mexican Americans.

A smaller and lesser known, but perhaps better organized, type of Mexican-American advocacy organization includes business groups such as the Hispanic Chamber of Commerce and Association of Mexican Empresarios. Such organizations represent the interests of a growing Mexican-American business class. Although the specific policy priorities of these groups differ from those of Mexican-American public interest groups substantially, and often conflict with them when it comes to ideology and economic philosophy, both types of groups emphasize the need to expand opportunities for Mexican Americans through greater inclusion and influence in various facets of the economy and society.

There is one very prominent Mexican-American labor organization. The United Farm Workers (UFW) is a union devoted to addressing the labor interests of migrant workers. This organization is relatively unique among the organizations we examined—not to mention among American labor organizations. Its leadership, which included the late César Chavez and Dolores Huerta, is also among the most recognizable in the history of Chicano politics.

Finally, Mexican-American interest groups that focus primarily on immigrant issues and programs offering immediate assistance constitute a fourth type of group. A good example is Mexicans and Americans Thinking Together (MATT), which pursues programs oriented toward assisting mostly adult immigrants in the United States with efforts to assimilate. These programs include help obtaining official documents such as birth certificates, educational programs that teach English and financial literacy, and for some, repatriation to Mexico.[69] Although this latter type of organization appears most clearly associated with developing linkages and alignment between Mexican Americans and Mexico, the footprint of such organizations in the Mexican-American community is also substantially smaller than those of other types of groups.

The domestic orientation of most Mexican-American interests stands in contrast with some of the most prominent examples of effective diaspora lobbying. Both Israeli-American and Cuban-American lobbies, for example, are noteworthy for their influence over U.S. foreign policy. Mexican-American interests possess several key characteristics that appear to limit their potential for such influence compared with the most successful diaspora lobbies. These include the geographic dispersion and diversity of the community, low rates of political participation, and limited political resources.[70] Furthermore, there is little evidence that the cultural ties Mexican immigrants maintain with Mexico translate into political ties.[71] Although the large size of the Mexican-American population presents opportunities for influence that other diasporas lack, the diversity of this population, and of its interests, limit cohesive action. Mexican-American interests exist in many different issues, and are not animated by narrow objectives like those of AIPAC or CANF. Mexican-American interests also enjoy relatively little support in non-Latino communities, at least in part because Mexican Americans exercise limited political influence outside districts in which they comprise majorities.[72] Even in districts where Mexican Americans comprise majorities, low participation rates and limited representation constrain political influence.[73]

The registered lobbying activities of Mexican-American organizations are quite limited, suggesting that their ability to influence policymaking through formal direct lobbying may also be limited.[74] As table 7.2 on page 154 illustrates, some of the most prominent Mexican-American organizations spend relatively modest sums to hire registered lobbyists, at least compared to organizations such as AIPAC, which spent between $850,000 and $3.39 million annually on pro-Israel lobbying with registered firms between 1998 and 2015.[75] NCLR, which represents a coalition of more than 260 Latino advocacy organizations across the country, led other Mexican-American advocacy organizations by spending an average of $340,000 on registered lobbyists between 1998 and 2016.[76] The organization also reportedly pursued the broadest issue agenda, emphasizing Latino interests in issues ranging from consumer product safety to education to immigration to health care to veteran's affairs.[77] NCLR's largest annual lobbying expenditures—more than $500,0000 a year between 2006 and 2010—coincided with the return of Democratic Party control in Congress. The organization's expenditures fell by more than 50 percent with the return of Republican control.

With the exception of 2001, the Hispanic Association of Colleges and Universities (HACU) spent an average of $140,000 on registered lobbying between 2000 and 2016, and addressed issues related to education (including for programs focused on agricultural sciences) and federal support for Hispanic Serving Institutions. MATT, an advocacy organization associated with Altos Hornos de Mexico, a major Mexican Steel producer, spent an

Table 7.2. Direct Lobbying Expenditures by Major Mexican American Advocacy Organizations Since 1998 (in Thousands of Dollars)

Organization	Years	Max	Min	Avg.	Issue(s) Lobbied
LULAC	2006–07, 2009–10	$20	$0	$7.5	Civil Rights and Civil Liberties; Immigration; Health
American G.I. Forum	2007–09	$0	$0	$0	Veterans Affairs; Taxes; Energy & Nuclear Power; Fuel, Gas & Oil; Health
United Farm Workers	2002–16	$80	$0	$21	Immigration; Labor, Antitrust & Workplace; Health; Agriculture
MALDEF	1998–2016	$252	$0	$62	Education; Government; Immigration; Labor, Antitrust & Workplace; Civil Rights & Civil Liberties; Welfare; Health; Taxes; Constitution; Federal Budget & Appropriations; Housing; Telecommunications; Finance; Environment & Superfund; Radio & TV Broadcasting; Economics & Economic Development; Law Enforcement & Crime; Defense; Medicare & Medicaid; Agriculture; Family, Abortion & Adoption
NCLR	1998–2016	$580	$129	$340	Consumer Product Safety; Economics & Economic Development; Education; Health; Immigration; Taxes; Law Enforcement & Crime; Housing; Education; Government; Finance; Housing; Federal Budget & Appropriations; Civil Rights & Civil Liberties; Labor, Antitrust & Workplace; Agriculture; Transportation; Telecommunications; Banking; Unemployment; Energy & Nuclear Power; District of Columbia; Disaster & Emergency Planning; Family, Abortion & Adoption; Arts & Entertainment; Religion; Veterans Affairs; Homeland Security; Retirement; Welfare; Media Information & Publishing; Small Business; Trade

SVREP				—	
NALEO	2010–11, 2013–15	$170	$30	$86	Federal Budget & Appropriations; Education; Civil Rights & Civil Liberti Liberties
U.S. Hispanic Chamber of Commerce	2002–03, 2005–16	$120	$9	$55	Small Business; Economics & Economic Development; Immigration; Taxes; Trade; Finance; Health; Housing; Government; Banking; Education
HACU	2000, 2002–16	$375	$10	$140	Agriculture; Federal Budget & Appropriations; Education
MATT	2007–09, 2013–16	$180	$30	$113	Federal Budget & Appropriations; Education; Immigration; Education; Federal Budget & Appropriations; Trade; Foreign Relations

*Data collected from the Center for Responsive Politics, available at OpenSecrets.org.

average of $113,000 annually between 2007 and 2009, and in 2013 and 2016, on registered lobbyists.[78] As mentioned earlier, MATT's initiatives focus primarily on programs for immigrants, and are more oriented to promoting linkages between Mexican Americans and Mexico than most other Mexican-American advocacy organizations. Their Washington, DC operations focus mostly on federal appropriations and education policy that affects their programming, and frequently targets officials in the Mexican embassy as well as in Congress.[79]

NALEO, an organization that represents Latino interests in seeing Latinos elected and appointed to government positions, pursues a modest ongoing lobbying effort centered on budgetary issues, education, and civil rights issues. The Hispanic Chamber of Commerce also pursues a relatively modest ongoing lobbying effort, one that has been sustained almost uninterrupted since 2002, to emphasize Latino interests in a range of business related issues. Generally speaking, the organization hues toward a neoliberal economic agenda, but also emphasizes the need for greater investment in Latino education, health care, and immigration reform.[80] The largest Mexican-American organizations by membership are some of the smallest spenders when it comes to registered lobbying, consistent with research highlighting the tendency of narrow, economically focused interests to dominate such activities.[81] The United Farm Workers union spent an average of $21,000 annually between 2002 and 2016 on registered lobbying. LULAC has not spent more than $20,000 on registered lobbying. Like a number of other Mexican-American organizations, including CHCI, NALEO, MALDEF and the G.I. Forum, a large share of LULACs resources go directly toward promoting educational access for Latinos through scholarships and other programming, instead of to direct lobbying.[82]

Conversations with a number of Mexican-American advocacy organization representatives, along with our own observations as former congressional staffers, reveal that data on formal representation by registered lobbyists provides only part of the picture when it comes to direct lobbying conducted by the organizations. Many Mexican-American advocacy groups maintain offices in Washington, DC, and send their own delegations, who are not registered lobbyists, to meet with members of Congress and congressional staffers. This is a cost-effective strategy for most of these organizations because they may lack the resources to hire registered lobbyists, because they pursue agendas that are far broader than could realistically be outsourced to paid representatives, and because they are populated by professional activists who can carry out many of the direct lobbying tasks themselves.

In contrast to their working relationships with Mexican interests, relationships between Mexican-American members of Congress and Mexican-American advocacy groups are often close. Although neither the former congressional representatives nor the interest group representatives we interviewed argued that Mexican-American representatives constituted automatic supporters of Mexican-American advocacy group initiatives, they generally acknowledged the importance of shared ethnicity to access, and often worked together. Many Mexican-American members and congressional staffers meet regularly enough with representatives from LULAC, MALDEF, NCLR, and other organizations that they are on a first-name basis. The domestic policy agendas pursued by Mexican-American advocacy groups frequently dovetail with the political and electoral agendas of Mexican-American members of Congress. The organized activities of the Congressional Hispanic Caucus (CHC) help to cultivate these connections. The CHC divides its policy agendas among several task forces, including task forces on civil rights; diversity and inclusion; education and labor; health and retirement security; financial services, manufacturing, and commerce; health care; and immigration.[83] Many of these agendas correspond closely with the agendas of Mexican-American advocacy organizations.

The close working relationships between Mexican-American representatives and advocates stems in part from the existential closeness of many members to those types of organizations. For example, all Mexican-American members of Congress are nominal members of NALEO, which was founded by former Mexican-American Representative Edward R. Roybal (D-CA) in 1976. Roybal, a cofounder of the Community Service Organization (CSO) in Los Angeles early in his political career, also helped found the CHC in 1976.[84] The CHC has its own 501(c)(3) organization, the Congressional Hispanic Caucus Institute (CHCI), which pursues a mission to educate and empower future Latino leaders.[85]

Many Mexican-American representatives have had experience working with advocacy organizations prior to their congressional careers. Former Representative Henry B. Gonzalez (D-TX) helped to found the Pan American Progressive Association (PAPA), an organization for empowering Mexican Americans in San Antonio, prior to running for elective office.[86] Democratic Representative Raúl M. Grijalva (AZ) worked as a community organizer and was an official in Arizona's La Raza Unida Party.[87] Democratic Representative Ruben Gallego, also of Arizona, helped to organize the group Citizens for Professional Law Enforcement in response to the anti-immigrant policing policies of Sheriff Joe Arpaio.[88] Representative Tony Cárdenas (D-CA), son of a migrant farm worker, has a close relationship with the United Farm Workers, and has sponsored legislation supported by the organization.[89]

Cooperation between Mexican-American representatives and Mexican-American advocacy organizations assists both the efforts of organizations to advance their agendas and the efforts of representatives to effectively represent local and national Mexican-American constituencies. Research shows that group consciousness and feelings of linked fate between Mexican-American representatives and constituents might elicit obligations on the part of Mexican-American representatives to serve Mexican-American interests.[90] Advocacy organizations can assist those efforts in important ways both by keeping representatives informed about developments in policy and public opinion, and by generating public support for representatives' legislative initiatives.[91] So just as having legislative champions in Mexican-American representatives appears to be a part of the advocacy strategy for Mexican-American organizations, those organizations may serve a mutually beneficial role that helps to link descriptive representation by Mexican Americans in Congress to substantive representation for Mexican Americans in legislative agendas.

While there is evidence of an active direct lobbying strategy by Mexican-American interests, indirect lobbying by these organizations through campaign expenditures appears extremely limited. Most organizations lack the resources to contribute large sums to campaigns, and therefore are minor players from the campaign finance perspective. In fact, among the organizations we examined, only the Hispanic Chamber of Commerce, which has made just over $19,000 in campaign donations over the past fifteen years, has a recent donation record. The Hispanic Chamber rarely gives more than one or two campaign donations per election cycle, usually in small amounts to individuals at the congressional level. The vast majority of their donations have been to Democrats. In 2016, they made their largest presidential contributions to date, totaling $8,095, to Hillary Clinton.[92]

We also found very limited evidence that Mexican-American advocacy organizations endorse candidates, including for president. For example, the Hispanic Chamber of Commerce had long followed a tradition of not endorsing presidential candidates. This changed in 2016 when the organization made two endorsements during the primary campaign (Hillary Clinton for Democratic nominee, and John Kasich for Republican nominee) and later endorsed Hillary Clinton during the general election campaign.[93]

Rather than engage in partisan electioneering, Mexican-American advocacy groups have historically focused their indirect lobbying efforts on grassroots mobilization. LULAC, for example, has cultivated civic participation by Mexican-American citizens since its founding.[94] The Southwest Voter Research and Education Project has registered more than 2.5 million Mexican-American voters since 1974.[95] The United Farmworkers union is well known for organizing strikes and boycotts of grapes and other crops in order to bring attention to the plight of migrant workers.[96] Chicano activists even formed their own political party, La Raza Unida. The party scored electoral victories in Crystal City, Texas, and a number of other Texas jurisdictions, and ran candidates in multiple southwestern states in the early 1970s.[97]

For a number of reasons, Mexican-American mobilization efforts generally have yet to translate the growing potential of Mexican-American political influence into an enduring reality. Foremost, Mexican Americans continue to lag behind Anglos on most socioeconomic measures, and therefore lack resources widely associated with political participation.[98] The population remains relatively young and disproportionately noncitizen, further impeding Mexican-American electoral influence. Institutional barriers, including restrictive voting laws compound these deficits.[99] Finally, gerrymandering schemes often limit Mexican-American electoral influence. Although majority-minority districting has increased the overall numbers of Mexican Americans elected to Congress, such plans have also arguably diminished their overall influence by packing Latino supermajorities into small numbers of districts that border districts where Latinos are not a significant electoral presence.[100] These circumstances collectively breed a climate of "two-tiered pluralism" that leaves Mexican Americans without proportionate influence in political participation, representation, and policy agenda setting.[101] Still, events such as the 2006 immigration protests, the increasing presence of Latinos on the ballot, and the galvanizing events of the 2016 presidential campaign appear to promote the types of solidarity and mobilization that might assist Mexican Americans in overcoming those barriers.

Although activity by the Mexican-American business lobby is not overwhelming, some evidence suggests that these organizations are achieving their objectives to expand business opportunities for Latinos. For example, a recent Hispanic Chamber of Commerce study concludes that the number of Hispanic-owned businesses increased by more than 57 percent between 2007 and 2015, to 4.07 million.[102] The same study found that approximately half of Hispanic business owners are middle class or wealthier, and more than half of Hispanic business growth was among Spanish dominant or bilingual business owners. These developments indicate growing potential for cross-border investment and economic partnership based on cultural and linguistic ties.

The overall picture of Mexican-American lobbying in the United States is one of substantial activity, but little coherence and limited influence. Influence is probably greatest when interests are relatively narrow and focused, and have appeal outside the Mexican-American community, such as some interests represented by Mexican-American business organizations. Broader civil rights concerns—including those associated with enhancing Mexican-American inclusion and influence in politics, society, and even in the business community—face greater challenges. A growing number of Mexican-American champions in Congress, namely, the Mexican-American and other Latino members of the CHC, offer a critical conduit through which Mexican-American interests gain lobbying access. While CHC numbers and influence are growing, it is important to note that this group is unlikely to exercise substantial unilateral influence in Congress both because the group is small and because its Democratic membership is currently in the legislative minority. The group therefore generally requires the cooperation of non-Latino representatives to achieve its goals.[103] Ultimately, advancing major Mexican-American agendas will require both expanding Mexican-American influence beyond their group of legislative champions and more legislative representation in positions of institutional power.[104]

A second critical observation is that Mexican-American organizations generally focus on domestic concerns of the constituencies they represent. This differentiates them in important ways from other major diaspora lobbies that focus narrowly on U.S. foreign policy toward ethnic countries of origin. It also makes Mexican-American agendas more pan-ethnic than those of some other diasporas. In many ways, the political agendas advanced by Mexican Americans are one and the same with those advanced as part of a larger Latino-interest agenda.[105] Clearly, Mexican-American interests in immigration differ fundamentally from those of two other major Latino subgroups, Cuban Americans and Puerto Ricans. But anti-immigrant xenophobia and ethnic discrimination appears to largely transcend fundamental differences with commonly shared civil rights concerns. Those concerns go beyond discrimination against immigrants per se to include educational, health, and other socioeconomic deficits. Thus, as the largest Latino subgroup, Mexican-American interests have become in many ways interchangeable with the concerns of the broader Latino community.

Conclusion

The policy agendas and political strategies of Mexican Americans rarely align with or even overlap those of Mexico. To the extent that Mexican-American organizations act as surrogates for Mexico's policy interests, it often occurs on business and trade issues and through the advocacy of Hispanic business organizations such as AEM or the Hispanic Chamber of Commerce. At other times, and recently in particular, Mexican-American civil rights interests align with Mexico's economic interests in maintaining positive global impressions of Mexicans. The evolving nature of Mexico's orientation toward its diaspora has reflected some recognition of the importance of a growing elite demographic in the Mexican-American community. However, there appears to be little coherent strategy as of yet to harness the economic opportunities this development provides.

The vast majority of Mexican Americans are represented by organizations whose agendas hold only tangential interest for Mexican economic policies, and focus primarily on domestic political issues related to Mexican-American needs as a politically and socioeconomically disadvantaged minority in the United States. Clearly, as the Mexican-American community grows in terms of numbers and influence, the linkages between Mexican and Mexican-American objectives have the potential to strengthen. We anticipate that this will occur primarily within the growing Mexican-American business class. This population possesses not only the resources desired by a Mexican government hungry for direct investment, but also—by virtue of their socioeconomic status—the luxury of being able to concern themselves with Mexican policy interests in addition to their own immediate domestic policy objectives.

Overall, Mexican Americans constitute a unique and interesting case among other political diasporas. They are, at once, less connected to political concerns in their ethnic country of origin and more united in pan-ethnic political struggle than are most other diasporas in the United States. Far from posing the threat to American foreign policy some have predicted, Mexican Americans appear steadily focused on domestic political concerns and political agendas they hold in common with other Latinos. Their greatest successes likely occur not strictly in the realm of ethnic politics, but rather in areas of relatively narrow concern to business owners and investors—interests shared without regard to ethnic demographic. In sum, Mexican Americans are not significant advocates for Mexico, nor is Mexico more than a coincidental advocate for most Mexican-American interests. Instead, both parties might be dubbed opportunistic partners—seizing opportunities when interests coincide but sharing little in terms of strategy or coordination.

Notes

1. Rodolfo O. de la Garza, "Interests Not Passions: Mexican-American Attitudes toward Mexico, Immigration from Mexico, and Other Issues Shaping

U.S.-Mexico Relations," *The International Migration Review* 32(2) (1998): 401–422; Rodolfo O. de la Garza, "Introduction," in *Latinos and U.S. Foreign Policy: Representing the Homeland?* eds. Rodolfo O. de la Garza and Harry Pachon (Lanham, MD: Rowman & Littlefield., 2000); Samuel P. Huntington, "The Erosion of American National Interests," *Foreign Affairs* (Sept./Oct. 1997): 28–49.

2. Harry Pachon, Rodolfo De la Garza, and Adrian Pantoja, "Foreign Policy Perspectives of Hispanic Elites," in *Latinos and U.S. Foreign Policy: Representing the Homeland?* eds. Rodolfo De la Garza and Harry Pachon (Lanham, MD: Rowman & Littlefield, 2000); Harry Mohar, "Relations with the Mexican Diaspora," in *Latinos and U.S. Foreign Policy: Representing the Homeland?* eds. Rodolfo De la Garza and Harry Pachon (Lanham, MD: Rowman & Littlefield, 2000), 125–130; James M. McCormick, "Ethnic Interest Groups and American Foreign Policy: How Influential?" in *Interest Group Politics*, 9th ed., eds. Allan J. Cigler, Burdett A. Loomis, and Anthony J. Nownes (Washington, DC: CQ Press, 2016), 249–281.

3. Mohar (2000); Carlos Gonzalez Gutierrez, "Decentralized Diplomacy: The Role of Consular Offices in Mexico's Relations with Its Diaspora," in *Bridging the Border: Transforming Mexico-U.S. Relations*, eds. Rodolfo O. de la Garza and Jesus Velasco (Lanham, MD: Rowman & Littlefield, 1997), 49–68; de la Garza (2000).

4. Jean-Michel. Lafleur, "Regime Change in Mexico and the Transformation of State-Diaspora Relations," in *Policies and Ideologies of Emigrant Engagement*, ed. Michael Collyer (New York: Palgrave, 2013), 1–19.

5. Ibid.

6. Lafleur (2013); David Gutiérrez, *Walls and Mirrors: Mexican Americans, Mexican Immigrants, and the Politics of Ethnicity* (Berkeley: University of California Press, 1995).

7. Lafleur (2013); Gutiérrez (1995).

8. Lafleur (2013), 154.

9. Ibid.

10. Ronald L. Mize and Alicia C.S. Swords, *Consuming Mexican Labor: From the Bracero Program to NAFTA* (Toronto: University of Toronto Press, 2011), p. xxxiii.

11. Craig A. Kaplowitz, *LULAC, Mexican Americans, and National Policy* (College Station: Texas A&M University Press, 2005), 18–23.

12. Benjamin Marquez, "The Politics of Race and Assimilation: The League of United Latin American Citizens 1929–1940," *Western Political Quarterly* 42(2) (1989): 355–337.

13. Galarza (1964), 41–46; Gutiérrez (1995).

14. Galarza (1964), 47; Lafleur (2013); Gutiérrez 1995.

15. Galarza (1964), 47–48.

16. Ibid., 50.

17. Gutiérrez (1997); Kaplowitz (2005).

18. Ibid.

19. Gutiérrez (1997); Galarza (1964).

20. Galarza (1964), 70; Mize and Swords (2011), 25–41.

21. Kaplowitz (2005).

22. Richard B. Craig, *The Bracero Program: Interest Groups and Foreign Policy* (Austin: University of Texas Press, 1971).

23. Alarcón and McKinley (1992); Ros (1993).

24. Patricia H. Hamm, "Mexican-American Interests in U.S.-Mexico Relations: The Case of NAFTA" (Working Paper no. 4. University of California, Irvine, 1996).

25. Denise Dresser, "Exporting Conflict: Transboundary Consequences of Mexican Politics," in *The California-Mexico Connection*, eds., Abraham F. Lowenthal and Katrina Burgess (Stanford, CA: Stanford University Press, 1993); Hamm (1996).

26. De la Garza (1998).

27. Cathryn L. Thorup, "The Politics of Free Trade and the Dynamics of Cross-Border Coalitions in U.S.-Mexico Relations," *The Columbia Journal of World Business* (1991), 12–26; Hamm (1996).

28. Amy Skonieczny, "Constructing NAFTA: Myth, Representation, and the Discursive Construction of U.S. Foreign Policy," *International Studies Quarterly* 45 (2001): 433–454; Mizc and Swords (2011); Angeles M. Villareal, *NAFTA and the Mexican Economy*, CRS Report RL34733 (Washington, DC: Congressional Research Service, 2010).

29. Carlos Gustavo Villela, *Understanding Institutionalized Collective Remittances: The Mexican Tres Por Uno Program in Zacatecas*. Bochum Studies in International Development 64 (Logos Verlag, 2014); authors' interview with Enrique Berruga, August 18, 2016; Villareal (2010); Gutiérrez (1997).

30. Authors' interview August 18, 2016.

31. Matt A. Barreto, Sylvia Manzano, Ricardo Ramirez and Kathy Rim, "Mobilization, Participation, and Solidaridad: Latino Participation in the 2006 Immigration Protest Rallies. *Urban Affairs Review* 44(5) (2009): 736–764; Chris Zepeda-Millan and Sophia J. Wallace, "Racialization in Times of Contention: How Social Movements Influence Latino Racial Identity," *Politics, Groups, and Identities* 1(4) (2013): 510–527.

32. "Full Text: Donald Trump Announces Presidential Bid," *Washington Post*, June 16, 2015. Accessed at washingtonpost.com

33. Martin Farrer, "Two Former Mexican Presidents Compare Donald Trump to Hitler," *The Guardian*, February 27, 2016. Accessed at theguardian.com

34. Alexandra Alper, "Mexican President Says Won't Pay for Trump Wall, Makes Hitler Warning," *Reuters*, March 7, 2016. Accessed at reuters.com

35. Jorge Castañeda, "Mexican Politician Calls for 'Strong Campaign' against Trump in Viral Ad-Video," *The Guardian*, March 11, 2016. Accessed at theguardian.com

36. Elise Foley, "Hispanic Chamber of Commerce Trolls Donald Trump by Endorsing Hillary Clinton at GOP Convention," *Huffington Post*. July 20, 2016. Accessed at huffingtonpost.com

37. Jens Manuel Krogstad and Mark Hugo Lopez, "Hillary Clinton Won Latino vote But Fell Below 2012 Support for Obama," *Pew Research Center*, November 29, 2016. Accessed at pewresearch.org; Francisco Pedraza and Bryan Wilcox-Archuleta, "Donald Trump Did Not Win 34% of the Latino Vote in

Texas. He Won Much Less," *Washington Post,* December 2, 2016; *Latino Decisions:* latinovote2016.com

38. Pachon, de la Garza, and Pantoja (2000).

39. Shain (2000); Mohar (2000); Lafleur (2013).

40. De la Garza (1998).

41. Todd A. Eisenstadt, "The Rise of the Mexico Lobby in Washington: Even Further from God, and Even Closer to the United States," in *Bridging the Border: Transforming Mexico-U.S. Relations,* eds., Rodolfo O. de la Garza and Jesus Valasco (Lanham, MD: Rowman & Littlefield, 1997), 89.

42. Ibid., 93.

43. Ibid., 94.

44. Department of Justice, National Security Division. 2001. "FARA Reports to Congress," *Foreign Agents Registration Act: Semi-Annual Reports to Congress* (2014). Accessed at fara.gov

45. Ibid., 102–107.

46. These representatives included Xavier Becerra (D-CA), Ed Pastor (D-AZ), Lucille Roybal-Allard (D-CA), and Esteban Torres (D-CA).

47. Eisenstadt (1997), 109.

48. Authors' interview April 21, 2016.

49. Authors' interview, May 24, 2016.

50. Authors' interview April 29, 2016.

51. Department of Justice, National Security Division (2001). "FARA Reports to Congress," *Foreign Agents Registration Act: Semi-Annual Reports to Congress* (2014). Accessed at fara.gov

52. "Investor Relations," *Televisa.* Accessed August 1, 2016, www.televisair. com

53. International Court of Justice, "Avena and Other Mexican Nationals (*Mexico v. United States of America*)," *International Court of Justice,* March 31, 2004. Accessed at icj-cij.org

54. Emily Stephenson, "How Ted Cruz Win in Supreme Court Hurt U.S.-Mexico Relations," *Reuters.* April 6, 2016. Accessed at reuters.com

55. Ibid.

56. Ibid.

57. Laurence Shore, Mildred Ojea, and Robert Rothkopf, "U.S. District Court Confirms Arbitral Award against Pemex That Was Nullified at Its Seat," *Arbitration Notes.* September 18, 2013. Accessed at hsfnotes.com

58. Mexico Tourism Board, "Mexico Tourism: Facts and Statistics," *Journey Mexico.* December 28, 2015. Accessed at journeymexico.com

59. Authors' interview August 18, 2016.

60. Ibid.

61. Ibid.

62. Authors' interview June 20, 2016.

63. Instituto Nacional de Migracion, "Programa de Repatriacion," *Programa de Repatriacion.* Accessed August 1, 2016 at www.gob.mx; authors' interview July 27, 2016.

64. William Booth, "Latin American Leaders Assail U.S. Drug 'Market,'" *Washington Post*, December 19, 2011.

65. Christopher Ingraham, "Why Mexico's Drug Cartels Love America's Gun Laws," *Washington Post*, January 14, 2016.

66. Ken Ellingwood, "U.S. Shares Blame for Mexico Drug Violence, Clinton Says," *Los Angeles Times*, March 26, 2009.

67. Ibid.

68. Eisenstadt (1997), 117.

69. Authors' interview August 18, 2016.

70. McCormick (2016).

71. De la Garza (1998).

72. Ibid.

73. Rodney Hero, *Latinos and the U.S. Political System: Two-Tiered Pluralism* (Philadelphia: Temple University Press, 1992).

74. All data on Mexican-American registered lobbying were collected by the Center for Responsive Politics and is available at opensecrets.org. See Center for Responsive Politics, "Influence & Lobbying: U.S. Hispanic Chamber of Commerce" (2016).

75. See Center for Responsive Politics (2016) and "American Israel Public Affairs Committee" at opensecrets.org

76. National Council of La Raza, "NCLR Affiliate Network" (2016). Accessed at nclr.org

77. Center for Responsive Politics, "Influence & Lobbying" (2016).

78. Richard Webner, "Mexican Steel Baron Finds Favor at Home, Opposition in Texas," *Houston Chronicle*, August 31, 2013. Accessed at houstonchronicle.com

79. Center for Responsive Politics, "Influence & Lobbying" (2016); authors' Interview July 27, 2016.

80. "Advocacy," *United States Hispanic Chamber of Commerce* (2016). Accessed at ushcc.com

81. Kay Lehman Scholzman and John T. Tierney. *The Organized Interests and American Democracy* (New York: Harper and Row, 1986)

82. "Education," *League of United Latin American Citizens* (2016). Accessed at lulac.org.

83. Walter C. Wilson, "The Congressional Hispanic Caucus and Immigration Reform," *Extensions: A Journal of the Carl Albert Congressional Research and Studies Center* (Summer, 2013): 11.

84. Jacqueline Burns, Erin Hromada, Kathleen Johnson, Kenneth Kato, Joshua Litten, and Barry Pump, *Hispanic Americans in Congress, 1822–2012* (Washington, DC: Committee on House Administration, 2013), 410–415.

85. Congressional Hispanic Caucus Institute, "What We Do," *Congressional Hispanic Caucus Institute*. Accessed August 1, 2016, at chci.org

86. Burns et al. (2013), 400.

87. Raul Grijalva, "Biography," *Congressman Raul M. Grijalva*. Accessed August 1, 2016, at grijalva.house.gov; Armando Navarro, *La Raza Unida Party* (Philadelphia: Temple University Press, 2000).

88. John Celock, "Joe Arpaio Opponents Form Super PAC to Unseat Arizona Sheriff," *Huffington Post*. Accessed September 25, 2012, at huffingtonpost.com

89. United Farm Workers, "Farm Workers Travel to Washington, DC to Outline Vision for Immigration Policy Reform as Negotiations Reach Critical Stage," *United Farm Workers, Press Releases*, April 5, 2013. Accessed at ufw.org; United Farm Workers, "United Farm Workers Statement on Rep Tony Cardenas Proposed Amendment to the Republican Budget," *United Farm Workers, Press Releases*, April 2, 2014. Accessed at ufw.org

90. Walter C. Wilson, "Latino Congressional Staffers and Policy Responsiveness: An Analysis of Latino Interest Agenda-Setting," *Politics, Groups, and Identities* 1(2) (2013): 164–180; Michael Minta, *Oversight: Representing Black and Latino Interests in Congress* (Princeton, NJ: Princeton University Press, 2011).

91. John R. Wright, *Interest Groups and Congress: Lobbying, Contributions, and Influence* (Boston: Allyn & Bacon, 1996), 187–188.

92. Center for Responsive Politics, "Influence & Lobbying" (2016).

93. Foley (2016).

94. Kaplowitz (2005); Marquez (1989).

95. "About SVREP," *Southwest Voter Registration Education Project*. Accessed August 1, 2016, at svrep.org.

96. David Bacon, "Legacy of the Delano Grape Strike, 50 Years Later," *San Francisco Chronicle*, September 16, 2015. Accessed at sfchronicle.com

97. Navarro (2000).

98. Sidney Verba, Kay Lehman Scholzman, and Henry E. Brady, *Voice and Equality* (Cambridge, MA: Harvard University Press, 1995).

99. Bill Hobby, Mark P. Jones, Jim Granato, and Renee Cross, "The Texas Voter ID Law and the 2014 Election: A Study of Texas's 23rd Congressional District," Hoppy Center for Public Policy (Houston, TX: Baker Institute for Public Policy, 2015).

100. Wilson, Walter. *From Inclusion to Influence: Latino Representation in Congress and Latino Political Incorporation in America* (Ann Arbor: University of Michigan Press, 2017).

101. Hero (1992).

102. Geoscape, "Hispanic Businesses and Entrepreneurs Drive Growth in the New Economy: 3rd Annual Report," U.S. Hispanic Chamber of Commerce (2015). Accessed at http://ushcc.com

103. Wilson, Walter. *From Inclusion to Influence*.

104. William Curtis Ellis and Walter Clark Wilson, "Minority Chairs and Congressional Attention to Minority Issues: The Effect of Descriptive Representation in Positions of Institutional Power," *Social Science Quarterly* 94(5) (2013): 1207–1221.

105. Chris F. García and Gabriel Sanchez. *Hispanics and the U.S. Political System* (Upper Saddle River: Pearson, 2008); Stella M. Rouse, *Latinos in the Legislative Process: Interests and Influence* (New York: Cambridge University Press, 2013).

Chapter 8

Congress and the Politics of the
End of the Cuba Embargo

PATRICK J. HANEY

This chapter analyzes ethnic lobbying of Cuban Americans with specific focus on the dynamics between Congress and the executive branch over the embargo policy toward Cuba and its potential end. After a brief recap of the working parts of the embargo from the 1980s and the emergence of the Cuban American National Foundation (a powerful Cuban-American organization), the chapter mostly focuses attention on Congress: its rise in embargo politics in the 1990s, particularly in the Cuban Democracy Act in 1992 and the Helms-Burton Act in 1996, the way Presidents Bill Clinton and George W. Bush fought back to retain control over policy, the Barack Obama era that moved toward normalization, the changing nature of the lobbying environment that has surrounded Capitol Hill, and ends with some discussion of the changes to Cuba policy made by President Donald J. Trump. Ultimately, a fast-evolving Cuban-American community that was also rapidly receding in political clout, shifting national opinion on the embargo, a divided Republican Party, and other changing political dynamics led us to the point where the embargo is perhaps on its last legs. President Trump can dial back the clock, but he will find it difficult as the embargo has been overcome by events. Ultimately, however, Congress still has a key role to play thanks to its efforts in the 1990s to codify the embargo into law. Events may still alter this trajectory, but here the focus is on the role of Congress on the path toward the "end" of the Cuban embargo.

Congress, Ethnic Lobbying, and Foreign Policy

The politics of U.S. policy toward Cuba is not only fascinating in its own right—and ever-evolving—but also speaks to two different conceptual puzzles that help inform debates at the heart of democratic governance in foreign affairs. One puzzle deals with the over-arching issue of this volume, namely, how are we to understand ethnic lobbying in the American political system?[1] Empirically, as shown throughout this volume, ethnic lobbying has been on the rise, but *normatively* is that a good thing for democracy, as for example Anne-Marie Slaughter argues, or is it potentially dangerous to the unity of the Republic, as Tony Smith suggests?[2] Another puzzle focuses on whether or not congressional activism in foreign affairs is really "less than meets the eye," as Barbara Hinckley so compellingly argues, or if there are significant avenues of influence for Congress and its members when it comes to trying to steer the ship of state, as James Lindsay persuasively shows.[3] The case of the Cuban embargo offers an interesting window into these issues, and the chapter concludes by asking what this case tells us about these puzzles.

Discussions of the politics of the Cuban embargo often focus on the powerful pro-embargo interest group, the Cuban American National Foundation (CANF),[4] the largest and perhaps most influential ethnic lobby group on Cuba policy during the 1980s and 1990s, and the Free Cuba PAC that ran side by side with it for many years. More recently, the focus has perhaps shifted to the Cuban-American members of Congress themselves as guardians of the embargo, and the influential U.S.-Cuba Democracy PAC, which started in 2003 and has become a major player in election seasons since.[5] Another common theme is to focus on the electoral politics that lurk over the embargo policy, as when Brent Scowcroft, former National Security Adviser to Presidents Gerald Ford and George H.W. Bush, commented that Cuba "is a domestic issue for the United States and not a foreign policy issue. It focuses more on votes in Florida than it does on what to do with Castro."[6]

Thus, while many focus on the ethnic lobbying and campaign contributions aspect of the story, another common element is to focus on how the locus of politics of the embargo shifts over time and with who controls the presidency—first from the ethnic interest group that championed its cause (along with a welcoming White House in the Reagan years), to the Cuban Americans in Congress who moved the embargo from the realm of executive orders to law, and now mostly to successive presidential administrations who use their power to limit or expand the embargo's reach. There is, in short, a little bit of everything in this case.[7]

While the case of the Cuban embargo may be unique, with heavy doses of ethnic lobbying, electoral politics and campaign finance, presidential power, and congressional entrepreneurialism, given our increasingly hyper-partisan political system[8] perhaps it is useful to think of it less as an extreme example and more of a harbinger of things that might come. This is a clear case of "intermestic" politics, in which the issues are simultaneously international and domestic,[9] and we are likely to see an intensification of these dynamics in the coming years, not an amelioration of them.

Background: Ethnic Lobbying and the Cuban Embargo

Fidel Castro came to power in 1959 as part of the revolution in Cuba, and within a year the Eisenhower and then Kennedy administration began to put in place the U.S. embargo of Cuba. The "embargo" is not one single policy but really a package of policies that change over time, sometimes stronger, sometimes weaker. The embargo includes no formal diplomatic recognition and no embassy (although it was reopened by President Obama); a ban on trade and commercial activity with Cuba, although some sales of food and medicine have been allowed since 2000; a ban on travel to Cuba by most Americans unless licensed to go under certain circumstances (which President Obama mostly lifted and President Trump has aimed to restrict somewhat); restrictions on Cuban-Americans' travel and aid to their family members still in Cuba (which President Obama also lifted); a policy on under what circumstances Cubans fleeing the island may enter the United States, the so-called "wet foot/dry foot" policy (lifted by President Obama just before leaving office); and radio and TV broadcasting to the island. The embargo, codified into law in 1996 in the Helms-Burton Act (or Cuban Liberty and Democratic Solidarity Act), has evolved over time and has been the subject of significant lobbying and debate.

The embargo seemed set in stone in the 1960s, especially in the context of the Cold War with Cuba as an ally of the Soviet Union—which posed an existential threat to the United States—and with the disaster of the failed Bay of Pigs invasion, through which the United States hoped to overthrow the Castro government, and the nightmare of the Cuban Missile Crisis that surely clarified the stakes of the Cold War. Nevertheless, there were attempts to make relations more normal in the 1970s. President Ford and Secretary of State Henry Kissinger tried to induce an opening with Cuba, which largely failed, and the Carter administration loosened some of the travel restrictions and opened an "interests section" for the United States inside the Swiss Embassy in Cuba (and Cuba opened one in the

Swiss Embassy in Washington, DC). Any hope for further opening ended with the Mariel Boatlift in 1980, when 125,000 Cubans took to the waters of the Florida Straits and headed for the Sunshine state.

In 1980, the entire lobbying environment around the Cuban embargo changed. First, Ronald Reagan won the White House promising to be far more confrontational with the Soviets in Cuba and across Central America. Second, a new interest group was formed—the Cuban American National Foundation—led by the charismatic Jorge Mas Canosa.[10] Together CANF and the Reagan team rattled off a series of policy successes in the 1980s that made CANF the envy of just about every lobby group in town, ethnic or otherwise. Radio Marti was founded, broadcasting signals to Cuba, followed later by TV Marti. The National Endowment for Democracy was formed, and CANF was a key partner in carrying out democracy promotion activities in the hemisphere. CANF helped coordinate the settling of Cuban exiles in America, and worked with the Reagan team to tighten the grip of the embargo and even to take the battle to Cuban forces in a civil war in Africa.[11] Jorge Mas Canosa took on legendary status as a lobbyist and wielder of influence in Washington, DC, and many members of Congress wanted to visit Miami for fundraisers.

When the Cold War ended between 1989 and 1991, however, an interesting debate erupted: should the embargo end? One side said yes, that now was the time to work with Cuba for democratic and market-based reforms on the island, while embargo hardliners urged not just its continuation but its strengthening—do not help someone up when they are down: now was the time when the embargo could finally really strangle the Cuban economy and regime, with no sponsor in Moscow to prop them up.[12] This was also a key period for the embargo because of the election of the first Cuban-American member of Congress: Representative Ileana Ros-Lehtinen (R-FL) was elected in a special election in 1989. A future governor of Florida and brother of a president, Jeb Bush, chaired her campaign. Other Cuban Americans from Florida and New Jersey would soon join Ros-Lehtinen. CANF would no longer just be lobbying Congress; now Cuban Americans were *in* Congress and were determined to legislate on the embargo. Today there are eight Cuban Americans in the House of Representatives and Senate, from Florida, New Jersey, Texas, and West Virginia.

The Cold War Ends, and Congress Gets Engaged

The 1992 presidential campaign was the first of a series of campaigns that would pit two futures of the embargo against one another, and frame the power of the White House and Congress over the embargo. A bill called the Cuban Democracy Act had been introduced in Congress, and President George H.W. Bush opposed the bill—not so much because it would tighten the embargo but because the bill would mean that Congress was calling the shots on the substance of our foreign policy, something Bush saw as the president's purview. With Bush opposed to the bill, CANF's leader Mas Canosa negotiated with Bill Clinton's campaign to get his approval of the bill.[13] Clinton liked the politics. "The point was not to win a majority of the Cuban vote but to get a bunch of campaign money, to outflank Bush on the right, and to make Bush spend time and money in Florida, which should [have been] a gimme state for Republicans."[14] He also liked the policy; the CDA would provide ways to get "hard" on the Castro regime but to be "soft" on the Cuban people by opening up people-to-people contacts—allowing the president to calibrate policy over time. Clinton did not win Florida, but he won the election, winning six times as many Cuban-American votes as Michael Dukakis had four years earlier; he would win Florida in his re-election campaign in 1996.

This is a key period in the development of the ethnic lobbying environment around the embargo. CANF had achieved incredible policy successes, forged a partnership with the Reagan White House, and helped elect Cuban Americans to Congress. But the fruits of that success were in some ways the start of their undoing. The Cuban Americans in Congress did not need lobbying, and they lobbied their own colleagues directly—relying on congressional logrolling to help move embargo legislation. The members still needed CANF for ideas and information, and money, but they became the drivers of policy on the Hill, and now CANF had to react to this environment—which included a Clinton White House that was more hostile to their positions.

A new legislative initiative on the embargo emerged after Republicans took control of the House and Senate in the November 1994 elections. It should be noted, too, that this bill was constructed on the Hill, largely outside CANF's grasp—reflecting this new lobbying environment with Cuban Americans themselves now in Congress; it was not a case that the Cuban-American lobbying community was weaker, but that the agenda was being carried forward by Cuban-American legislators in a vastly different environment.

Gluing together different pieces of legislation that had been around the Hill for some time, the Helms-Burton Act sought to significantly tighten the embargo by clamping down on foreign businesses that do business in Cuba and on executives in those businesses who might wish to visit the United States. The most controversial part of the bill was its Title III, which would create a "right to sue" in U.S. courts for U.S. nationals with property in Cuba that was seized after the revolution and that was being used by foreign companies.[15] The prospect of Cuban Americans taking foreign companies to court in Miami for "trafficking" in stolen property was, depending on one's point of view, either a master stroke as a way to extend the embargo's grip or a looming diplomatic disaster.

The Clinton team had largely beaten back the offending parts of Helms-Burton when the Cuban Air Force shot down two planes over the Florida Straits in February 1996, killing four. The planes were flown by members of the group Brothers to the Rescue, who regularly flew to look for rafters in danger, and on occasion would fly over Cuba and drop anti-Castro leaflets. This action led to calls for an American response—including perhaps using force against the bases that launched the attack. In this environment, the Helms-Burton bill was front and center, with its deletions restored. Negotiators in Congress clamped down more by codifying into law the parts of the embargo that up to that time had existed through executive order, not legislation.

The Clinton administration had little room to negotiate. They did get a "waiver" on the right to sue, but it was not the ordinary waiver, where a president could waive enforcement if the president said that it was in the national security interests of the United States to do so. This waiver actually had two parts—the usual national security part, but also a part where the president would have to justify to Congress that a democratic transition was underway in Cuba, and that the waiver would facilitate that process. With the 1996 re-election (and Florida's electoral votes) looming, Senator Jesse Helms (R-NC) famously said that the waiver was "Clinton proof," meaning not even Bill Clinton (who in Helms's eyes had a willingness to be fast and loose with the truth) would dare execute the waiver. Clinton did execute the waiver every six months (as did every president who followed, including George W. Bush, who promised to "fully enforce" Helms-Burton). Asked about the decision to execute such a waiver, when on its face it was difficult to justify, Alan J. Kreczko, special assistant to the president and legal adviser for the National Security Council during this period, said doing so emerged less from the administration's concern about Cuba policy than it did from a "preserve the president's institutional prerogatives policy,"[16] setting the stage for later moves by Clinton that would alter the outlines of the embargo but that were also significantly about regaining power over Cuba policy that was perhaps lost in this episode.

In 1998, Clinton instituted a variety of reforms to the embargo policy, timed to coincide with the visit to Cuba by Pope John Paul II.[17] Clinton expanded the family travel and remittance policies, reestablished humanitarian flights to the island, and then in 1999 went further to develop "people to people" contacts, to broaden the ways that Americans could get licenses to travel to Cuba, and to support the sale of food and medicine to the island—as well as a Baltimore Orioles baseball game on the island. How Clinton had the power to do this, having signed Helms-Burton, was a matter of some debate. Many found the action to be outside his powers;[18] the Clinton team thought otherwise. White House official James Dobbins argued that, "Helms-Burton codified the embargo, and at the same time it codified the president's licensing power; that is, it codified a process by which there was an embargo to which exceptions could be granted on a case-by-case basis, by the president, in cases in which it was deemed to be consistent with U.S. policy."[19] However one might interpret the move, it certainly appeared that Clinton had decided to act as if Helms-Burton never happened and that he was proceeding under the previous policy of the Cuban Democracy Act.

In 2000, Congress passed and Clinton signed the Trade Sanctions Reform and Export Enhancement Act, which increased the sale of food and medicine to Cuba. These transactions would be difficult: Congress required cash up front, which limited the reach of the legislation. Still, the template for increased economic activity between the United States and Cuba was in place, and Act followed shifts in the political environment around the embargo, as support for ending the decades-old policy became more bipartisan, as big business, agriculture, and pharma came to see the embargo as a hindrance to economic growth in the United States, and as the Cuban-American community became more open to engagement with the island.

At the same time that these dynamics were evolving, the powerful CANF was quickly falling apart. Jorge Mas Canosa died in 1997, and in addition to a leadership vacuum, CANF fell victim to a string of additional bad news. In 1998, allegations were made that CANF—formed in part to take the policy battle to Washington, DC, rather than the paramilitary battle that had been waged on the streets of Miami in the 1970s—supported the terrorist acts in Cuba of Luis Posada Carriles. As controversy ensured, many of its members left CANF for a new rival organization, essentially eroding the power of the group. In 1999 and 2000, CANF was engaged on the ground in Florida to try to keep the young Elian Gonzalez—who had washed up alive after everyone else on a boat perished, including his mother—in Florida with relatives rather than returning him to his father in Cuba. Federal agents took Elian and returned him to his father in spring 2000, just as the election season heated up. CANF seemed to accept that the momentum was shifting against the embargo and that it no longer had the clout it once had, and moved toward campaigns to educate the American public more so than a legislative agenda.[20] But perhaps all would not be lost for CANF, as Al Gore lost Cuban-American voters in Florida, lost Florida officially by 527 votes, and with it, lost the White House.[21]

With George W. Bush, the embargo supporters on the Hill and in Florida and New Jersey had a like-minded President. The lobbying action would shift away from CANF in 2003, however, and toward a new PAC that targeted not just embargo supporters with campaign cash, but also new members and new candidates for office who had yet to take a position on the embargo: the U.S.-Cuba Democracy PAC, formed to create support for the embargo. Bush tightened the rules around the embargo just as the 2004 election season kicked off, and worked with Republican leadership to make sure that the "travel ban," which prohibited travel by Americans to Cuba because it forbade their ability to spend money in Cuba, remained in place.[22]

It was at this time that the travel ban really became ground zero for the embargo. Presidents might loosen restrictions on family remittances and travel (Clinton) or tighten them (Bush), but ending the travel ban became the way to end the embargo through the back door. Recall that the legislation passed in 2000 allowing the sale of food and medicine in Cuba required cash up front; if the travel ban were lifted, then Americans could easily go to Cuba, spend dollars, which would then be able to be used to pay for more transactions. In essence, ending the travel ban became a way to make the embargo obsolete, albeit still on the books. Bipartisan support for ending the travel ban, which is embedded in the annual appropriations for the Department of Treasury—essentially forbidding Treasury, which enforces the embargo, from spending money to enforce the ban—was growing in the first Bush term. A showdown loomed and came to a head in the 2004 budget deal.

The House and the Senate used identical language in the 2004 Treasury appropriations bill that would have banned money from being spent to enforce the travel ban, and was headed for a presidential veto. Normally, a conference committee would not focus on parts of a bill that passed both houses with identical language, but this case was different. Then House Majority leader Tom Delay (R-TX), a strong supporter of the embargo, stacked the committee with travel ban proponents. In a committee staff meeting, the Cuba travel provision was struck from the bill. Senator Michael B. Enzi (R-WY) commented, "There was no vote taken. Poof, it just disappeared into the congressional ether."[23] That was as close as the travel ban came to a legislative death. Bush won re-election in 2004, and a relatively tight embargo policy continued through his second term.

The electoral politics of the embargo that developed in the 2000s and beyond are fascinating in many respects, but especially in the way that they show that what matters is not who *can* vote, but who *actually* votes. In 2004, the rules that Bush tightened were widely unpopular except among the hardest of hardliners. Many depicted the rule changes, which limited family visits and the amount of money Cuban Americans could send to their family in Cuba, and redefined "family" as only the nuclear family—no more cousins—as cruel and harsh, and anti-family. They were unpopular nationally, in Florida, and among many Cuban Americans.[24] Bush's standing in the polls among all Cuban Americans fell twenty points, to the level where Clinton had defeated Bush's father.[25] But the moves were popular among Cuban Americans who voted! Even while the percentage of all voters in Florida, and all Hispanic voters in Florida, diminished, embargo supporters flocked to the polls for Bush, delivering victories in 2000 and 2004,[26] showing once again that a small but motivated set of voters can carry the day over a larger more diffuse set of voters and nonvoters. It was prescient of the dynamic visible in 2016, when Obama's opening to Cuba was quite popular, but not on Election Day—when it (literally) counted.

The End is Near. Or Is It?

The 2008 election seemed to be a watershed in the history of the connection between the embargo and presidential elections in Florida. Barack Obama won the White House—and won Florida—without tacking to the right on the embargo. While he did not call for its outright repeal, he did promise to relax Bush's restrictions, and it was clear that Obama would seek to broaden connections between the United States and the island. And Obama appeared on solid ground, both in terms of general public opinion and the opinion of the quickly-evolving Cuban-American community.[27] Obama won approximately 35 percent of Cuban-American voters in Florida, and would go on to win just shy of a majority of these voters in the 2012 re-election race.[28] The tide seemed to have turned on the embargo, leaving it as a relic trapped in a time warp.

Pro-embargo forces would not give up without a fight, and the U.S.-Cuba Democracy PAC poured money into congressional races in 2008 and 2012 to try to bolster their side—with some impressive wins.[29] The PAC spent $1 million in the 2008 cycle,[30] but receipts fell off in 2010 (below their 2006 midterm election level of activity) and for the 2012 re-election cycle, spending over $400,000 in 2012 and then again in 2014. The writing seemed to be on the wall. The best the embargo's supporters could do on the Hill, it seemed, was stall for time.[31]

In his second term, President Obama launched a series of changes to the rules around the embargo that left in place only a shell of the decades-old policy. Bolstered by majority support in public opinion, bipartisan support in Congress, the support of many state governors, and big business, Obama set about to all but end the embargo.[32] In a series of steps, Obama legalized nearly all but purely tourist travel to the island, eased banking rules and the rules on family travel and remittances, restored diplomatic ties (although he did not succeed in an effort to place an ambassador in Havana), re-opened the embassy in Havana, and visited the island in March 2016. Days before leaving office, Obama also ended the "wet foot/dry foot" policy, in place since 1994, that gave special status to Cubans who arrive on U.S. soil, but would send back Cubans rescued at sea—meant as a way to deter Cubans from fleeing the island in such a dangerous manner.[33] Obama's moves found popular majorities in the country and among Cuban Americans.

In the 2016 election cycle, the opening to Cuba at first seemed like settled policy, with both Hillary Clinton and Donald Trump supportive of Obama's moves. During the campaign, Trump said that while he would have negotiated a better deal, what Obama had done was "fine" and that fifty years was "long enough."[34] In the lobbying environment, a new pro-engagement PAC entered the scene seeking to offset the work of the pro-embargo U.S.-Cuba Democracy PAC, called the New Cuba PAC; they raised almost half a million dollars in 2016, competing closely with the receipts and spending of the U.S.-Cuba Democracy PAC.[35] The embargo had been abandoned by big business, by the general public, by members of both parties, and by most Cuban Americans

Then things got interesting. The Clinton campaign seemed to struggle with Hispanics as the race there tightened,[36] and Donald Trump saw an opening. In September, Trump went to Miami and threw in with the embargo hardliners, promising to overturn Obama's reforms.[37] Trump seemed to be betting, as had others, that even though the portion of Hispanic voters in Florida who were Cuban-American had shrunk over time, he could turn out this constituency in high numbers, higher than other more left-leaning Hispanics, and perhaps get a win in the state that at one time seemed out of reach given its demographic shifts.[38] It was perhaps reminiscent of Bill Clinton's gamble in 1992. As we know, Trump won Florida, won Cuban-American voters, and won the election. Now the pressure is on him to turn back the Obama clock on Cuba policy. A key member of Trump's transition team for Treasury (which enforces the embargo) was Mauricio Claver-Carone, the head of the U.S.-Cuba Democracy PAC and a proponent of allowing Helms-Burton's "right to sue" to go into force; a second was Carlos Diaz-Rossilo, a Cuban-American political scientist who had taught at Harvard and who was now on the White House staff. Another on the State transition team was a key staffer for Rep. Ros Lehtinen. Trump was also lobbied by several former diplomats to act quickly.[39] Vice President Pence said during the transition that Trump would in fact dial back Obama's reforms,[40] and Representative Mario Diaz-Balart (R-FL), the brother of one of the key architects of the Helms-Burton law, has said that he expects the Trump administration to roll back Obama's changes, saying, "I would expect it to happen pronto."[41] Perhaps ironically, on the cusp of Trump's inauguration as president, Obama's Cuba policy was widely popular.[42]

Conclusion

In the 1990s, one of the metaphors used to describe the different ways that change could come to the island was a "hard landing" or "soft landing." A hard landing was envisioned as an overthrow of the Castro regime, with anger fueled by a rigorous and perhaps more multilateral embargo policy than the one in existence then. Elements of such a hard landing might include violence in Cuba and mass migration heading across the Florida Straits—a sort of Mariel on steroids. A soft landing would evolve more slowly over time, with the political system in Cuba gradually evolving to allow more elements of market-based capitalism, more avenues for free expression, and political pluralism, allowed by the Cuban government as a way to try to forestall more dramatic political change. In a soft landing, the Castro brothers would eventually either die or leave power willingly, opening the door to normalization with the United States. Commenting on this debate and speaking the day after the Republicans took the House of Representatives in 1994, Senator Jesse Helms (R-NC) famously said, "Whether Castro leaves Cuba in a vertical or horizontal position is up to him and the Cuban people . . . but he must—and will—leave Cuba."[43] For years this was one of the key differences that lay behind the policy preferences of different presidents: the interest in, and tolerance for risk associated with, a hard landing. Republican presidents, from Ronald Reagan to George W. Bush, were generally more willing to provoke a hard landing, and risk its potential dangers, than were Democratic presidents from Bill Clinton to Barack Obama. All the while, the lobbying environment essentially circled around this baseline.

The focus on this debate, however, might have missed the way things have played out over time: that the embargo would stay, sometimes tighter and sometimes looser, but stay; like the proverbial Energizer Bunny, it would just keep going and going, and everyone would just keep adjusting to each other. Clinton would loosen the embargo, Bush would tighten it, Obama would loosen it. All the while, the embargo became increasingly toothless as more and more people and products moved across the Straits. CANF evolved, and the Free Cuba PAC disappeared; the U.S.-Cuba Democracy PAC looked like it was losing steam but came roaring back in 2016. The views of the Cuban-American community also changed significantly. A degree of political change would come to the island as Fidel Castro receded from the scene, passing away in November 2016, and Raul Castro, Fidel's brother, promised to turn power over to a new generation of leadership. In many ways, the idea of the embargo would outlive the reality of the embargo.

In a speech in Miami on June 16, 2017, President Trump announced that he will use his unilateral power of the pen to dial back Obama's general ratcheting toward normalization with Cuba.[44] Trump will direct the Treasury Department to alter the travel restrictions so as to not allow individual "people to people" educational trips, which critics see as tourism. He will also prohibit business activity with military enterprises—which control much of Cuba's tourism sector. Once the new rules come out, Americans likely will not be able to stay at hotels owned by these enterprises. The Trump administration is also likely to monitor compliance with the travel rules very closely once they are issued by the Office of Foreign Assets Control (OFAC) at Treasury, which handles sanctioned regimes. It is interesting to note that even some Cuba policy hardliners are not happy with these changes for not going far enough; there is also a chance that these actions would actually harm the creation of markets and civil society in Cuba by shutting off the flow of cash to individuals and giving the regime an excuse for clamping down again.[45] It will also be interesting to see if Cuba policy will continue to draw President Trump's attention or if this is a "one and done" policy payoff to his supporters.[46] He did, after all, find his pro-embargo voice late in the campaign as Florida's electoral votes came into focus. And this is not the first time that the embargo is like a pendulum—swinging from one end to the other as the parties change power in the White House. Still, even with these changes, the pendulum's center point has shifted toward normalization.

By way of concluding this chapter, let us return to the two puzzles with which this chapter began, in reverse order. What does the case of the Cuban embargo tell us about congressional power in the area of foreign policy? Is Congress a central player, or a toothless giant? There is some evidence here on both sides. On the "more smoke than fire" side, Congress has allowed the executive branch to alter the embargo in significant ways that frankly push the meaning of the Helms-Burton Act. The president has used a very narrow (on its face) "licensing" power embedded in that Act with respect to family travel and remittances to alter the broad outlines of the embargo. Only Congress can repeal it, having codified the embargo into law, but Presidents Clinton and Obama, through executive orders, made that action far less weighty than it at first appeared. The ability of Congress to restrain the executive branch, determined to pursue a different course, is shown here to be limited. With little ability to sue in the courts, and unless there is enough support in both houses to take on the budget or nominations in the Senate as a way to punish a noncompliant president, Congress has been largely on the sidelines, as Hinckley might have expected but in ways that few would have predicted in 1996 after Helms-Burton was signed into law. The "protect the power of the presidency" policy certainly won out in this case, with little matching ethos on the Hill to vigorously defend the power of Congress.

At the same time, however, the case of the embargo also offers a blueprint for how Congress can get engaged on substantive foreign policy questions when it wishes to do so, and offers some warnings about what loopholes to avoid—loopholes that a willing president might later exploit. Congress did vote to codify the embargo into law in the Helms-Burton Act, largely over the policy preferences of the president—an extraordinary step in the area of foreign policy. Similar examples in the modern era are few and far between. In that sense, this case is by definition an extreme case of congressional activism in substantive foreign policy. That very legislation, however, also included in it language that could later be exploited by presidents who wished to loosen the embargo. Members of Congress and prospective policy entrepreneurs would be wise to learn from this experience and legislative explicitly and in detail—although that might also make it more difficult to build a winning coalition.

As for what this case tells us about the value of ethnic lobbying in the American political system, we should ponder the possibility that the American political system has evolved (purposefully or not) to spur exactly this type of activity—to value money in politics, to reward small but loud factions, to provide multiple doors through which special interests of all types might walk, and to forge a connection between electoral politics and public policy. There is certainly nothing illegal in this story, and while the empirical facts may not answer the broader normative question of whether ethnic lobbying is good for the Republic or undermines it, it is hard to deny that the pattern of politics visible in this case is as American as apple pie.[47]

Notes

1. For background beyond this volume, see Mohammed E. Ahrari, ed., *Ethnic Groups and U.S. Foreign Policy* (New York: Greenwood, 1987); Patrick J. Haney, "Ethnic Lobbying in Foreign Policy," in *The International Studies Encyclopedia*, ed. Robert A. Denemark (United Kingdom: Wiley-Blackwell, 2010), 1677–1693; Patrick J. Haney, "Ethnic Lobbying in the Obama Administration," in *U.S. Foreign Policy Today: Renewal?*" eds. Steven W. Hook and James M. Scott (Washington, DC: CQ Press, 2011), 77–92; David M. Paul and Rachel Anderson Paul, *Ethnic Lobbies and U.S. Foreign Policy* (Boulder, CO: Lynne Rienner Publishers, 2009); Eric M. Uslaner, "All Politics are Global: Interest Groups in the Making of Foreign Policy," in *Interest Group Politics* (4th ed.) eds. Allan J. Cigler and Burdett A. Loomis (Washington, DC: CQ Press, 1995), 369–391; Paul Y. Watanabe, *Ethnic Groups, Congress, and American Foreign Policy: The Politics of the Turkish Arms Embargo* (Westport, CT: Greenwood, 1984).

2. Anne-Marie Slaughter, "America's Edge: Power in the Networked Century," *Foreign Affairs* 88, 1 (Jan./Feb., 2009): 94–113; see also Yossi Shain, *Marketing the American Creed Abroad: Diasporas in the U.S. and their Homelands* (New York: Cambridge University Press, 1999); and Tony Smith, *Foreign Attachments: The Power of Ethnic Groups in the making of American Foreign Policy* (Cambridge, MA: Harvard University Press, 2000).

3. Barbara Hinckley, *Less Than Meets the Eye: Foreign Policy Making and the Myth of the Assertive Congress* Chicago: University of Chicago Press, 1994); James M. Lindsay, *Congress and the Politics of U.S. Foreign Policy* (Baltimore, MD: Johns Hopkins University Press, 1994).

4. See William LeoGrande, William, "The Cuba Lobby," *Foreign Policy*, April 12, 2013, http://foreignpolicy.com/2013/04/12/the-cuba-lobby; "The Fading of Fidel," *The Economist*, January 17, 1998, 13; Walter Russell Mead, "Mutual Assured Stupidity: Washington's Cuba Policy is Made in Miami," *The New Yorker*, March 11, 1996, 9–10; Patrick J. Haney and Walt Vanderbush, "The Role of Ethnic Interest Groups in U.S. Foreign Policy: The Case of the Cuban American National Foundation," *International Studies Quarterly* 43 (1999): 341–361.

5. See particularly Trevor Rubenzer, "Campaign Contributions and U.S. Foreign Policy Outcomes: An Analysis of Cuban-American Interests," *American Journal of Political Science* 55(1) (2010): 105–116; Trevor Rubenzer, "Ethnic Minority Interest Group Attributes and U.S. Foreign Policy Influence: A Qualitative Comparative Analysis," *Foreign Policy Analysis* 4 (2008): 169–185; Jonathan C. Smith, "Foreign Policy for Sale? Interest Group Influence on President Clinton's Cuba Policy, August 1994." *Presidential Studies Quarterly* 29 (1998): 207–220.

6. Quoted in Frank Davies, "White House Considers Plan for Commission to carry Out a Bipartisan Review," *Miami Herald*, November 24, 1998; see also Walt Vanderbush and Patrick J. Haney, "Cuba Policy: The Electoral Connection," paper presented at the Western Social Science Association, April 12, 2003.

7. For background, see Philip Brenner, *From Confrontation to Negotiation: U.S. Relations with Cuba* (Boulder, CO: Westview Press, 1988); Daniel P. Erikson, *Cuba Wars: Fidel Castro, the United States, and the Next Revolution* (New York: Bloomsbury Press, 2008); Patrick J. Haney and Walt Vanderbush, *The Cuban Embargo: The Domestic Politics of an American Foreign Policy* (Pittsburgh, PA: University of Pittsburgh Press, 2005); Donna R. Kaplowitz, *Anatomy of a Failed Embargo: U.S. Sanctions against Cuba* (Boulder, CO: Lynne Rienner, 1998); Morris H. Morley and Christopher McGillion, *Unfinished Business: America and Cuba After the Cold War, 1989–2001* (New York: Cambridge University Press, 2002); Lars Schoultz, *The United States and the Cuban Revolution: That Infernal Little Cuban Republic* (Chapel Hill: The University of North Carolina Press, 2009); Maria de los Angeles Torres, *In the Land of Mirrors: Cuban Exile Politics in the United States* (Ann Arbor: University of Michigan Press, 1961).

8. Thomas E. Mann, and Norman J Ornstein, *It's Even Worse Than It Looks: How the American Constitutional System Collided with the New Politics of Extremism* (New York: Basic Books, 2012).

9. Bayless Manning, "The Congress, the Executive and Intermestic Affairs: Three Proposals." *Foreign Affairs* 55 (1977): 306–324; Philip Brenner, Patrick J. Haney, Walt Vanderbush, "Intermestic Interests and U.S. Policy Toward Cuba," in *The Domestic Sources of American Foreign Policy*, 5th ed., eds. Eugene R. Wittkopf and James M. McCormick (Lanham, MD: Rowman & Littlefield, 2008), 65–80.

10. G. Fonzi, "Who is Jorge Mas Canosa?" *Esquire* (January 1993), 86–89, 119–122.

11. See Haney and Vanderbush (2005).

12. See Morley and McGillion (2002).

13. Jane Franklin, *Cuba and the United States* (New York: Ocean Press, 1997), 290; Ann Bardach, "Our Man in Miami," *The New Republic*, October 3, 1994, p. 20; and former Clinton administration official telephone interview with author, June 1, 1998.

14. Former Clinton administration official telephone interview with author, June 1, 1998; Patrick J. Haney and Walt Vanderbush, "Strange Bedfellows: Cuba Politics and Policy in the Clinton Administration," paper presented at the Presidential Conference on William Jefferson Clinton, Hofstra University, New York, November 2005.

15. Patrick J. Kiger, *Squeeze Play: The United States, Cuba, and the Helms-Burton Act*. Washington, DC: The Center for Public Integrity, 1997); Haney and Vanderbush, *The Cuban Embargo: The Domestic Politics of an American Foreign Policy.*

16. Alan J. Kreczko, telephone interview with author, June 18, 2002; Haney and Walt Vanderbush, "Strange Bedfellows: Cuba Politics and Policy in the Clinton Administration."

17. It ended up coinciding as well with revelations of a Clinton extramarital affair with a former White House intern.

18. Keep in mind that President Clinton was impeached by the House of Representatives and tried in the Senate, but not for this.

19. Special State Department Briefing: U.S.-Cuba Relations. *Federal News Service*, January 5, 1999.

20. See Henriette Rytz, *Ethnic Interest Groups in U.S. Foreign Policy-Making: A Cuban-American Story of Success and Failure* (New York: Palgrave Macmillan, 2013), 149.

21. See William Schneider, "Elian Gonzalez Defeated Al Gore." *The Atlantic*, May 2001, http://www.theatlantic.com/politics/nj/schneider2001-05-02.htm

22. Ryan Lizza, "Havana John," *The New Republic*, July 26, 2004: pp. 10–11; Christopher Marquis, "Bush's Allies Plan to Block Effort to Ease Ban on Cuban Travel." *New York Times*, November 13, 2003; Kirk Nielsen, "Politics and Policy: With Its Severe New Cuba Regulations, the Bush Administration Alienated Some Miami Exiles, but Not the Ones Who Matter," *Miami New Times*, July 29, 2004, http://www.miaminewtimes.com/2004-07-29/news/politics-and-policy; Wes Allison, "Bush Cuba Policy Stirs Backlash in S. Florida." *St. Petersburg* Times, May 22, 2004, http://www.sptimes.com/2004/05/22/news_pf/State/Bush_Cuba_policy_stir.shtml

23. Frank Davies and Nancy San Martin, "GOP Leaders Kill Provision to End Ban on Travel to Cuba," *Knight-Ridder Newspapers*, November 13, 2003; Frank Davies, "Cuba Travel Battle Looms," *Miami Herald*. October 31, 2003.

24. See Christopher Marquis, "Get-Tough Policy on Cuba May Backfire Against Bush." *New York Times*, July 24, 2004, http://www.nytimes.com/2004/07/29/us/get-tough-policy-on-cuba-may-backfire-against-bush.html

25. See Tamara Lush and David Adams, "Bush's Cuban American Support Slips." *St. Petersburg Times*, August 27, 2004, http://www.sptimes.com/2004/08/27/Decision2004/Bush_s_Cuban_American.shtml

26. Lizza, 2004; Nate Cohn, "Why the Cuba Issue No Longer Cuts Against Democrats in Florida." *New York Times*, December 17, 2014, https://www.nytimes.com/2014/12/18/upshot/why-the-cuba-issue-no-longer-cuts-against-democrats-in-florida.html

27. See David Rieff, "Will Little Havana Go Blue?" *New York Times Magazine*, July 13, 2008, http://www.nytimes.com/2008/07/13/magazine/13CUBANS-t.html; Evan Perez, "Cuba Sanctions Likely to Ease: As Candidate, Obama Said He Would Lift Restrictions on Family Visits, Remittances," *Wall Street Journal*, November 7, 2008, http://online.wsj.com/article/SB122602004920007191.html; Damien Cave, "Democrats See Cuba Travel Limits as a Campaign Issue in Florida," *New York Times*, June 1, 2008, http://www.nytimes.com/2008/06/01/us/01florida.html; Damien Cave, "U.S. Overtures Find Support Among Cuban Americans," *New York Times*, April 20, 2009, http://www.nytimes.com/2009/04/21/us/21miami.html; Lesley Clark, Lesley, "Money Affects Cuba Policy," *Miami Herald*, November 16, 2009, http://www.miamiherald.com/news/southflorida/story/1335580.html; the Cuba Study Group, *Lifting Restrictions on Travel and Remittances: A Case for Unilateral Action* (Washington, DC, 2008), www.cubastudygroup.org

28. See Perez, "Cuba Sanctions Likely to Ease"; Jens Manuel Krogstad, "After Decades of GOP Support, Cubans Shifting toward the Democratic Party," Pew Research Center, June 24, 2014, http://www.pewresearch.org/fact-tank/2014/06/24/after-decades-of-gop-support-cubans-shifting-toward-the-democratic-party

29. See Ian Swanson, "Hard-line Cuba PAC Makes Inroads with House Freshmen," *TheHill.com*, September 21, 2007, 1–3.

30. Based on data available on OpenSecrets.org

31. See Cohn, "Why the Cuba Issue No Longer Cuts."

32. J.P. Faber, "Seeds of Change," *Cuba Trade Magazine*, September 5, 2016.

33. Julie Hirschfeld Davis and Frances Robles, "Obama Ends Exemption for Cubans Who Arrive without Visas," *New York Times*, January 12, 2017, https://www.nytimes.com/2017/01/12/world/americas/cuba-obama-wet-foot-dry-foot-policy.html?

34. Jeremy Diamond, "Trump Backs U.S.-Cuba Diplomatic Relations." *CNN*, September 15, 2015, http://www.cnn.com/2015/09/08/politics/donald-trump-cuba-diplomatic-opening

35. Mimi Whitefield, "PACs For and Against Cuba Embargo Bring in Big Money," *Miami Herald*, January 28, 2016.

36. Trip Gabriel, "Hillary Clinton Struggles to Gain Traction in Florida, Despite Spending," *New York Times*, September 17, 2016, http://nyti.ms/2cXdrwj

37. Marc Caputo, "In Miami, Trump Morphs Back into a Cuba Hardliner," *Politico*, September 16, 2016.

38. See Andres Oppenheimer, "Shift Among Cuban American Voters Could Deliver Florida to Donald Trump," *Seattle Times*, November 5, 2016.

39. Patricia Mazzei and Nora Gámez Torres, "Former Diplomats Urge Trump to Undo 'Unlawful' Obama Cuba Policy," *Miami Herald*, January 4, 2017, http://www.miamiherald.com/news/nation-world/world/americas/cuba/article124590444.html

40. Ben Weyl, "Pence: Cuba Executive Orders Will Be Overturned," *Politico*, October 14, 2016.

41. Congressional Quarterly, "Hardliners Lean on Trump to Close Cuba Opening," *CQ Magazine* (December 5, 2016). http://library.cqpress.com/cqweekly/weeklyreport114-000004996154

42. Alec Tyson, "Americans Still Favor Ties with Cuba after Castro's Death, U.S. Election," Pew Research Center, December 13, 2016.

43. Quoted in Matthew Rees, "Jesse at the Helm," *The Weekly Standard*, July 1, 1996, http://www.weeklystandard.com/jesse-at-the-helm/article/8748

44. See Fact Sheet on Cuba Policy. https://www.whitehouse.gov/blog/2017/06/16/fact-sheet-cuba-policy

45. See especially Julia Sweig's comments quoted in Jake Meth, "How Trump Could Embolden Cuba's Hardliners," *Fortune.com*, November 30, 2016.

46. See, e.g., Arturo Lopez-Levy, "Trump's Restrictions on Cuba Are a Detour, Not the Future," *Foreign Policy in Focus*, July 14, 2017, http://fpif.org/trumps-restrictions-on-cuba-are-a-detour-not-the-future

47. See the classic in the field, E.E. Schattschneider, *The Semi-Sovereign People* (New York: Holt, Rinehart, and Winston, 1960).

Chapter 9

Vietnamese Americans and the Socialist Republic of Vietnam

The Grassroots Lobby Takes on the Corporatized State

CHRISTIAN COLLET

On March 14, 2014, Representative Edward R. Royce (R-CA), introduced H.R. 4254, the Vietnam Human Rights Sanctions Act, a bill that sought "to impose sanctions on Vietnamese government officials who are complicit in human rights abuses committed against the people of Vietnam." It was far reaching. The bill promised to prevent anyone—from the prime minister to a cop on the street—from potentially visiting the United States, or having their American assets frozen if they were identified as being responsible for human rights violations. Anywhere. Within a week and a half, Orange County Supervisor Janet Nguyen, the highest-ranking elected Vietnamese-American in California, in the midst of a run for the California State Senate, claimed 1,500 supportive signatures on a petition at www.hr4254.com, while the largest Vietnamese-American lobby group in the Washington, DC, area, Boat People SOS (BPSOS), distributed talking points on the measure in advance of the fifth annual "Vietnam Advocacy Day" (VNAD), in which hundreds descended on Capitol Hill for a day of group lobbying. On Facebook, an H.R. 4254 page "liked" nearly a thousand times urged support for the bill because "the situation in Vietnam has never been as dark as in the 39 years since the Communists took over."[1] Back in Nguyen's district, the City Council of Garden Grove unanimously backed the bill, with one member declaring before a crowd of flag-waving Vietnamese Americans, "We're sending a profound message that (the city) is a communist-free zone." An analysis on Radio

185

Free Asia joined in, claiming that Representative Royce privately believed the chance for the bill's passage was "rất cao"—"very high."[2]

Four months later, Royce chaired the House Foreign Affairs Committee's first hearing on the measure, in which Janet Nguyen, BPSOS President Nguyễn Đình Thắng, and members of the Congressional Caucus on Vietnam testified on behalf of the legislation. After Royce remarked on his own travels to the country, in which he had "seen first-hand the length that the secret police will go to in order to stifle any form of free speech," Representative Chris Smith (R-NJ), took the microphone. A long-time human rights stalwart, Smith cautioned the hearing room that "there is an active effort to suppress this legislation," noting that the Socialist Republic of Vietnam (SRVN) had recently retained The Podesta Group, one of K Street's most recognized public relations firms. "No wonder," he concluded, "the Senate won't take it up." Hanoi's public response came shortly after. An article posted on the People's Public Security Force website, the main police and security force of Vietnam, denounced H.R. 4254 as a "ridiculous" bill and itself a violation of the Universal Declaration of Human Rights. Congress, the author argued, would ultimately reject it.[3] After the single committee hearing, H.R. 4254 quietly died.

The story of H.R. 4254 is significant, not for its outcome (which, as we will see, was routine), but because of the means by which activists quickly rallied behind the legislation—and because of the lurking elephant in the room: Hanoi. Only two decades prior, Vietnamese Americans were nary a national political force, but instead a parochially beset group consumed by a bitter re-election of the community's lone elected councilmember and just beginning to emerge socioeconomically from the hardship of the war in Vietnam. The Vietnamese government, moreover, hardly seemed primed for a rise to Washington, DC power, having just negotiated with the Clinton administration to end the crippling U.S.-led trade embargo, with an economy roughly one hundred times smaller than that of California's and an embassy that had not yet opened. Yet, by 2014, the struggle between the old adversaries—the refugees from the former Republic of (South) Vietnam (RVN), their congressional supporters, and the Socialist Republic of Vietnam (SRVN)—had moved past the war and on to Capitol Hill. The SRVN won the skirmish over H.R. 4254, but the battle would continue.

This chapter is about how the conflict between Vietnamese Americans and the SRVN has unfolded in Washington, DC—and around the world—and the strategies that grassroots activists have used to gain support for their broad and ambitious agenda: democratization in Vietnam. I begin with a brief history of the Vietnamese diaspora, giving emphasis to the stages of politicization of the American community and the changing, as well as paradoxical, nature of its relationship with the SRVN. I then turn to five elements that feature in the group's grassroots lobby, focusing on the ways in which organizations, demonstrations, elections, money, and media forge to contest the SRVN in public spaces, symbolically and sometimes literally. Following this, I move to an analysis of the outcomes of these efforts, looking at 382 pieces of legislation before Congress between 1981 and 2014 for evidence of Vietnamese-American or SRVN influence. I conclude with a reflection on the findings.

History and Goals

The beginning of the Vietnamese American-SRVN conflict lies at the end of the war in Vietnam when, on April 30, 1975, communist forces from the North captured the capital of what was then the South, Saigon (now Ho Chi Minh City), and proceeded to unify the country under a new government led by the Communist Party of Vietnam (CPV), as outlined in table 9.1 on page 188. Although U.S. forces had formally withdrawn from Saigon two years prior, the Americans had left behind a huge cultural and economic footprint—as well as a significant number of government employees that had stayed to advise RVN officials. As communist tanks breached Saigon's perimeter, President Gerald Ford ordered a series of dramatic airlifts to extricate the American personnel—as well as more than 130,000 Vietnamese civilians with ties to both the United States and RVN. Running against nativist public opinion back in the United States, Ford's policy was to welcome and assist the "new arrivals," but to disperse them around the country so as to minimize the possibility for enclave politics and a disproportionate impact on any particular area. Within five years, the plan had come undone: half of the refugees had resettled in California and Texas, providing the seeds for the growing and vibrant Little Saigons that are seen today in Orange County, San Jose, and Houston. Owing to their ties with Washington, DC officials and the RVN embassy, refugees also resettled around the Seven Corners area in Arlington, Fairfax, and Falls Church, Virginia, where they remained connected to political affairs.

The Birth of Exile Politics

As the SRVN made its world debut, a triumphant and doctrinaire CPV, led by Lê Duẩn, began to integrate the South with the North by applying socialist economics and undertaking a dramatic Marxist makeover to a Westernized Saigonese society. It proved catastrophic. Measures to prohibit

Table 9.1. The trajectories of Vietnamese Americans and the Socialist Republic of Vietnam.

	Vietnamese Americans	Socialist Republic of Vietnam/U.S. Relations
1975	Approximately 130,000 refugees airlifted from Saigon, processed and dispersed across the United States.	War in Vietnam ends when capital of South Vietnam, Saigon is captured by forces from the North. Regime begins process of socialist construction in the South to reunify the country.
1976–1980	Internal migration leads to growth in extant communities in California and Texas. Exile politics emerges. 1980 census counts 261,729 Vietnamese in the United States. Median household income is $12,545. More than 1 in 4 are on public assistance and roughly 9 in 10 are noncitizens.	The Socialist Republic of Vietnam (SRVN) is born and faces immediate U.S.-led trade embargo. Vietnam joins the United Nations. Discussions aimed at normalizing relations with the U.S. break down. CPV implements dramatic social and economic change to the South. Invades Cambodia and faces incursion from China. Thousands flee by boat and land.
1981–1985	Arrival of Boat People under the Orderly Departure Program leads to growth and service economy diversification in enclave areas. First wide-circulation Vietnamese newspapers emerge in Orange County.	Vietnam struggles with postwar recovery, faces massive inflation and food shortages. U.S. and SRVN relations remain hostile. Border clashes with China continue.
1986–1990	The first "Little Saigon," in Orange County, CA, is recognized as a business district. Significant growth in co-ethnic organizations occurs. Community demonstrations increase as early signs of transnational engagement are seen as economic support for the SRVN. Members of Congress representing Orange County become more vocal in opposition to Hanoi. 1990 census counts 614,547 with median household income at $29,772. Roughly 4 in 10 are now U.S. citizens.	Đổi Mới is introduced at the 6th Party Congress of the Communist Party of Vietnam (CPV) ushering in market reforms and new approach to foreign relations. First summit between the United States and Vietnam since 1973. Progress is made on accounting for American POWs/MIAs. Vietnam withdraws from Cambodia. Vietnam's per capita income stands at $98.

1991–1993	Third wave of immigration from Vietnam peaks following the Amerasia Homecoming Act and Humanitarian Operations (HO) programs. First Vietnamese American elected to public office in city of Westminster, CA. Vietnamese media diversifies into broadcast television and radio.	G.H.W. Bush Administration offers Hanoi a "roadmap" to normalized relations with the United States. Tourism to Vietnam increases as organized travel ban from United States lifted. Vietnam adopts new constitution. Bush grants permission for companies to open offices in Vietnam.
1994–1998	Demonstrations spike in number in response to opening of trade and business relationships with Vietnam.	Clinton Administration lifts trade embargo, consular agreement is reached, and normalization of bilateral relations in announced. Vietnam joins ASEAN. GDP growth reaches postwar high (9.5%). Debt agreement reached with United States. United States and Vietnam officially exchange ambassadors.
1999–2005	Display of Ho Chi Minh portrait in Westminster provokes 54 days of unrest, attracting tens of thousands. 2000 census counts 1,169,672 with a median household income of $45,085. Candidates begin to emerge for public offices. Grassroots efforts begin to have other Little Saigons recognized, to institutionalize the former South Vietnam flag as the "official" flag of the community and declare cities as "communist free" zones. Direct flights from begin from United States to Vietnam. First Vietnam Human Rights Act (VNHRA) introduced in the House by Chris Smith (R-NJ).	Vietnam's per capita income reaches $433. Bilateral trade agreement (BTA) reached and signed into public law by President George W. Bush. U.S. and Vietnamese ministry and diplomatic officials make visits to both countries, culminating in Prime Minister Phan Văn Khải's historic visit to Washington, DC.

continued on next page

Table 9.1. Continued.

	Vietnamese Americans	Socialist Republic of Vietnam/U.S. Relations
2006–2009	Joseph Cao (R-LA) wins election as first Vietnamese American to serve in the U.S. Congress. Westminster becomes the first U.S. city council with a Vietnamese American majority.	Permanent normalized trade relations (PNTR) is passed by Congress and signed by President Bush. Vietnam joins World Trade Organization. Vietnam and the United States open first joint defense dialogue.
2010–2014	2010 Census counts 1,632,717, making Vietnamese the fourth largest Asian group in the United States. Median income reaches $53,400, above the U.S. average. Roughly 3 in 4 are U.S. citizens.	President Obama announces Comprehensive Partnership, where United States and SRVN would cooperate on military, economic, environmental, and education initiatives.
2015–2016	American Community Survey (2015) estimates population at 1,710,547 and individual per capita income at $24,670. World Bank estimates $7.5 billion sent in remittances from the United States to Vietnam. Stephanie Murphy (D-FL) becomes second Vietnamese American and first Vietnamese American woman eleced to the U.S. House.	Communist Party General Secretary Nguyễn Phú Trọng makes historic visit to Washington, DC. GDP growth rate is 6.7% and per capita income reaches $2,111. Vietnam and the United States sign Trans Pacific Partnership (TPP). Obama announces full lifting of U.S. arms embargo.

Sources: World Bank, http://www.worldbank.org/en/country/vietnam/overview#1 (accessed January 23, 2017); Pew Global, http://www.pewglobal.org/interactives/remittance-map (accessed January 23, 2017); American FactFinder, factfinder.census.gov; Ong and Meter (2008); Furuya and Collet (2009); U.S. Embassy in Vietnam, https://vn.usembassy.gov/our-relationship/policy-history/chronology-of-us-vietnam-relations (accessed January 23, 2017); SRVN Embassy in the United States, http://vietnamembassy-usa.org/vietnam-us-relations/timeline (accessed January 23, 2017).

commercial activities were introduced, assets of suspected capitalists were frozen, and those who had been tied to the RVN suffered discrimination and, in the worst cases, forced to endure hard labor in reeducation camps. When Vietnam invaded Cambodia to oust the Khmer Rouge in 1978, and China invaded Vietnam in retaliation a year later, it triggered a second mass exodus of refugees who fled by boat into the South China Sea and Gulf of Thailand. More than 700,000 Boat People eventually resettled in the United States between 1978 and 1988. Having endured tremendous hardship in Vietnamese society, and living in fear of repatriation, the Boat People arrived younger and with fewer resources than their well-educated and skilled 1975 predecessors. Their arrival was a second layer of politicization for Little Saigons, as they provided numbers and energy to support the intense anti-communism that had migrated with the exiled 1975 government and military leaders.

It was at this juncture, during the 1980s, that Vietnamese America entered a period of extreme—and oftentimes violent—exile politics, in which the Little Saigons in California, in particular, grew rapidly and became hotbeds of activism organized around the shared cause of overthrowing the CPV and reclaiming the homeland.[4] As shadow governments formed in Orange County—now "the capital of overseas Vietnamese," according to newspapers—the community's "mainstream" political identity began to emerge in ethnic media, cultural events, and scores of young organizations and businesses that embraced their new independence in the United States and the memory of the fallen RVN. Consonant with refugee ambitions, and in the face of efforts by the Ronald Reagan and George H.W. Bush administrations to resolve lingering war issues (such as accounting for POW/MIAs), conservatives representing this area, including Representatives Royce, Robert K. Dornan (R-CA), and Dana Rohrabacher (R-CA), began to chide Hanoi on the House floor and hire Vietnamese-American students as aides. In 1992, the first Vietnamese American was elected to a public office in the small city of Westminster, but as a business-oriented moderate tied to those who wanted relations with Hanoi, he was soon engulfed by activists who considered him too soft on the CPV. A poll released in 1994 by the Los Angeles Times showed three in five Vietnamese Americans in Southern California had an "unfavorable" view of the SRVN (with only one in ten seeing it favorably) and a plurality believing the government should be overthrown. At the same time, a majority favored the Clinton administration's decision to remove the nineteen-year-old trade embargo—even as very few told pollsters they would ever do business themselves or invest in the country.[5]

Transnationalism and the Democratic Transition

The contradictions were Vietnamese-American politics in a nutshell: even as political attitudes were crystallizing in resistance to the SRVN, economic bridges were beginning to open between Little Saigon and Vietnam. The new path ushered in by the lifting of the trade embargo had been precipitated in 1986, when, in the face of economic collapse and starvation, the CPV offered a series of dramatic reforms under the banner of Đổi Mới ("renovation"). Along with a market-style economy and a new foreign policy to make "more friends, fewer enemies,"[6] Đổi Mới brought with it new efforts by the SRVN to actively court the diaspora into national reconstruction—a group that the CPV had previously wished away as "traitors" and "enemies" who fled the country. Now the largest and wealthiest among them, and more than 600,000 strong (according to the 1990 Census), Vietnamese Americans were coveted for remittances, investments, tourism, and intellectual contributions. As the SRVN actively worked toward normalization of bilateral relations with Washington, DC, community politics, particularly in California, became volatile. This was facilitated by a third immigration wave flowing into Little Saigons from reeducation camps under the Humanitarian Operations (HO) program—an aging group that had seen their lives decimated by imprisonment under the SRVN. With this layer in place, the community soon became engulfed by regular street demonstrations and direct efforts to confront Hanoi and Washington, DC-led engagement policies in public spaces.

The transformative event occurred during Tết, the Vietnamese Lunar New Year, in early 1999. As Washington, DC and Hanoi were putting the final touches on the first bilateral trade agreement (BTA), a little-known shopkeeper in Westminster placed a portrait of CPV founder and icon, Hồ Chí Minh, on the front of his video store. This was perceived by Vietnamese-American activists as an act of provocation and potential subversion by the SRVN. For fifty-four days, the store drew crowds as large as ten thousand and provoked intense debates across the diaspora over communism, free speech, and community leadership. As the protests spilled over to other sites later in the year, youth groups and community lawyers organized registration drives that reached tens of thousands of new voters.[7] This, combined with the eventual passage of the BTA by Congress in 2001—seen by activists as a political defeat—provoked the sense among an emergent class of well-educated, professionals that the political energies of overseas Vietnamese ought to be channeled away from expressive anti-communist dissent—and toward the development of a cohesive, co-ethnic voting bloc.

Normalization and the Strategic Shift from Overthrow to Identity Politics and the Language of Human Rights

Between 2000 and 2008, as scores of SRVN officials and delegations came to the United States, including an historic visit by Prime Minister Phan Văn Khải, at least sixty Vietnamese-American candidacies were mounted for local and state elective office in California alone, resulting in several wins and new platforms for speaking out against the SRVN. Ostensibly, the agenda of the young politicians, like the activists themselves, was diverse: as a predominantly first generation and Vietnamese-speaking population now about 1.1 million strong (according to the 2000 census), Vietnamese Americans continued to face economic barriers and cited domestic concerns—education, crime, and health care—as top policy priorities. At the same time, as shown in surveys conducted in California between 2000 and 2004, "fighting communism" and continuing to put pressure on the SRVN were also important concerns, ranking higher among those who were most politically active.[8] Importantly for the new representatives, two in three registered voters agreed that it was "very" or "somewhat important" to have people in office who "will fight the government of Vietnam"—more important than their language abilities or their ideological beliefs.[9]

Accordingly, group strategies began to shift away from exile politics toward a savvier approach that blended identity affirmation and cultural institutionalization with the globally resonant language of human rights. As the United States and SRVN moved forward toward full normalization with the passage of permanent normal trade relations (PNTR) and increasing defense and security coordination, at the local level, Vietnamese-American officeholders pursued symbolic measures—like erecting signs demarcating "Little Saigon" across the United States and ordinances recognizing the display of the former yellow flag of the RVN, now rebranded as the "Vietnamese American Freedom and Heritage Flag" around the world.[10] A more controversial effort was a campaign to declare certain cities as "communist free zones." Resolutions enacted in 2012 in Garden Grove, Westminster, and neighboring Santa Ana, representing more than 500,000 residents, declared that any visit by SRVN officials in city boundaries would not be welcome and that those coordinating such visits must give several days advance notice before their arrival.

Although confrontational strategies persist, one can witness a dovetailing between the human rights language of artists, writers, and U.S. government officials and recent activist campaigns in the United States. This is exemplified by a petition drive launched in 2012 on the Obama administration's "We the People" website. Spearheaded by the overtly political Saigon Broadcasting Television Network (SBTN), whose Garden Grove-based president is composer and entertainment producer Trúc Hồ, the petition implored Obama to use Vietnam's desire to join the Trans-Pacific Partnership (TPP) as leverage to compel the SRVN to release its "detained or imprisoned human rights champions." Powered by SBTN's reach, and Trúc Hồ's music, the petition spread quickly across student and activist groups and generated 130,000 signatures in just four days. Shortly thereafter, the Administration honored the petition's request and met with two hundred Vietnamese Americans to discuss U.S.-SRVN relations. Outside the White House, another thousand stood holding signs proclaiming "Human Rights for Vietnam."[11]

The Grassroots Lobby and the Corporatized State

Taken together, we can depict these efforts—and Vietnamese-American politics generally—as a grassroots lobby, where diasporic activists and co-ethnic institutions aim to influence policy by framing media narratives, persuading public preferences,[12] and demonstrating symbolic and substantive political strength through organization building, campaigns, demonstrations, fundraising, and voter mobilization. Grassroots lobbying is generally defined in the literature as *indirect* efforts directed at citizens, not policymakers;[13] but, as we saw in the examples of the BPSOS-led VNAD or the 2012 petition drive, community-derived mobilization campaigns also manifest as a *direct* form of citizen contact with members of Congress and administration officials. Among Vietnamese Americans, thus, indirect and direct mobilization is part of the same grassroots-driven strategy.

In a grassroots lobby (simplified in figure 9.1), the relevant actors are rooted within and on the periphery of the American electoral process. Candidates, political action committees (PACs), and tax-exempt 527 groups, as well as voters and partisans, can be thought of as operating in the *electoral* realm. At the same time, numerous groups, activists, and donors in *civil* society straddle the nonpartisan boundaries between politics, group advocacy, humanitarianism, art, and community service and are an important backbone to any concerted mobilization effort. These include 501(c) and non-governmental organizations based in the United States and abroad that define interests and raise awareness, provide news and analysis, and generally assume a posture of representing the group. In this model, ethnic and social media play a crucial role in linking the diaspora together by providing platforms for information dissemination,

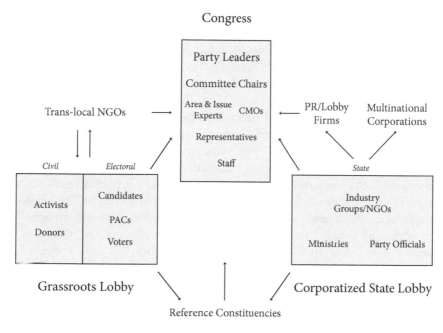

Figure 9.1. The main actors in grassroots versus corporatized state congressional lobbies.

entertainment, dialogue, organization, and mobilization. Although Vietnamese activists in the United States exercise more direct power at local levels, their orientations, agenda, and actions are, in an age of open U.S.-SRVN relations, transnational. As such, many of the disparate entities that constitute the Vietnamese-American lobby can be considered "trans-local" in the sense that they operate well *beyond* the corridors of Washington, DC, but seek to influence those working *within*, by mobilizing co-ethnics and reference constituencies across the United States, in Vietnam, and around the world.

As Vietnamese Americans typically pursue strategies for maximizing visibility, the SRVN's approach remains, like other Asian governments, low key. This can be attributed to the constraints imposed by historical memory in the United States of the Vietnam war and Vietnam (the country), forty years past, continuing to evoke strong sentiments among Americans[14] and some members of Congress—as well as the uneasy relationship the SRVN has had with a diaspora that now send billions of dollars in remittances, but continues to support political activities that seek to undermine Hanoi's interests and the CPV's legitimacy. Another factor behind the SRVN's understated approach is simply that the CPV is new to the game of Washington, DC politics: after two decades of civil war, and a quarter-century of hostile relations and international isolation, Hanoi is playing catchup to develop a political stature that is internationally competitive and consonant with its new foreign policy ambitions.

Even as much of the U.S.-SRVN relationship transpires quietly and beyond the public, at critical junctures—key diplomatic exchanges and discussions over trade and defense agreements—the sensitive politics of "Vietnam" are on display. Akin to China, who also struggles with a mixed image, the sum of SRVN efforts to influence American policymakers can be viewed as a corporatized state lobby (see figure 9.1) that relies on a coterie of elite actors—state-backed industry groups and NGOs, multinational corporations, and Washington, DC lobbyists—to work on behalf of Hanoi by proxy.[15] In recent years, as high-level visits and ritualized, critical discussions of Vietnamese affairs on Capitol Hill have increased, the SRVN has started to evolve into a more of a regular, professionalized presence in Washington, DC. University lectures, op-eds, and roundtables at think tanks have all been employed to facilitate the government's message within what Kent Calder calls the "penumbra of power."[16] More recently, the SRVN has retained established public relations firms such as The Podesta Group (and Parven Pomper Strategies—now Akin Gump, which has direct interests in Vietnam) for media relations and congressional liaising.[17] The SRVN also engages in direct and indirect contacts with prominent Vietnamese Americans, including elected officials,[18] and uses state media channels online to advertise diasporic returns, contributions to the homeland, and progress in Hanoi's diplomatic and economic agenda. Although things are changing quickly—state broadcaster Vietnam Television (VTV) has opened offices in Washington, DC, New York, and Los Angeles—the controversy that can surround these interactions often compels a gradual approach toward the more politicized Little Saigons that relies on intermediaries and representatives.

Organizational Proliferation and Diffusion

Vietnamese-American organizations have proliferated, across the country and around the world, constituting a genuine diaspora network collectively capable of affecting policy in a wide variety of domestic and international locales. As table 9.2 shows, Vietnamese Americans differ from Cuban Americans in the sense that, at least to this point, they have generally channeled greater resources into tax-exempt 501(c)3s and individual candidate committees than into political action committees (PACs) or 527s. Searches of a database of IRS 990 disclosure forms (required of

Table 9.2. Comparing Vietnamese American and Cuban American Organizational Strength

	Vietnamese American					Cuban American				
	Organization	Established	Location	Receipts/ Revenue	Year of Filing	Organization	Established	Location	Receipts/ Revenue	Year of Filing
PACs* (active)	Human Rights for Vietnam PAC		Garden Grove, CA	$11,609	2016	New Cuba PAC		Washington, DC	$483,537	2016
						U.S.-Cuba Democracy Political Action Committee		Hialeah, FL	$507,773	2016
527s**	Vietnamese American Political Action Committee		Anaheim, CA	$22,560	2016	Cuban Americans for a Better Florida PAC		Fort Lauderdale, FL	$5,600	2016
	Vietnamese American Leadership PAC/VAL PAC		Santa Ana, CA	Unknown	2007	Cuban Americans for Change, Inc.		Coral Gables, FL	Unknown	2004
	Vietnamese American Democratic Caucus		San Jose, CA	Unknown	2001	Nueva Esperanza de Cuba, Inc.		Miami, FL	$1,788	2011
	Republic of Vietnam Warrior Federation of San Diego		San Diego, CA	Unknown	2002	U.S.-Cuba Now Political Action Committee		Tampa, FL	Unknown	2011
	Congregation of Vietnamese Buddhists		Unknown	Unknown	2008					
501(c)(3)s***	Vietnamese Community of Orange County Inc	1992	Santa Ana, CA	$4,759,593	2015	Cuban American National Council Inc.	1974	Miami, FL	$2,809,409	2014
	Boat People SOS	2003	Falls Church, VA	$3,162,990	2014	Cuban Museum Inc	1998	Coral Gables, FL	$2,403,110	2014
	Vietnam Assistance for the Handicapped	1991	McLean, VA	$2,455,394	2015	Foundation for Human Rights in Cuba Inc	1996	Miami, FL	$2,005,155	2014
	Vietnamese Buddhist Center Inc.. Chua Viet Nam	1995	Sugar Land, TX	$1,586,323	2014	Medical Education Cooperation with Cuba	1998	Decatur, GA	$1,265,931	2014
	Bach Viet Association Inc.	1984	Sacramento, CA	$957,726	2014	Center for Cuban Studies Inc.	1971	New York, NY	$815,035	2014
	Viet Blind Children Foundation Blind Vietnamese Children Foundation	2000	San Francisco, CA	$429,058	2016	Cuban American National Foundation Inc.	1983	Miami, FL	$790,629	2015

continued on next page

Table 9.2. Continued.

	Vietnamese American					Cuban American				
	Organization	Established	Location	Receipts/ Revenue	Year of Filing	Organization	Established	Location	Receipts/ Revenue	Year of Filing
501(c)(3)s***	Global Community Service Foundation	1995	Fairfax, VA	$363,304	2014	Cuban Classical Ballet of Miami Inc.	2008	Miami, FL	$598,724	2015
	Viet Toc Foundation Inc.	2002	Silver Spring, MD	$316,248	2014	The Sarasota Cuban Ballet School Inc.	2014	Sarasota, FL	$544,186	2015
	Vietnamese Cultural Center Trung Tam Van Hoa Viet Nam	1996	Westminster, CA	$248,508	2014	American Friends of the Ludwig Foundation of Cuba	2000	New York, NY	$451,595	2014
	Lua Viet Youth Association Inc.	1997	Marlboro, NJ	$189,635	2015	National League of Cuban American	1980	Fort Wayne, IN	$437,392	2015
	Vietnamese Community of Houston and Vicinity Inc. To Chuc Cong Dong Nguoi Viet Quoc	2002	Houston, TX	$186,220	2015	Cuban American Bar Association Probono Project Inc.	2007	Miami, FL	$384,905	2014

*Source: Federal Elections Commission (http://www.fec.gov/finance/disclosure/candcmte_info.shtml)

**Source: Internal Revenue Service (https://forms.irs.gov/app/pod/basicSearch/search?execution=e4s1)

***Source: National Center for Charitable Statistics (http://nccsweb.urban.org/PubApps/search.php?1). Represented are the ten largest groups in terms of reported revenue.

all tax-exempt organizations) maintained by the National Center for Charitable Statistics[19] yields 307 Vietnamese groups in California alone; by comparison, a companion search of Cuban organizations in Florida yields 67. Taken together, the 307 reported a combined $20,794,193 in income over 2014–2015 and assets of $43,270,454. The sixty-seven Cuban groups had $11,711,221 and $13,832,776, respectively.

Vietnamese-American organizations, therefore, represent a paradox: as they outnumber and financially outweigh Cuban-American organizations, most would agree that they collectively pack a weaker punch. Some of this might be attributed to the head start Cuban exiles had in organization building (the first major wave arrived in 1959) and the charisma of particular leaders such as Jorge Mas Canosa. More importantly, Cuban Americans enjoy the significant advantage of concentration. As figure 9.2 illustrates, more than four of every ten Cuban Americans during the period of the 113th Congress (2013–2015) resided in one of three Miami area districts; all, as the figure shows, were represented by a Cuban American. The largest Vietnamese concentrations, by contrast, were about 10 percent—in California's 19th and 48th congressional districts in San Jose and Northwest Orange County, respectively. The former was represented by

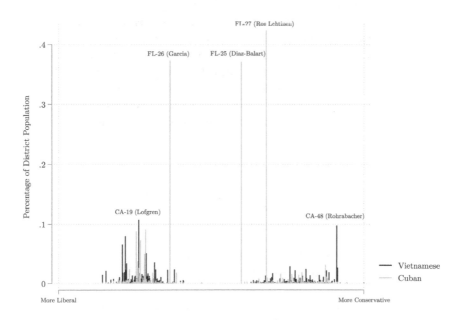

Figure 9.2. Vietnamese American and Cuban American population distribution across House districts by ideology of representative, 113th Congress (2013–2015).

Democratic Representative Zoe Lofgren, a rank-and-file liberal Democrat; the latter was represented by Representative Rohrabacher, one of Congress' most conservative Republicans. Cuban Americans, therefore, not only benefit from easier access to Washington, DC power by way of favorable districts, Cuban-American representatives themselves hew toward the ideological center, facilitating potential coalitions. Those representing the largest shares of Vietnamese Americans have, with one exception (noted below), been non-Vietnamese. More significantly, their representatives in Congress are virtually poles apart ideologically—a disincentive to collaboration and coalition building.

Vietnamese efforts are likely to remain on a different trajectory from Cuban Americans due to rapid changes in the U.S.-SRVN relationship and Vietnamese civil society[20]—driven in the background by the assertion of Chinese power—as well as the global nature of the overseas community. Less than half of the estimated four million Vietnamese diaspora lives in the United States, compared to nine in ten of overseas Cubans.[21] Although some groups, such as the SBTV-backed Human Rights for Vietnam PAC (HRV-PAC),[22] reflect a more traditional electoral-influence strategy, well-heeled and established community entities more often adopt a politically muted posture behind which human rights and democracy campaigns are undertaken as part of an (ostensibly) broader humanitarian agenda. This includes groups such as BPSOS that have grown political out of an original refugee resettlement and social welfare role, as well as newer groups, such as Vietnamese Overseas Initiative for Conscience Empowerment (VOICE), that emphasize the transnational nature of their cause and an agenda to empower Vietnamese civil society directly. Taken together, the diverse and diffuse array of groups operating on behalf of Vietnamese-American interests often give the lobby the feel of a social movement aiming for broad societal change more than a professionalized force with a discrete set of instrumental goals.

Inside versus Outside Tactics: Demonstrations as Confrontation

As BPSOS' Thắng explains, events like VNAD are relatively new attempts to position Vietnamese Americans as Washington, DC insiders, because for decades the community has been defined by its "outsider" tactics.[23] During the era of exile politics that began around 1980, Vietnamese in the United States began to use demonstrations as a means of directly confronting the SRVN government and to intimidate Vietnamese Americans deemed sympathetic to the regime. The numerous protest events in and around Little Saigons, U.S. government offices, and SRVN consulates—one study tabulated more than one hundred in Southern California alone between 1975 and 2001[24]—have attracted considerable media attention for their boisterous and colorful displays, as well as the controversy they invite from inside and outside the Vietnamese-American community. In doing so, they continue to give activists a reliable tool for reaching reference publics—and for conveying to Hanoi and the diaspora a symbolic unity and the image of group power. Even the VNAD—an ostensible move to the inside—has attempted to maximize this image of Vietnamese America as a mass resistance movement, with news reports on overseas Vietnamese media showing activists gathering, and then descending *en masse*, on congressional offices and meeting in groups with representatives.[25]

As protests sometimes turn toward co-ethnics—as a coercive tool for enforcing discipline around the anti-Hanoi agenda—they remain controversial as a tactic. Most events revolve in some way or another around a strategic attempt to influence Vietnamese affairs or U.S.-SRVN relations. Community mobilization, as noted above, increases at specific diplomatic junctures, such as when the two governments took steps toward the first bilateral trade agreement (BTA) and normalized trade relations (NTR) in 2000 and 2001.[26] Surveys confirm that Vietnamese Americans are more likely than other Asian Americans to use this tactic, believing that such acts have a significant impact on Hanoi.[27] But where efficacy has proven to be a crucial variable behind Vietnamese-American grassroots energy, the direct effectiveness of the protest strategy on policy outcomes in Congress is highly debatable.[28] At the same time, there is little doubt that Hanoi sees the protests as a nuisance, as the events regularly draw official denunciations of U.S.-based protest leaders as reactionaries stirring up social unrest among co-ethnics. This alone tends to give activists sustenance and ongoing support, as they can claim success even as bilateral relations continue apace.

In recent years, one group that has used protests strategically, San Jose-based Việt Tân (or Vietnam Reform Party), has drawn particular ire from the SRVN. Việt Tân grew out of a militant organization called the National United Front for the Liberation of Viet Nam (NUFLVN) whose founder, former South Vietnamese Navy Admiral Hoàng Cơ Minh, collected considerable sums during the 1980s from Little Saigons to lead a small, armed resistance to the SRVN on Vietnam's Thai border. (Like many of his generation and status, Minh had significant ties to Washington, DC's elite.) Việt Tân has since attempted to distance itself from the NUFLVN's original call for insurgency and, as stated on its website, pledges to "establish democracy and reform the country through peaceful means."[29] As part of this evolution, garnering support from Washington,

DC has taken on a higher priority. Two of its leaders, Diem Do (Đỗ Hoàng Điềm) and Dan Hoang (Hoàng Tứ Duy), are the group's complete activists: leading demonstrations, supporting a Vietnamese-American PAC, donating thousands to congressional candidates of both parties, and, on multiple occasions, being invited to give congressional testimony. For their efforts, Do and Hoang are also, as of this writing, designated as terrorists by Vietnam's Ministry of Public Security (MPS), as the SRVN, long suspicious of Việt Tân, blames them for inciting protests in Ho Chi Minh City and Hanoi in 2016 following demonstrations in San Jose that openly called for Vietnamese public resistance.[30]

Campaigns, Votes, and Money: Instruments of American Democracy as the Symbols of Group Power

In 1996, two Vietnamese Americans held political office in the United States—both at the city level. As of the 2016 elections, Vietnamese Americans were the mayors of and held council majorities in Westminster and Garden Grove, and held seats on the San Jose and Houston city councils and in the California and Texas legislatures. The transformation has led local reporters to dub the community as "a political machine rivaled only by the Cubans in Miami."[31] The underlying causes of the transformation are a "perfect storm" of socioeconomic growth, high naturalization rates, young, creative leadership, strong group identity, and a unifying cause that together has forged and mobilized a bloc of voters.

Much of what we know about Vietnamese-American voters is based on local studies and surveys. In Orange and Santa Clara counties, Vietnamese Americans comprise about 6 and 8 percent of voters, respectively (as of 2016); in some jurisdictions, such as Westminster city, more than 40 percent of voters are of Vietnamese descent. There is evidence that voters vote as a bloc for co-ethnic and Asian candidates, particularly in contexts when voters perceived co-ethnic candidates to be under threat.[32] In some elections, Vietnamese Americans have been shown to turn out at significantly higher rates than other groups,[33] although longitudinal studies suggest that this is highly context- and elite-driven.[34] As Vietnamese Americans show a high propensity to articulate a hybrid "ethnic American" identity,[35] candidates themselves have honed effective mobilization strategies that appeal to co-ethnics and "mainstream" voters simultaneously, by weaving the widely shared refugee experience and flight from "Communist Vietnam" into a narrative of the "American Dream."[36] More significantly, they have shown the ability to dramatically outraise and outspend their opponents.[37] This reflects the considerable financial clout that can be generated by co-ethnic networks of families, business and professional elites, and community organizations.[38] Vietnamese-American political and financial muscle has had ripple effects on local and state politicians; after years of keeping the community at arm's length, elected officials have become increasingly attentive in recent years to cultural events, community outreach, and as we will see below, issues related to U.S.-SRVN relations.

Although Vietnamese Americans have become increasingly formidable at the local and regional level, their ability to win congressional races—due in part to unfavorable districts—has been put to the test. As table 9.3 on page 204 shows, at least twenty-six candidates of Vietnamese descent have run for the House or Senate since 1994, raising a total of $5.6 million and more than $840,000 from co-ethnic donors. On two occasions—in Louisiana in 2008 and Florida in 2016—they have been successful. Both wins could be considered unconventional in that they involved upsets of long-serving incumbents and came outside of major Little Saigons in California and Texas. Joseph Cao (Cao Quang Ánh), a Republican, became the first Vietnamese American to serve in Congress after surprising a scandal-plagued Representative William Jefferson (D-LA) in the majority–African American second congressional district in New Orleans. Democrat Stephanie Murphy's (Đặng Thị Ngọc Dung) defeat of incumbent long-time Representative John Mica (R-FL) in 2016 made her the second. Where Cao, a Jesuit in training whose father was held in prison camps, represents classic community conservatism—Vietnamese-American voters and politicians in the 1980s and 1990s affiliated heavily with the Republican Party—Murphy represents an emergent progressive strand: one that is younger, more panethnic, and focused on domestic issues.[39] As table 9.3 shows, Vietnamese-American money played a greater role in Cao's races than Murphy's—and increased dramatically *after* his surprise victory during his re-election bid (from 8.8% to 26.3%). This illustrates how grassroots mobilization is not only *candidate* driven, but *incumbency* driven—especially when the representative is perceived, as Cao was, to be attentive to key community interests related to Vietnamese affairs. During his single term in the House, Cao, a former lawyer for BPSOS, was involved in multiple pieces of legislation that sought to chastise the SRVN, restrict funding to Vietnam, and recognize the achievements of Vietnamese Americans.

Vietnamese and Social Media: Arenas for Mobilization and Contestation

All grassroots lobbies rely heavily on media, but in this case, the primary vehicles are Vietnamese language outlets, print and broadcast, web platforms,

Table 9.3. Vietnamese American Candidates for Congress and Co-Ethnic Money, 1994–2016*

Candidate	Party	Year	State	Office	District	% Viet Pop	Total Receipts^	Total Itemized Individual Contributions	Total Co-Ethnic Contributions**	Co-ethnic (as %) of itemized individual contributions**	Votes^	Vote %	Outcome
Nguyen, Chung H	D	1994	CA	House	46	~5.8	$10,275				121	0.7%	Lost as write-in candidate in Democratic Party primary for seat held by Republican incumbent Robert Dornan
Ly, Binh	R	1994	FL	House	19	~0.1	$50,144				9,368	39.7%	Lost in Republican primary to Peter Tsakinakis
Dao, Linh Kieu	I	1995	CA	House	15	~1.7	$0				4,922	5.3%	Lost in special election to fill unexpired term of Norm Mineta
Pham, Long Kim	R	1998	CA	House	45	~4.0	$6,825				6,486	8.4%	Lost in Republican primary to incumbent Dana Rohrabacher
Dao, Linh	R	1998	CA	Senate		~1.0	$0				29,241	1.0%	Lost in Republican primary to Matt Fong
Vu, Joe	R	2000	TX	House	29	0.9	$58,996				29,606	25.6%	Lost in general election to incumbent Gene Green
Pham, Long Kim	R	2000	CA	House	45	8.0	$9,499				10,942	10.9%	Lost in Republican primary to incumbent Dana Rohrabacher
Nguyen, Tuan A.	R	2002	NC	House	4	0.2	$7,869				78,095	36.2%	Lost in general election to incumbent, David Price
Nguyen, Tan D.	D	2004	CA	House	46	9.3	$46,858				14,349	32.6%	Lost in Republican primary to incumbent Dana Rohrabacher
Tran, Giannibicego Hoa	R	2006	TX	House	22	2.3	$17,500				2,434	2.1%	Lost in Special Election to fill unexpired term of Tom DeLay
Tran, Hong Thi	D	2006	WA	Senate		1.0	$40,688				33,124	5.3%	Lost in Democratic primary to incumbent Maria Cantwell

													Won, defeating incumbent Bill Jefferson (D)
Cao,	Anh "Joseph"	R	2008	LA	House	2	1.9	$242,530	$140,687	$12,400	8.8%	33,132 49.5%	**Won, defeating incumbent Bill Jefferson (D)**
Van,	Quoc Ba	D	2008	FL	House	8	0.5	$14,756	$9,805	$205	2.1%	1,219 3.7%	Lost in Democratic primary to Alan Grayson
Nguyen,	Kelly Ann	R	2010	GA	House	5	0.2	$13,432	$5,872	$1,700	29.0%	5,937 40.4%	Lost in Republican primary to Fenn Little
Nguyen,	Tan D	R	2010	CA	House	47	11.0	$45,100	$42,000	$42,000	100.0%	3,876 19.7%	Lost in Republican primary to Van Tran
Pham,	Quang X	R	2010	CA	House	47	11.0	$296,253	$75,540	$2,750	3.6%	0 0.0%	Withdrew before Republican primary
Cao,	Anh "Joseph"	R	2010	LA	House	2	2.4	$2,079,914	$1,052,714	$276,427	26.3%	43,378 33.5%	Lost in general election to Cedric Richmond
Tran,	Van	R	2010	CA	House	47	11.0	$1,404,741	$941,968	$352,610	37.4%	37,679 39.3%	Lost in general election to incumbent, Loretta Sanchez (D)
Lowe,	Thuy	R	2014	FL	House	5	0.5	$49,045	$19,441	$5,390	27.7%	6,451 37.0%	Lost in Republican primary to Glo Smith
Tran,	Stanford	R	2014	RI	House	1	0.1	$19,724	$6,050	$700	11.6%	2,483 27.6%	Lost in primary election to Cormick Lynch
Quang,	Tue Phan	R	2014	CA	House	11	0.6	$118,694	$84,517	$61,609	72.9%	57,160 32.7%	Lost in general election to Mark DeSaulnier
Tran,	Minh	I	2016	WA	Senate		1.0	$0#					Did not compete
Cao,	Joseph	R	2016	LA	Senate		0.8	$0#				21,011 1.0%	Lost to John Neely Kennedy in Blanket Primary
Nguyen,	Bao Quoc	D	2016	CA	House	46	5.0	$270,569#	$203,362	$71,968	35.4%	30,193 29.9%	Lost in general election to Lou Correa
Lowe,	Thuy	R	2016	FL	House	10	0.7	$34,436#	$9,650	$500	5.2%	107,423 35.1%	Lost in general election to Val Demings

continued on next page

Table 9.3. Continued.

Candidate	Party	Year	State	Office	District	% Viet Pop	Total Receipts^	Total Itemized Individual Contributions**	Total Co-Ethnic Contributions**	Co-ethnic (as %) of itemized individual contributions)	Votes^	Vote %	Outcome
Murphy, Stephanie	D	2016	FL	House	7	0.3	$777,543#	$405,509	$15,085	3.7%	180,372	51.5%	Won, defeating incumbent John Mica (R)
Totals:							$5,615,391	$2,997,115	$843,344	28.1% (average)	749,002	22.7% (average)	

Files from 1988–2016 were downloaded, merged, and surname coded per methods described in Collet (2005).
*Derived from the FEC's "Candidate Master List" (http://www.fec.gov/finance/disclosure/ftpdet.shtml).

Files from 1988-2016 were downloaded, merged and surname coded per methods described in Collet (2005).
**Derived from surname coding of individual contribution files.
No candidates prior to 1994 were identified.

^Figures derived from Candidate's Two Year Summary Files. 2008–2016 information (http://www.fec.gov/finance/disclosure/candcmte_info.shtml.)
Pre-2008 files downloaded from http://www.fec.gov/finance/disclosure/PostCycleSummaryDataFiles.shtml

**Derived from surname coding of individual contribution files.
^Figures derived from Candidate's Two-Year Summary Files, 2008–2016 information (http://www.fec.gov/finance/disclosure/candcmte_info.shtml.)
^^Votes and results sourced from state election websites, Ballotopedia and Wikipedia.

As of October 19, 2016.
~ Derived from 1990 Summary Tape File 1 (STF 1)—100-percent data. Others derived from American Community Survey 1-year estimates for appropriate year.

As of October 19, 2016.

and increasingly social media.[40] Since the arrival of Saigon's first wave of evacuees in 1975, ethnic newspapers and radio have played a crucial role in community politics by stoking and enforcing the group's anti-SRVN identity; it is no coincidence that some of the most heated controversies in the community have revolved around media outlets and whether news reports, journalists and broadcasters have sufficiently towed the appropriate political line on Hanoi. The pressure to conform has left behind a community media that often remain, like SBTN, openly and proudly anti-communist. Ethnic/diaspora media in the United States are generally more advocacy-minded anyway, but the politics of Vietnamese diaspora media combined with their pliability gives activists frequent, unfiltered, and often favorable exposure for their messaging. The cause of human rights also benefits more generally from the political tone of cultural events and entertainment programming, where variety shows, dramas and documentaries repeatedly reinforce the themes of loss and suffering at the hands of communism and the successes of co-ethnics in the free, democratic West.[41] Activist messaging is further aided by Washington, DC, with congressionally funded democratization programs, such as Voice of America (VOA) and Radio Free Asia (RFA), reaching Vietnamese citizens directly with regular news of activist campaigns and critical reports on the SRVN.[42]

For NGOs and individual activists, the more hotly contested terrain is cyberspace. As internet penetration has grown in Vietnam, Facebook and YouTube usage in particular, activists have been blessed with an invaluable set of resources for transnational organization, not just for mobilizing co-ethnics in the United States and abroad to challenge Vietnamese authorities, but for bypassing them altogether and engaging with Vietnamese citizens. The SRVN's attempts to control information are, if weaker than China's, notorious nonetheless: Vietnam earns perpetually low ratings from Freedom House and Reporters Without Borders for vaguely worded and harshly enforced laws and the imprisonment of bloggers and street activists who have been openly critical of the regime or attempted to mobilize on the streets.[43] Through such actions, the SRVN has stifled serious opposition domestically but, at the same time, given Việt Tân, VOICE, the related Viet Path Movement, and others a cause célèbre around which they are able to mobilize and unify co-ethnics, and gain attention from Washington, DC officials. Reaching millions through their Facebook pages alone, these trans-local groups document, oftentimes with citizen reports and photos, dissent and abuse in Vietnam and invite a steady flow of criticism toward SRVN officials. Combined with the several platforms offered by the U.S. government—the CCV, VOA, RFA, the Commission on International Religious Freedom (CIRF), and the Lantos Human Rights Commission[44]—activists are enjoying unprecedented opportunities to organize and mobilize.

Is Anyone Winning? Jostling for Influence over
U.S.-SRVN Policy in Congress

Although it is common to hear activists talk of "victory" over "the communists," when it comes to the ability of an ethnic group to influence congressional action, notions of winning and losing are rarely so cut and dried. As John J. Mearsheimer and Stephen M. Walt explain in the context of U.S.-Israeli affairs,

> [o]ne cannot measure the influence of an interest group simply by looking at whether it "won" or "lost" a particular policy dispute. The real question is what the outcome would have been had interest group pressure been absent. After all, an interest group may lose a specific policy battle but still force policymakers to water down their goals or expend lots of political capital in order to overcome its opposition. In short, there is no simple linear relationship between "lobbying activities" and "policy outcomes" in the real world; thus gauging a lobby's clout requires paying careful attention to the process by which decisions and outcomes were reached.[45]

There are at least two ways to approach the dilemma of measuring Vietnamese-American "clout." The first considers the extent to which members of Congress are attentive to Vietnamese-American interests, which we can define simply in zero-sum terms as the frequency with which representatives and senators sponsored legislation that might be deemed favorable to Vietnamese Americans and/or unfavorable to the SRVN. The second looks at member voting behavior on legislation where the SRVN's interests or reputation were at stake. It is here that we can look specifically at bills and resolutions that came to a contested floor vote and assess whether the Vietnamese-American population in a member's district may have played a significant role in shaping the outcome. Size, or "numerical significance," has long been identified by scholars of ethnic lobbies as a potentially critical variable in determining group influence—in part, because of the perceived electoral threat they pose to members.[46] Examining the proportion of Vietnamese Americans in each member's district in juxtaposition to other factors, like ideology and perceptions of electoral threat, allows us to put that to a direct test.

Gauge 1: Attentiveness to Vietnamese-American Issues

Using a corpus derived from Congress.gov,[47] 382 pieces of Vietnam-related legislation were captured for analysis: 241 bills and 141 resolutions introduced between 1981 and 2015. This works out to about twenty-two measures coming before Congress every two-year session. Of the bills, more than two-thirds originated in the House, and about 15 percent became public law—a significantly higher rate of passage than the three to seven percent average for all bills. This owes to the fact that most were foreign authorizations or appropriations bills that included provisions regarding aid to or programs in Vietnam. The remainder were a mixture of laws dealing with immigration (e.g., the Amerasian Homecoming Act; Vietnamese Reeducation Prisoner Settlement Act) and POW/MIAs (e.g., Bring them Home Alive Act).

The bills that died give us an indication of how group and state interests collide in U.S.-SRVN relations. Among the more than two hundred that did not pass were scores of proposals that sought to restrict interactions with the SRVN or otherwise endeavored to promote democracy. The thrust of legislation through the 101st Congress (1989–1991) addressed residual issues from the war (immigration, resettlement, debts), but began to turn during the 102nd (1991–1993) Congress as the George H.W. Bush administration outlined its "roadmap" for bilateral relations. Among the first of these were measures such as the Freedom First for Vietnam Act, which sought to prohibit Bush from lifting the trade embargo unless the Communist Party agreed to "free and fair elections." Or the philosophically titled, Dornan-authored, "To encourage liberty inside the Socialist Republic of Vietnam," which aimed to prohibit any "military presence and political indoctrination programs" in the presence of a U.S. citizen if they were to visit Vietnam in a cooperative capacity. About one of every five unsuccessful bills in the corpus carry the words "freedom," "democracy," or "human rights" in the title—most appearing after the 106th Congress (1999–2001) when the embargo was lifted.

More telling are resolutions—the nonbinding expressions of chamber sentiments that, for symbolic reasons, carry significant weight in foreign policymaking (see, e.g., the Armenian-American case).[48] Because regular bills can face significant barriers to passage—and because the appropriations process has become increasingly opaque[49]—resolutions present ethnic groups with a unique opportunity to gain the backing of the U.S. government. They also present congressional foreign policy entrepreneurs with a vehicle for advertising and credit-claiming in response to critical constituencies.[50] Thirty-five, or about 25 percent, of the 141 resolutions in the corpus were adopted by one or both chambers; simple resolutions (which can be passed more easily by "suspension of the rules" in only one chamber) had an even higher rate of success, with 29 percent passage in the House and 46 percent in the Senate. Nearly all of these single-chamber measures were critical of Hanoi, featuring titles such as *Calling on the*

Government of the Socialist Republic of Vietnam to release imprisoned bloggers and respect Internet freedom. (H.Res. 672., Representative Loretta Sanchez [D-CA], in the 111th Congress [2009–2011]). Despite this, the SRVN enjoyed a handful of history-making victories through these symbolic measures. One was H.J.Res. 51 by Representative Richard Armey (R-TX) in the 107th Congress (2001–2003), a more powerful joint resolution that authorized Vietnam NTR status and was signed by President George W. Bush. But even as H.J. Res. 51 passed (88 to 12) in the Senate, the House coupled the measure with a 401 to 1 vote in the same session on H.R. 2833, Representative Smith's Vietnam Human Rights Act (VNHRA), which sought to make aid to Vietnam contingent on "substantial progress" on human rights. That VNHRA failed to gain a hearing in the Senate (then and since) is indicative of how group-homeland state conflicts can play out in the American bicameral system: grassroots-influenced human rights supporters gaining a foothold in the House, but meeting resistance from engagement and trading forces in the Senate.[51]

Research demonstrates that co-ethnic representatives are more likely to sponsor bills of group interest as the size of the ethnic group increases, but less is known about whether this also affects out-group representatives.[52] When we tabulate the sponsors of the legislation in the corpus, we get mixed results. Between the 108th (2003–2005) and 113th (2013–2015) Congresses, Representative Smith sponsored ten bills—the most in the corpus. The Vietnamese population in Smith's New Jersey district is less than 0.4 percent. Moreover, the multiple appropriations bills over this period were authored by committee chairs or party leaders (e.g., Representative Benjamin A. Gilman [R-NY], who chaired the House International Relations Committee, Senator Patrick J. Leahy [D-VT], a longtime member of the Appropriations Subcommittee on State Department, Foreign Operations and Related Programs, and Representative James T. Kolbe [R-AZ], who chaired the Foreign Operations, Export Financing, and Related Agencies Subcommittee who directly represented few Vietnamese-American constituents). A Vietnamese-American presence is felt in bills sponsored by Representative Cao, as well as those by California Representatives Lofgren, Rohrabacher, and Sanchez, but their collective output—ten bills over twenty years—only equals Smith's and, more significantly, none was successful. Only one bill signed into law—H.R. 1840, by former Representative Thomas M. Davis (VA), which extended refugee status to the children of former political prisoners—can be traced to both a significant Vietnamese constituency and the presence of a direct lobbying campaign.[53]

When it comes to resolutions, the evidence for Vietnamese-American influence is stronger. Consider figure 9.3, which shows the eleven resolu-

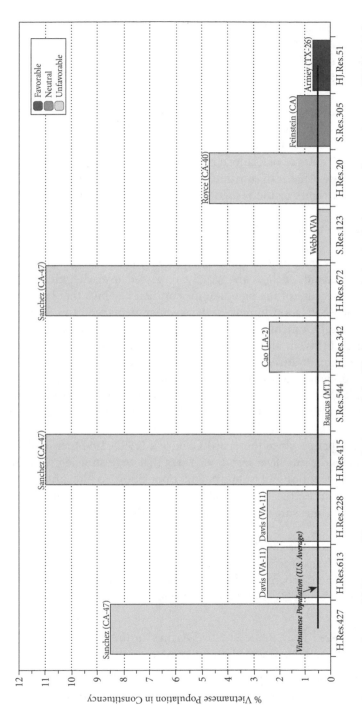

Figure 9.3. Successful Vietnam/Vietnamese resolutions and the Vietnamese population in their sponsor's constituency, 107th–111th Congresses (2001–2011).

tions that passed the House or Senate between the 107th (2001–2003) and 111th (2009–2011) Congresses. Of the nine that were unfavorable to the SRVN, seven were sponsored by representatives whose Vietnamese American-constituencies were significantly larger than the national average—in the case of Sanchez's three measures (all sternly chastising the country's human rights record), the second largest Vietnamese congressional district in the United States. The approved resolutions by Davis and former Senator James H. "Jim" Webb (D-VA), Cao, and Republican Representative Royce of California can also be read as a potential response to Vietnamese-American constituents, as each dealt, in one way or another, with human rights or the recognition of group achievements.

Gauge 2: Constituency Influence on Contested Roll Call Votes

Relatively few measures in the corpus came down to floor votes. Several of those that did, such as the VNHRA, passed overwhelmingly. As we have seen, because of the potential for conflict, key bills that have moved the U.S.-SRVN relationship forward have been managed carefully by party leaders and senior members in a process that has steered around grassroots opposition. (This, in and of itself, could be taken as a sign of grassroots influence, though attributing it decisively to Vietnamese-American pressure is the challenge.) By the same token, the measures that are critical of the SRVN—and presumably reflect activist efforts—are sometimes passed with little dissent in the House, but go on to wither on the Senate's vine.

Nonetheless, since the 103rd Congress (1993–1995), at least twelve bills or amendments have seen floor votes that were sufficiently contested to indicate coalitions of support and opposition to the normalization policy pursued by the United States (see appendix A). Among these are four votes on measures deemed *favorable* to the SRVN:

- *Amendment S.1263 to S.1281*, by Senator John F. Kerry (D-MA) in the 103rd Congress (1993–1995), which stated that sufficient progress had been made on locating the remains of American POWs to warrant an end to the embargo (*passed*, 62 to 38);

- *H.J.Res.51*, by Representative Armey in the 107th Congress (2001–2003), as stated above (*passed*, 88 to 12);

- *H.R.5602*, by Representative Jim Ramstad (R-MN) in the 109th Congress (2005–2007), which sought to authorize permanent NTR, or PNTR, to Vietnam (*passed*, 228 to 161, but failed to gain a necessary 2/3 vote under the rule); and

- *H.R.6406*, by Representative William "Bill" Thomas (R-CA) in the 109th Congress (2005–2007), a second effort to authorize PNTR for Vietnam (*passed*, 212 to 184);

as well as eight votes deemed *unfavorable*:

- *Amendment S.1266 to S.1281*, by Representative Robert Smith (R-NH) in the 103rd Congress (1993–1995), a countermeasure to Kerry's amendment that endeavored to force President Bill Clinton to report on Vietnam's human rights progress prior to lifting the trade embargo (*failed*, 42 to 58);

- A motion by Senator Judd A. Gregg (R-NH) to table Amendment S.3276 (Kerry), in the 105th Congress (1997–1999) that would have blocked efforts to continue funding the U.S. embassy in Hanoi (*failed*, 34 to 66);

- Five joint resolutions by Rohrabacher across the 105th to 107th Congresses (1997–2003) (*H.J.Res.120, H.J.Res.58, H.J.Res.99, H.J.Res.101, and H.J.Res.55*) that sought to express opposition to PNTR (*failed*, 163 to 260; 130 to 297; 91 to 332; 91 to 338; and 91 to 324); and

- *H.R.1587*, by Representative Smith in the 108th Congress (2003–2005), the VNHRA of 2004, which sought to limit increases in nonhumanitarian assistance contingent upon human rights stipulations and provided supplemental appropriations for pro-democracy initiatives, such as Radio Free Asia transmissions (*passed*, 323 to 45).

Using logit regression equations, an effort was made to isolate the effect of Vietnamese-American constituencies on these votes, while controlling for other factors that might shape the outcome—ideology, the race of the representative or senator, his or her military service, expertise in foreign policy (as evidenced by service on the House Foreign Affairs or Senate Foreign Relations Committees) and the overall perception of electoral threat (as indicated by the closeness of their most recent election). The general hypothesis is that, all things being equal, as the Vietnamese-American constituency *increases*, so will the probability of a "nay" vote on favorable measures and a "yea" on unfavorable measures.

The results (shown fully in appendix B) reveal that the strongest evidence for Vietnamese-American influence is in the five unsuccessful Rohrabacher measures in opposition to PNTR—votes that also appear to be driven by support from House conservatives. All things being equal, the models predict that a one percentage point increase in the representative's Vietnamese constituency increases the odds of voting "yea" on these measures from 34.6 to 55.2 percent. This translates into a high probability (>.70) of support with as little as 4 percent Vietnamese in the district. By contrast, on the two votes on PNTR itself (the bills by Representatives Armey and Ramstad), where we expected a *negative* effect produced by Vietnamese-American constituents, we find one: but it is too weak to be considered statistically meaningful. What this tells us is that Vietnamese Americans had the numerical strength to mobilize a significant and persistent symbolic countermeasure to PNTR, but ultimately lacked the muscle to defeat PNTR itself. Conservative ideology coalesced with Vietnamese Americans to drive the vote on the Rohrabacher measures, but it played a less powerful role in the Ramstad and Thomas measures. Rather, it appears as if representatives of color and those with military service records in the House aligned with Vietnamese Americans against the bills—a logical, if unusual, coalition given the impact of trade on minority communities (and labor unions) and the longtime reservations that some veterans have had with regard to the SRVN.

The other votes in the analysis do not yield strong results. On VNHRA, the influence of Vietnamese-American constituents was in the expected positive direction, but again, the effect cannot be distinguished from that which might have been produced by chance. In the Senate, it appears as if the impact of a larger Vietnamese population may work in the *opposite* effect. On the Kerry Amendment that gave congressional backing to lifting the trade embargo, an increase in the state Vietnamese population leads to a *higher* probability of support; similarly, on the Smith countermeasure, the effect is negative. As the vote on the Kerry Amendment was also explained by senators' ideology, this tells us that greater concentrations of Vietnamese Americans in heavily Democratic states such as California, Hawaii, and Massachusetts may have a countereffect on activists' grassroots efforts to coalesce with conservatives in House districts. This may help to explain why activists have found it difficult to gain greater support for human rights measures (and direct opposition to the SRVN) in the Senate—and why Vietnamese Americans have, in recent years, turned increasingly to liberals such as Representatives Sanchez and Lofgren—and Democrats generally—to give voice to their human rights and democratization agenda.

Conclusion: Washington, DC and the
Conflict between Identity and Survival

Brantly Womack highlights a tension in Vietnamese society, a "yin and yang dialectic between identity and survival," that is reflective of a state that has been forced throughout history to navigate the reality of living asymmetrically as the smaller party in the proximity of a more powerful Chinese neighbor.[54] The tension between identity and survival can also shed light on the motives behind Vietnamese Americans and the SRVN in American politics: the former, a young and dispersed, but emergent, group that is flexing its political identity as it mobilizes for change in the homeland; the latter, facing its own threats internationally—from territorial issues with China to economic competition—finding itself in cooperation with a former enemy as it attempts to survive in the international system. As this chapter has endeavored to show, the diaspora and homeland state are inextricably bound to one another, yet increasingly in collision, as both lobby Washington, DC to support their respective and ambitious agendas. As it stands now, Washington, DC reconciles this tension by supporting *both*: bilateral relations move forward "from above," even as democratization continues to be pressed "from below."[55]

Echoing Mearsheimer and Walt, this makes any attempt to discern clear winners or losers a self-defeating empirical exercise. The growing U.S.-SRVN partnership has represented a dramatic turn in history, but it has largely moved along the steady trajectory as it was first laid out by the Bush administration. The relevant question raised by this chapter is whether the trajectory has been, or is being, altered by the efforts of Vietnamese Americans. This is a recognized challenge,[56] given that critical foreign policy decisions are often made out of public view—and because multiple interests are lobbying Congress on issues related to Vietnam at any given time. A search of the Center for Responsive Politics database, OpenSecrets.org, reveals 182 clients—from the National Pork Producers Council to Amnesty International USA—lobbying the government on a Vietnam-related issue since 2006.[57] Evaluating the effectiveness of the Vietnamese-American lobby thus requires putting their efforts in the broader context of American pluralism—as well as considering the general "convergence of interests," or receptiveness, that Washington, DC, and human rights–oriented members of Congress, such as Smith, may have to their cause.[58]

With these caveats in mind, the evidence presented here seems clear: Vietnamese Americans, working at the grassroots, are making a difference in terms of raising the attention given to human rights and democratization in Vietnam. Spread across congressional districts, and split by two polarized parties, activists have encountered major "defeats," but have been able to marshal small size into a focused, effective electoral threat nonetheless—a feat that, in turn, has led to increased responsiveness from Congress and the introduction of strongly worded resolutions calling on the SRVN to release detainees and democratize its political institutions. In the 1990s, Vietnamese-American activism and group-influenced resolutions were insufficient to block the Bill Clinton and George W. Bush administrations' desire to open and expand bilateral trade. But since then, the evidence suggests that Democratic representatives have been at least as vigorous as Republicans in calling for scrutiny of the SRVN. There are more avenues on Capitol Hill for Vietnamese Americans to speak out on human rights than there were before trade relations were established. The evidence suggests, ultimately, that activists are increasingly using those avenues and incorporating them into a multipronged strategy for growing their grassroots movement.

Notes

1. https://www.facebook.com/HR-4254-502994996468748 (accessed January 2, 2017).

2. Thy Vo, "Garden Grove Council Supports Viet Human Rights Sanctions," *Voice of OC*, 2014, http://voiceofoc.org/2014/08/garden-grove-council-supports-viet-human-rights-sanctions (accessed January 14, 2017); Chí Dũng Pham, "HR. 4254: Nước cờ thứ hai của thế 'triệt buộc,'" *Radio Free Asia Vietnamese*, March 27, 2014, http://www.rfa.org/vietnamese/ReadersOpinions/bandocviet-032714-pcd-03272014132508.html (accessed January 14, 2017).

3. Minh Đăng, "Cổ súy HR 4254–hành động lố nghịch," *Công an Nhân dân Online*, http://cand.com.vn/Su-kien-Binh-luan-thoi-su/Co-suy-HR-4254---hanh-dong-lo-nghich-269788 (accessed January 14, 2017).

4. For a discussion of this in the Cuban case, see Lisandro Perez, "Cuban Miami," in *Miami Now!* eds. Guillermo Grenier and Alex Stepick (Gainesville: University of Florida Press, 1992), 83–108.

5. Hiroko Furuya and Christian Collet, "Contested Nation: Vietnam and the Emergence of Saigon Nationalism in the United States," in *The Transnational Politics of Asian Americans*, eds. Christian Collet and Pei-te Lien (Philadelphia: Temple University Press, 2009), 56–76.

6. Carlyle Thayer, "Vietnamese Diplomacy, 1975–2015: From Member of the Socialist Camp to Proactive International Integration," presentation to the International Conference on Vietnam: 40 Years of Reunification, Development and Integration (1975–2015), Thủ Dầu Một University, Bình Dương province, Việt Nam, April 25, 2015.

7. Tini Tran, "Voter Campaign Targets Vietnamese," *The Los Angeles Times*, August 19, 1999. B1.

8. Christian Collet, "Minority Candidates, Alternative Media, and Multi-ethnic America: Deracialization or Toggling?" *Perspectives on Politics* 6(4) (2008): 707–728; Christian Collet and Nadine Selden, "Separate Ways . . . Worlds Apart? The 'Generation Gap' in Vietnamese America as Seen Through the *San Jose Mercury News* Poll," *Amerasia Journal* 29(1) (2003): 199–217.

9. Christian Collet, "Bloc Voting, Polarization and the Panethnic Hypothesis: The Case of Little Saigon," *Journal of Politics* 67(3) (2005): 907–933.

10. The flag campaign is not only one of the best examples to date of the diaspora's grassroots influence, it is one of the most offensive to Hanoi because activists often seek to displace or discredit Vietnam's current flag in the process. Having been thwarted by the SRVN and State Department in an initial effort in Virginia in 2003, activists quickly retooled; now, over one hundred localities, states and provinces, from Honolulu to Sydney, recognize the banner as the "official symbol of the Vietnamese American community." Nami Kim, "Letting Bayous be Bygones: Should Louisiana be Allowed to Mandate Use of the Pre-Socialist Vietnam Flag?" *Pacific Rim Law and Policy Journal* 14(1) (2005): 129–158.

11. Roaxana Kopetman, "Garden Grove to Vietnam: Don't Visit." *The Orange County Register.* November 30, 2012, http://www.ocregister.com/articles/vietnam-379317-grove-garden.html (accessed January 14, 2017); SBTN, Press Release: Human Rights for Vietnam. March 10, 2012; http://littlesaigoninside.blogspot.jp/2012/03/white-house-and-vietnamese-american.html (accessed January 16, 2017).

12. Michael Lipsky, "Protest as a Political Resource," *American Political Science Review* 62(4) (1968): 1144–1158.

13. See Anthony Nownes, *Interest Groups in American Politics: Pressure and Power*, 2nd ed. (New York and London: Routledge, 2013); Christine Barbour and Gerald C. Wright, *Keeping the Republic: Power and Citizenship in American Politics*, 7th ed. (Washington, DC: CQ Press, 2016).

14. A 2008 survey conducted by the Chicago Council on Global Affairs found Vietnam gaining a 16% "favorable" rating, a 26% neutral rating, and 33% "unfavorable" rating. Gallup, in 2002, found similarly mixed sentiments (46% favorable, 42% unfavorable).

15. See Robert Dreyfuss, "The New China Lobby." *The American Prospect* (Jan./Feb., 1997), http://prospect.org/article/new-china-lobby (accessed January 17, 2017); Kent Calder, *Asia in Washington: Exploring the Penumbra of Transnational Power* (Washington, DC: Brookings Institution Press, 2014).

16. Calder, *Asia in Washington: Exploring the Penumbra of Transnational Power*; see also Tuan Minh Ta, "The Future of Vietnam-U.S. Relations," April 14, 2010, https://www.brookings.edu/opinions/the-future-of-vietnam-u-s-relations (accessed January 12, 2017); Murray Hiebert, Phuong Nguyen, and Gregory B. Poling, *A New Era in U.S.-Vietnam Relations: Deepening Ties Two Decades after Normalization* (Washington, DC, and Lanham: Center for Strategic and International Studies, Rowman and Littlefield, 2014), https://csis-prod.s3.amazonaws.com/s3fs-public/legacyfiles/files/publication/140609HiebertUSVietnamRelationsWeb.pdf (accessed January 11, 2017).

17. Foreign Agent Registration Act (FARA) filings demonstrate the recency, timing, and nature of the SRVN's public relations efforts. Between 1996 and 2016, Vietnamese Ministries or the Embassy in the United States were registered on ten occasions to nine different firms. The embassy has retained the Podesta Group regularly since December 2013, totaling over $1 million in fees. See also Betsy Woodruff, "From Team Hillary to Vietnam Lobbyist." *The Daily Beast*, May 25, 2016, http://www.thedailybeast.com/articles/2016/05/25/from-team-hillary-to-vietnam-lobbyist.html (accessed January 8, 2017).

18. Although norms are changing, this remains somewhat taboo because of anti-SRVN sentiments among Vietnamese; as such, few are willing to publicly discuss such interactions.

19. Search parameters were the keywords "Viet," "Vietnam," and "Vietnamese" at nccsweb.urban.org on December 1, 2016. To render a final count, duplicate cases and chapters of Vietnam Veterans of America were eliminated. Cuban search terms were "Cuba" and "Cuban," respectively, as the database requires exact terms.

20. Carlyle Thayer, "Vietnam and the Challenge of Political Civil Society," *Contemporary Southeast Asia* 31(1) (2009): 1–27.

21. Susan Eckstein, *The Immigrant Divide: How Cuban American Changed the U.S. and their Homeland* (New York: Routledge, 2009).

22. HRV-PAC emerged in the 2012 election and, according to FEC filings, raised $147,196 during that cycle and made $49,000 in contributions, mostly to Democratic senators and representatives. In 2014, it raised an additional $177,158 but made far fewer contributions to federal candidates. In 2016, it made only $6,000 in donations.

23. Cindy Dinh and Bao Nguyen, "The Rise of the Vietnamese American Political Consciousness: Advocacy on Capitol Hill," *Asian American Policy Review* 25 (2015): 52–59. For a broader discussion of this dichotomy, see Frank R. Baumgartner, Jeffrey M. Berry, Marie Hojnacki, David C. Kimball, and Beth L. Leech, *Lobbying and Policy Change: Who Wins, Who Loses, and Why* (Chicago: University of Chicago Press, 2009), 154–158.

24. Như-Ngọc T. Ông and David S Meyer, "Protest and Political Incorporation: Vietnamese American Protests in Orange County, California, 1975–2001," *Journal of Vietnamese Studies* 3(1) (2008): 78–107.

25. Hòa Ái, " 'Ngày Vận Động Cho Việt Nam' tại Quốc hội Hoa Kỳ," Radio Free Asia. June 24, 2016, http://www.rfa.org/vietnamese/in_depth/vietnam-advocacy-day-2016-ha-06242016133510.html (accessed January 9, 2017).

26. Ông and Meyer, "Protest and Political Incorporation: Vietnamese American Protests in Orange County, California, 1975–2001."

27. Janelle Wong, Karthick Ramikrishnan, Taeku Lee, and Jane Junn, *Asian American Political Participation* (New York: Russell Sage, 2011); Christian Collet and Hiroko Furuya, "Transnational Effects on Racial and Ethnic Participation in the United States: The Role of Vietnam in the 'Protest-to-Politics' Incorporation of Vietnamese Americans," unpublished manuscript, 2004.

28. Doug McAdam and Yang Su, "The War at Home: Antiwar Protests and Congressional Voting, 1965 to 1973," *American Sociological Review* 67(5) (2002): 696.

29. http://www.viettan.org (accessed December 29, 2016).

30. Thayer, "Vietnam and the Challenge of Political Civil Society"; Sharon Simonson, "Bay Area Vietnamese Promote Uprising in Vietnam," SiliconValleyOneWorld, September 12, 2016, http://www.siliconvalleyoneworld.com/2016/09/12/bay-area-vietnamese-seek-to-inspire-uprising-in-vietnam-after-huge-fish-kill (accessed December 26, 2016); Trẻ Tuổi, "Terrorist group responsible for recent rallies in Ho Chi Minh City, police say," June 16, 2016, http://tuoitrenews.vn/society/34802/terrorist-group-responsible-for-recent-rallies-in-ho-chi-minh-city-police (accessed December 26, 2016); Reuters, "Vietnam Declares California-based Group Terrorist," October 8, 2016, http://www.reuters.com/article/us-vietnam-security-idUSKCN1271HZ (accessed December 28, 2016).

31. Charles Lam, "Little Saigon Politics Are Taking a Turn for the Liberal, With a New Generation of Activists." *OC Weekly* (2015), http://www.ocweekly.com/news/little-saigon-politics-are-taking-a-turn-for-the-liberal-with-a-new-generation-of-activists-6442736 (accessed January 19, 2017).

32. Collet, "Bloc Voting, Polarization and the Panethnic Hypothesis"

33. Emily Foxhall, Doug Smith, and Anh Do, "Voter turnout disparity was key in razor-thin O.C. supervisor race," *Los Angeles Times*, March 27, 2015, http://www.latimes.com/local/orangecounty/la-me-lost-election-20150328-story.html (accessed January 17, 2017).

34. Carole Jean Uhlaner and Danvy Le, "'The Role of Coethnic Political Mobilization in Electoral Incorporation: Evidence from Orange County, California," *Politics, Groups and Identities* (2015): 1–35. doi:10.1080/21565503.2015.1109527

35. Wong et al., *Asian American Political Participation*.

36. Collet, "Minority Candidates, Alternative Media, and Multiethnic America"

37. Collet, "Bloc Voting, Polarization and the Panethnic Hypothesis"

38. Wendy K. Tam Cho, "Contagion Effects and Ethnic Contribution Networks," *American Journal of Political Science* 47(2) (2003): 368–387.

39. Surveys taken as recently as 2008 have revealed Vietnamese Americans as more Republican identifying than other Asians, but independent and lacking partisan strength. Surname-coded data in Orange and Santa Clara counties reveal a steady decline in GOP registrations since 2006 (by the author), and more recent surveys suggest that voting for Democrats at the national level is increasing. See Kim N. Nguyen and James C. Garand, "Partisan Strength and Nonpartisanship among Asian Americans," *American Politics Research* 37(3) (2009): 375–408; Wong et al., *Asian American Political Participation*; Karthick Ramikrishnan and Taeku Lee, "The 2012 General Election: Public Opinion of Asian Americans in California," http://naasurvey.com/wp-content/uploads/2016/10/NAAS12-oct2-CA-election.pdf (accessed January 10, 2017).

40. For a discussion of the Cuban case, see Trevor Rubenzer, "Social Media Foreign Policy: Examining the Political Use of Social Media by Ethnic Identity Groups in the United States," *Politics* 36(2) (2015): doi:10.1111/1467-9256.12091

41. Nhi Lieu, *The American Dream in Vietnamese* (Minneapolis: University of Minnesota Press, 2011).

42. Ái, " 'Ngày Vận Động Cho Việt Nam' tại Quốc hội Hoa Kỳ."

43. Zachary Abuza, *Stifling the Public Sphere: Media and Civil Society in Vietnam* (Washington, DC: National Endowment for Democracy, International Forum for Democratic Studies, October 2015), http://www.ned.org/stifling-the-public-sphere-media-and-civil-society-in-egypt-russia-and-vietnam (accessed January 4, 2017).

44. The Lantos Human Rights Commission in 2012 launched the "Defending Freedoms Project" in which members of Congress adopt a "prisoner of conscience" and commit to publicly advocating on the captive's behalf. As of this writing, more Vietnamese had been sponsored than in any other country. https://humanrightscommission.house.gov/defending-freedom-project/adopted-prisoners-conscience (accessed January 16, 2017).

45. John J. Mearsheimer and Stephen M. Walt, "The Blind Man and the Elephant in the Room: Robert Lieberman and the Israel Lobby," *Perspectives on Politics* 7(2) (2009): 259–273.

46. Trevor Rubenzer and Steven B Redd, "Ethnic Minority Groups and U.S. Foreign Policy: Examining Congressional Decision Making and Economic Sanctions," *International Studies Quarterly* 54(3) (2010): 755–777.

47. The search parameters included all types of legislation between the 93rd (1973–1974) and 113th (2013–2015) Congresses, in which the keyword "Vietnam" appeared in the title or summary and fell into one of four designated policy areas: international affairs; economics and public finance; immigration; foreign trade and international finance (one policy term is assigned by Congress.gov to each measure). It should be recognized that this may have excluded bills of pertinence to Vietnamese Americans or the U.S.-SRVN relationship. If one removes the policy parameters, the total amount of "Vietnam" legislation numbers over one thousand, due to scores of bills and resolutions concerning U.S. veterans.

48. James M. McCormick, "Ethnic Interest Groups in American Foreign Policy," in *The Domestic Source of American Foreign Policy*, 6th ed., ed. James M. McCormick (Lanham, MD: Rowman and Littlefield, 2012), 67–87.

49. Rebecca K.C. Hersman, *Friends and Foes* (Washington, DC: Brookings Institution Press, 2000); Susan B. Epstein, *Department of State and Foreign Operations Appropriations: History of Legislation and Funding in Brief* (Washington, DC: Congressional Research Service, 2016), https://fas.org/sgp/crs/row/R44637.pdf (accessed January 10, 2017).

50. Ralph G. Carter and James M. Scott, *Choosing to Lead: Understanding Congressional Foreign Policy Entrepreneurs* (Durham, NC: Duke University Press, 2009); David R. Mayhew, *Congress: The Electoral Connection* (New Haven, CT: Yale University Press, 1974).

51. Some variation of the VNHRA has been introduced in every session since the 107th (2001–2002) and has found sponsors in the Senate. It has passed four times, with scant nay votes, in the House. The SRVN's public response to the bill, though its Washington, DC embassy and media organs, has included citing House members and NGOs in Vietnam who have spoken critically of the legislation. SRVN media explicitly attribute the bill to the "heavy influence" of the Vietnamese-American community. See *VietnamPlus*, "U.S. MP opposes mark-up of Vietnam human rights act," June 29, 2013, http://en.vietnamplus. vn/us-mp-opposes-markup-of-vietnam-human-rights-act/46461.vnp (accessed January 8, 2017).

52. Walter Clark Wilson, "Descriptive Representation and Latino Interest Bill Sponsorship in Congress," *Social Science Quarterly* 91(4) (2010): 1043–1062.

53. Mạch Sống, "Thượng Viện Hoa-Kỳ Đã Chấp Thuận Gia Hạn Tu Chính Án McCain–Davis Thêm Hai Năm (2007–2009) và Những Điều Cần Biết về Tu Chánh Án Này," September 7, 2007, http://www.machsong.org/modules.php?na me=News&file=article&sid=1090 (accessed January 8, 2007).

54. Brantly Womack, *China and Vietnam: The Politics of Asymmetry* (Cambridge: Cambridge University Press, 2006).

55. Ibid.

56. David Lowery, "Lobbying Influence: Meaning, Measurement and Missing," *Interest Groups & Advocacy* 2(1) (2013): 1–26.

57. Search undertaken on December 1, 2016, at https://www.opensecrets. org/lobby/lookup.php using the issue term "Vietnam."

58. Josh DeWind and Renata Segura, *Diaspora Lobbies and the U.S. Government* (New York and London: New York University Press, 2014).

Chapter 10

A View from the Hill

GREGORY C. MCCARTHY

On Capitol Hill, ethnic lobbying is no theoretical matter. Ethnic groups take their place alongside interests of every flavor and stripe. Their presence can occur as an appointment on a member of Congress' calendar, a large reception for members and staff, or a color-coordinated protest, silent or otherwise, at a committee hearing. Members' calculation of how much to heed ethnic lobbies rests on their own interest and the perennial questions of public relations, credit claiming, and political rewards, all ultimately serving the cause of re-election. Unlike virtually every other political controversy, the influence of ethnic lobbies, particularly in foreign policy, does not always break along party lines and is not entirely predictable in its political effect. Several examples from the last two decades, many based on personal observations, will be offered to demonstrate how ethnic lobbies are received by their targeted audience which is through a heavy use of former members of Congress, constituent mobilization and issue interest. Despite the potential liability of unsavory characteristics or political embarrassment, members of Congress interact with ethnic lobbies, most of which are sympathetic allies, others less obviously so.

Member Motivation

How and to what extent members of Congress embrace ethnic lobbies depends largely on individual motivation. David R. Mayhew's classic, *Congress: The Electoral Connection*, finds member calculation resting on credit claiming, position taking, and advertising.[1] All can be observed in Congress's interaction with ethnic lobbies. Lawmakers generally need political credibility to find their efforts worthwhile. Ethnic lobbies can provide this, in everything from "A Friend of Israel" award, for example, to a political action committee (PAC) contribution. If a policy position is popular, legislators can publicly take a position. This dynamic is seen in the Florida congressional delegation's embrace of the Cuban embargo (further discussion below). Seeking good policy is generally assumed, if individually defined, but its importance recedes behind the other goals. Lawmakers often seek to be identified taking a position, such as denouncing but not pulling out all procedural stops to blocking the Iranian nuclear deal, for example. If there is a risk associated with ethnic lobbies, the possible reward is policy entrepreneurship and a reputation for expertise. In the years before he emerged from a competitive race to chair the full House Foreign Affairs Committee in 2013, Representative Edward R. Royce (R-CA) immersed himself in the details of his African subcommittee chairmanship, a seemingly obscure and thankless task that gave him gravitas and credibility at the opportune time to claim the chairmanship.

There is an interest group for every cause, no matter how obscure, although success can be another matter. Groups' presence is no longer viewed as special pleading or the dreaded "special interest" of political hyperbole. The House of Representatives in particular has responded by creating a "caucus" for various causes that members can join painlessly.[2] Caucus membership gives lawmakers the opportunity for position taking.

In the realm of international affairs, ethnic lobbies tend to be associated with foreign governments. Foreign lobbying disclosure data reveals a peak in 1987 with a high of 916 lobbyists, with a decline in the mid-1990s, with only 360 registrations by the end of 2014.[3] Ethnic lobbies unapologetically advocate their own interests, implicitly assuming their interests and the national interest are aligned. This is occasionally challenged by a critic of a specific position, but self-interest, constituent interest, and national interest all blend together in practitioners' minds, to the extent they are considered at all. This trend was lamented by then House Majority Leader James C. "Jim" Wright in 1983, who said, "[t]here may be danger in the tendency of increasing numbers of people to think of themselves and their special interests first, and only second in terms of the national interest of the country."[4] Eric Uslaner argues, "foreign policy decisions increasingly reflect ethnic interests rather than some overarching sense of national interest."[5] That this is not viewed as a damning indictment gives a sense of the assumed nature of today's interest groups.

Despite the partisan hostility that characterizes today's Congress and politics generally, most members of Congress view themselves as genial quasi-celebrities, taking selfies and glad-handing with ease, as any viewer of the State of the Union can see. Interpersonal relations across party lines, while perhaps less cordial than a generation ago, are warmer than might be predicted. Accessibility, to those who have not witnessed members in their natural habitat, is surprisingly easy. Lawmakers, detectable by their quarter-sized official lapel pin with the number of the current Congress, are visible at public receptions, press conferences, walks to votes, constituent meetings, and so on.

Members and staff, along with former members and former staff as lobbyists, present a fluidity that makes sorting out the effect on the policy process difficult. The value of former members as lobbyists cannot be overestimated. Lobbies seek a coveted one-on-one meeting with a member of Congress, and former members go to the head of the line in likelihood of getting an appointment. Congress confers lifetime privileges on its members, to include floor authorization, avoiding metal detectors that the public and staff must endure, and exclusive Capitol dining room access, among other goodies. Although open lobbying on the floor of Congress was limited in 2007 ethics reforms, former legislators still have access that most lobbyists do not. As a part of the club, former members have instant credibility. As fellow practitioners, former members understand the constant pressure of fundraising and electoral politics. A major constraint is time since Congress has only a Tuesday-to-Thursday legislative schedule, during roughly half the possible work weeks in recent years.[6] Lobbyists also establish relationships with staff who work the issues on a daily basis and sometimes represent continuity. Partisan lines can blur. Today's congressional majority can be tomorrow's minority.

Ethnic lobbies, like other causes, have various tools at their disposal. Lobbies offer lunches or an evening Capitol Hill reception that tend to draw midlevel staffers, as senior staff are often too busy. These events build goodwill and familiarity and usually include "honoring" members of Congress and offering them the chance to address a group. Although lobbyist-purchased sit-down lunches were prohibited in successive gift bans last modified in 2007, one exception is an event that is "widely attended."[7] The goods are viewed as too dispersed to be a risk of corruption. The Center for a Free Cuba, for example, hosts such an occasional lunch on its issue. The Defense Forum Foundation offers similar events, notably on behalf of North Korean refugees, an ethnic lobby tragically underrepresented relative to other ethnicities. This group also sponsors staff delegation trips (STAFFDELs) to see the United Nations Mission for the Referendum in Western Sahara (MINURSO) mission in Western Sahara, a disputed area between Algeria and Morocco, a conflict otherwise largely overlooked.

Ethnic lobbies have also used think tanks in a slightly obscured fashion to advance their cause. The New York Times recently reported that a dozen prominent think tanks had received "tens of millions of dollars" from foreign governments that had not registered under the Foreign Agents Registration Act (FARA) required for conventional lobbying.[8] This opening allows invisible influence as respected opinion leaders shape the foreign policy discussion without disclosing some large funds. Another report found a prominent GOP figure, Ed Rogers, failed to report his being a hired Saudi advocate as he argued their case in the *Washington Post* and other outlets.[9] Additionally, former House Foreign Affairs Committee staffers David Adams and Ari Fridman, the latter just weeks removed from his job there, circulated talking points and suggested public hearing questions for committee staffers in emails to former coworkers on behalf of Saudi Arabia.[10] Longstanding relationships and hidden agendas advance the cause of ethnic lobbies, like all lobbies, and characterize the foreign policy milieu.

The Big Three Lobbies: AIPAC, Cuba, and Greece

The Israeli, Cuban, and Greek lobbies are generally considered the most powerful and even denounced as "too influential," as suggested below. But it is noteworthy that in recent history all have suffered significant setbacks to their causes, raising some doubt about their ostensible power. Even powerful lobbies can lose battles, and eventually clout.

The American Israel Public Affairs Committee (AIPAC) is the archetype ethnic lobby whose success is nearly unrivaled and fully explored elsewhere in this volume (chapter 4). AIPAC is closely aligned with the Israeli government and its prowess has been noted for decades. It places no worse than third in multiple assessments of all lobbies' strength.[11] AIPAC spends roughly $3 million per year on lobbying.[12] Its literature boasts that its annual convention "will be attended by more members of Congress than almost any other event, except for a joint session of Congress or a State of the Union address."[13] One of its primary efforts is sponsoring congressional delegation (CODEL) trips to Israel. This is a recurring event that includes dozens of lawmakers (and their spouses) annually. In August 2011 alone, CODELs including about 20 percent of the House went to Israel.[14] AIPAC can claim a generation-long education effort, and its nearly unanimous support in Congress is such that criticism of the lobby carries some political risk.

Most successful ethnic lobbies broaden their appeal beyond their ethnicity or natural allies. AIPAC began with the Jewish community, expanded when embraced by Christian evangelicals decades ago and now only a relative handful of members of Congress could be described as anything other than wholehearted supporters. Even dissenters on this topic have special circumstances. They tend to be driven by constituents, a large Arab diaspora in Michigan and Minnesota, for example, or the Islamic faith, or both.

But, even with this acknowledged stature, one cannot assume AIPAC's automatic success on favored issues. AIPAC's half-century goal of getting the United States to move its embassy from Tel Aviv to Jerusalem had, until recently, not gone beyond symbolism. The Jerusalem Embassy Act of 1995 recognized Jerusalem as Israel's capital but gave American presidents waiver authority on national security grounds to be declared every six months on the relocation of the U.S. Embassy matter. Every president exercised this authority, including President Donald J. Trump, until his December 2017 announcement that he would no longer. Despite commanding wide majorities on this topic in Congress at various times and in multiple fora, no previous administration has ever come close to taking this step.[15] AIPAC also suffered a significant setback in opposing the Obama administration's Iran nuclear deal, which the ostensibly opposed Trump administration has kept it mostly in place. The original defeat demonstrated the difficulty in overcoming presidential power, but it also raised some questions regarding the lobby's future.[16] Many principals blamed the failure on the heavy-handed and Republican-dominated approach by Israeli Prime Minister Benjamin Netanyahu and his Ambassador to the United States Ron Dermer in their lobbying of Congress in effecting a Netanyahu joint congressional address at the invitation of Republican leaders. Representative Stephen Cohen (D-TN), echoing a common view said, "Netanyahu should not get himself involved in American politics in the future, and AIPAC played a stronger hand than they should have."[17] The lobby may have suffered when its broadly appealing group became viewed as seeking support that was too narrow. Fitting for an influential organization, it had critics from the opposite perspective. While many thought AIPAC was too willing to wade into domestic American partisan politics, others thought it was not partisan enough in letting Democrats who supported the administration off the hook.[18] Counterintuitively, AIPAC did not seem overly concerned and found fundraising success from previous setbacks. One reporter noted, "after each of those fights, AIPAC's membership and fundraising spiked. In special interest politics, there's nothing like losing to enhance the bottom line."[19] But, another report concluded, "Washington insiders [are] wondering if the once-untouchable lobbying giant has suffered lasting damage to its near-pristine political reputation."[20]

The Cuban lobby's strength in Congress was virtually impregnable from the establishment of economic sanctions in the waning days of the

Eisenhower administration to as recently as 2014. William M. Leo Grande described it in 2013 as "the most powerful lobby in Washington . . . the Castro-hating right wing that has Obama's bureaucrats terrified and inert." He argued the "aggressive" lobby is "able to prevent rational debate about an anachronistic policy by intimidating anyone who dared challenge it."[21] The lobby's friends prominently included multiple Republican presidents and the Florida congressional delegation, led by House Foreign Affairs Committee Chair Ileana Ros-Lehtinen (2011–2013), herself a Cuban-born refugee. But the lobby's strength was not limited to Republicans or Floridians. New Jersey Democrats and ethnic Cubans, Senator Robert Menendez and Representative Albio Sires, are every bit as outspoken as their South Florida Republican colleagues.[22] All are encouraged by their constituents.

The Cuban lobby's strength may also be eroding. Its monolithic opposition to lifting the embargo is waning partly because younger voters appear to be outgrowing it. Two longtime observers cite a precipitous falloff in support for the embargo in Cuban exiles over the previous two decades.[23] Directly challenging the lobby's long-held clout, President Barack Obama normalized relations with Cuba in 2014 to bitter denunciations from the lobby, but little broader political fallout followed.[24] While the longstanding partial travel ban was voided and diplomatic relations restored, complete lifting of the embargo will require congressional approval.[25] The current unpopularity of trade agreements may make this harder than it might otherwise be, but the hold of the lobby has been gravely threatened.

The Greek lobby regularly tops lists of ethnic influence, but also struggles in some of its prominent causes. The Congressional Hellenic Caucus has 137 members, one third of the House.[26] One of its recent fights has been its attempt to keep a neighboring state from its desired name, the Republic of Macedonia.[27] Citing her membership in the Hellenic Caucus, the incoming top House Foreign Affairs Committee Republican, Ros-Lehtinen, opposed the Bush administration's 2004 decision to recognize Macedonia's preferred name, calling it "unresolved."[28] Ros-Lehtinen praised Greece's support for War on Terrorism efforts, implicitly suggesting it deserved an indulgence.[29] Conversely, the comparatively meager Macedonian lobby did not welcome her ascension to chair after the 2010 elections saying, "Of particular concern to [United Macedonian Diaspora] is Representative Ros-Lehtinen's co-sponsorship of anti-Macedonian resolutions in the last three sessions of Congress."[30] Years after the Department of State's recognition of the rename, several House members introduced a nonbinding resolution urging "finding a mutually-accepted name for [the Former Yugoslav Republic of Macedonia]."[31] The Greek lobby has persisted on this matter but has not prevailed. One author further wondered why the lobby had not even attempted to get Congress to address Greek financial insolvency.[32] The lobby also has not successfully marginalized its historic rival, Turkey, despite years of effort and some advantages (a closer culture and religion to the United States, for example). Despite being a large and prominent lobby generating issue mobilizations, major Greek policy victories are elusive.

Success breeds critics. David Paul and Rachel Anderson Paul found that in their survey of thirty-eight ethnic lobbies, only the Jewish, Cuban, and Armenian lobbies were criticized as too powerful in their interviews with several dozen anonymous congressional figures.[33] One prominent, controversial 2006 study, which became a book, *The Israel Lobby and U.S. Foreign Policy* by John J. Mearsheimer and Stephen M. Walt, has generated much commentary and is mostly beyond the scope of this chapter.[34] These critics generally argue that various ethnic lobbies advance their own interest at the expense of the national interest. How this can be assessed with any rigor is unclear. How much influence is "too much" for a specific group mostly depends on one's view of the specific question at hand. Ethnic groups presumably acquire influence legally and mostly advocate their cases publicly. Other groups and individuals are free to make their own case or criticize "the big three" in the open marketplace of ideas as the best antidote to possible undue influence.

Armenian Genocide Resolution from Behind the Curtain

The proposed Armenian Genocide resolution is a study unto itself (see chapter 6). More importantly, the lobby garnered more than half the House's *sponsorship* of a 2007 genocide resolution condemning the Ottoman Empire's activity in 1915.[35] The formidable Armenian lobby was up against the Turkish government, a key North Atlantic Treaty Organization (NATO) ally, and the best efforts of lobbyists former House Majority Leader Richard A. "Dick" Gephardt (D-MO) and Representative Robert L. "Bob" Livingston (R-LA), each with his own team. While the House Foreign Affairs Committee passed the resolution twenty-seven to twenty-one, it never made it to the House floor, resulting in a major victory for the Turkish lobby, albeit one that may have to be revisited.[36]

In the midst of this contentious and high-visibility debate, it was not unusual to see Bob Livingston utilizing his former-member privileges and milling about in the members' anteroom or along the staff wall of the House Foreign Affairs Committee hearing room, patiently explaining that the Ottoman Empire is not present-day Turkey and that atrocities occurred on both sides. Gephardt also enjoyed access to most Members' offices. One of his many visits was to Representative Dana Rohrabacher (R-CA), a senior member of the House Foreign Affairs Committee, not one of his natural allies or friends while he was in Congress. Conversely, some of his old Democratic Caucus colleagues were not pleased with his advocacy. A former ally, Representative Anna G. Eshoo (D-CA), Congress's only ethnic Assyrian, said of him, "Clearly this is not a principle of his. This is business."[37]

The full weight of Turkey's friends came through, with threats regarding Turkish airspace and basing for NATO (at the height of the Iraq surge during George W. Bush's presidency). All living former secretaries of state weighed in on Turkey's behalf.[38] The Turkish lobby succeeded in getting seventeen congressional cosponsors to take the awkward position of publicly withdrawing their support for the bill.[39] Gephardt's lobbying firm was paid $100,000 per month for his work during the period, and he arranged a meeting between Turkish parliamentarians and House Democratic leaders, as well as with the Turkish ambassador and a hostile Speaker Nancy Pelosi (D-CA).[40] Livingston was described as the "kingpin of Turkish advocacy," whose lobbying firm received $13 million from Turkey from 2000 to 2007. His team contacted 141 members of Congress in the five weeks before an aborted 2000 vote.[41] The late, respected former Representative Stephen J. Solarz (D-NY) abandoned the view he had while in Congress favoring the genocide resolution and received $400,000 to lobby against it.[42] One commentator has proclaimed, "Few niches of the Washington lobby are as lucrative as the foreign racket."[43]

MEK, India, Tibet, Pakistan, and More

The matter of the Mujahedin-e-Khalq (MEK) marks one of the more unusual recent chapters in foreign policy. A full discussion is beyond the scope of this chapter. Briefly, the MEK is a militant Iranian dissident group that was protected in a camp in Iraq from the time of the 1980s Iran–Iraq War until the fall of Saddam Hussein in 2003. Anticipating the U.S. withdrawal in 2011, the camp's residents were badly threatened and occasionally attacked by vengeful pro-Iranian Iraqis probably acting at the behest of their government. The United States felt a moral obligation to protect them. Complicating matters was their listing by the Department of State as a foreign terrorist organization (FTO) because of 1970s attacks, including on Americans.[44] The group's staunchest early advocate, Representative Ted Poe (R-TX), withstood criticism that he was supporting a "terrorist group" because of the FTO list. The MEK also faced questions for the exorbitant speaking fees it paid to prominent former officials, such as former New York Mayor Rudy Giuliani, to publicly endorse their cause. Others, such as former CIA Director James Woolsey, insisted they were not paid.[45] Despite also being criticized as an Islamic "cult," their cause was adopted across virtually the entire political spectrum, from President Trump's National Security Adviser John Bolton to former Vermont Governor and Democratic presidential candidate Howard Dean, and the group quickly became one of the most powerful ethnically-based lobbies.[46] Their man in DC was the ubiquitous, soft-spoken, and courteous Nasser Rashidi, officially of the National Coalition of Pro-Democracy Advocates, a self-described Iranian-focused "human rights advocacy group," whose office seemed to be out of the Rayburn House Office Building Cafeteria given how often he could be spotted there. The range of MEK supporters is difficult to assess completely (e.g., the Iranian American Community of Northern California hired the powerful Washington, DC law firm Akin Gump Strauss Hauer and Feld to lobby on its behalf).[47]

Denied by the Bush administration in several successive years, the Obama administration finally removed the group from the FTO list in September 2012. The Administration had the further difficulty of finding countries outside Iran or Iraq to take the group members who were unwelcome in both countries and had lengthy counterterrorism vetting obstacles to immigrating to America.[48] Their astonishing success at moving overwhelming majorities in Congress—removal from the FTO list and gaining protected status—represented an unusual confluence of circumstances that are unlikely to be replicated.

The Indian lobby also deserves mention in a volume like this, as it has almost consciously followed the AIPAC model. It succeeded in the late 1990s in getting a change of policy on the disputed territory of Kashmir.[49] But its heavy lift was overcoming late 1990s sanctions related to an unauthorized nuclear test. In 2008, the United States concluded a "123" nuclear deal that required hurdling multiple committee approval and answering objections from disarmament skeptics, among others.[50] The Indian lobby hired prominent former officials, many fresh from Bush administration national security circles, to make its case.[51] These efforts succeeded with relative ease. One of its prominent lobbyists boasted, "You haven't heard a lot from [India critic Representative] Dan Burton, right?"[52] At the White House East Room gathering for the agreement-signing ceremony October 8, 2008, attended by President George W. Bush, Vice President Richard Cheney, and Secretary of State Condoleezza Rice, the Indian diaspora was well represented, and it was clearly a day of great pride and celebrated as a major breakthrough.

The cause of Tibet represents another ethnic lobby with its appeal beyond its natural base. Like Israel, the MEK, and few others, Tibet's advocates have generated support beyond ethnic or religious identity, owing largely to their charismatic exiled leader. Judging by members' front offices, photos with the Dalai Lama exceed those with a pope and are about as coveted as with a president of one's own party. The International Campaign for Tibet is the lead lobbying group, and its specialized license plates are popular in Virginia and elsewhere, but their policy agenda is limited outside of boilerplate human rights, general goodwill, and symbolic affection. They notably do not confront China head-on or pose much criticism of the regime.

Lobbies' strength can sometimes be measured indirectly by presidential actions on foreign policy. In his second term, President Bill Clinton successfully pressed NATO expansion, requiring a treaty confirmation vote in the U.S. Senate. Two commentators cast his NATO enlargement proposals "largely as a bid to win Central and Eastern European ethnic votes."[53] In 1997, Canadian Prime Minister Jean Chrétien was overheard complaining that the NATO push was occurring because "ethnic voting blocs in the United States are pushing their cause."[54] Many NATO expansion critics are now revisiting their twenty-year-old objections in light of a rising Russia.

Ethnic lobbies can also be a liability. The gadfly maverick tendencies of Representative Dana Rohrabacher to seek his own solutions to Middle East and counterterrorism challenges led him to dealings with various Afghans and Arabs and have been criticized by national security hawks as cavorting with the enemy. His Russian dealings have apparently drawn FBI interest.[55] Representative Dan L. Burton (R-IN), then a self-appointed Pakistan expert and senior member of the House Foreign Affairs Committee, faced accusations from a Pakistan-hired lobbyist that he had threatened to cut off the lobbyist's access to House GOP leaders if the lobbyist could not raise him $5,000.[56] The lobbyist's firm makes almost $1 million a year representing Pakistan and had regular dealings with Burton. Burton was put on the defensive by the exchange as he was investigating President Clinton at the time as a prominent critic while Chair of the Government Reform Committee.[57] Surprisingly, some members of Congress will take risks with ethnic lobbies, including those with alleged terrorist ties that might be politically fatal in a different context. In addition to the MEK, hardline lawmakers sympathetic to the Cuban lobby were criticized for acquiescence in various administrations' unwillingness to extradite a suspected airline bomber who was an illegal alien living freely in Miami and "buoyed by the support of conservative politicians."[58] Representative

Peter T. King (R-NY), an Irish Republican Army (IRA) supporter, faced charges of hypocrisy as he investigated Islamic but not Irish extremism.[59] Ethnic lobbies' group solidarity can sometimes be a trump card.

Not all lobbying portfolios are high profile. Joe and Shirley DioGuardi are a husband and wife team representing ethnic Albanians and Kosovo in the Balkan controversies of the 1990s and after. Former Representative Joseph J. DioGuardi (R-NY) had a brief stint in Congress (1985–1989) but made a lifelong friend in House Foreign Affairs Committee Chairman Henry J. Hyde (2001–2007), based on their shared outspoken antiabortion Catholic profile. Hyde gave the DioGuardis an informal but exalted status in matters before the committee where they testified frequently. Their lobbying position was often controversial, but members (and most former members) testifying before committees generally benefit from bipartisan courtesy that keeps them from the adversarial inquisitions that other witnesses can face. The DioGuardis had a similar if slightly less effusive relationship with Hyde's successor as top Republican, Ros-Lehtinen.[60]

No study of foreign policy lobbying would be complete without Saudi Arabia, although it is not a traditional ethnic lobby in the sense of a concentrated diaspora or a large exile community. The legislative effort to allow 9/11 victims to sue the government of Saudi Arabia as indirectly responsible for the fifteen Saudis of the nineteen hijackers resulted in the first override of an Obama veto by a 97 to 1 vote in the Senate and 348 to 77 vote in the House of Representatives in September 2016.[61] A related controversy involves twenty-eight classified pages of the *9/11 Commission Report* that reference Saudi contacts. The Saudi effort to lobby Congress has largely arisen to address this. Saudi Arabia spent $11 million in direct lobbying in 2015, fourth among foreign nations.[62] One of its prominent hired guns was former Senator Norm Coleman (R-MN), who procured meetings with most of the leadership of the foreign policy committees.[63] Its ultimate success is unclear, but because of its strategic resources and location, it will remain a pivotal country and an important lobby.

The United Arab Emirates (spending $14.2 million), Germany ($12 million), and Canada ($11.2 million) are the top three countries ahead of Saudi Arabia in spending on direct lobbying of Congress in 2014.[64] None of these have a significant ethnic component.

Members as Ethnic Lobbyists

Representative Charles W. Boustany (R-LA) is ethnically Lebanese, as is Representative Darrell Issa (R-CA). Together with then Senator John E. Sununu (R-NH), this faction was informally led by a senior member of

Congress, then-Representative Nick J. Rahall (D-WV). These members became highly identified leaders of Lebanese ethnicity and of moderate Arab views. Issa and Rahall led an April 2003 CODEL to meet with Syrian President Bashar Assad. Representative Rahall raised some eyebrows when he effusively praised Assad's efforts publicly and privately.[65] Rahall later came under fire for his sister's $15,000-a-month lobbying contract with Qatar, which critics viewed as a ham-handed payment to him.[66] He ultimately lost re-election in 2014 but more for larger political trends in West Virginia and became a lobbyist as soon as the ban on this work for him as a former member of Congress expired.[67]

One of the more peculiar ethnic advocates is Portuguese and an otherwise influential member, House Intelligence Committee Chair Devin Nunes (R-CA). He has taken the unusual step of attempting to get defense assets for a base in the Azores, a Portuguese island used by the U.S. military in the mid-Atlantic. This has resulted in an "increasingly nasty war" between Nunes and senior Pentagon officials, according to one report.[68] One observer said,

> [Nunes's relationship with the] Portuguese government is extensive—and a private source of consternation for some congressional and defense staffers. Nunes sometimes visits his distant cousins on other islands in the archipelago during his frequent vacations there. During a visit just before the July 4 [2015] weekend, he attended a ceremony thrown in his honor by his ancestral village.[69]

This conduct would be typical for an average member of Congress, attempting to steer federal largess to his constituency. Atypical is that the constituency is *overseas*.

Some members are self-appointed representatives of an ethnic lobby. Representative Luis V. Gutiérrez (D-IL), an ethnic Puerto Rican, has become so outspoken on Latino issues that he has been called "the Martin Luther King of immigration reform."[70] Describing his activity the previous few years, an article says, "he has been touring the country, often speaking before large, cheering [Hispanic] crowds."[71] Yet, sometimes an ethnic lobby can have opposing sides' interests represented. Former Representative Connie Mack, IV (R-FL) was paid $40,000 to represent bondholders threatened if Puerto Rico defaults in its current debt crisis.[72]

Puerto Rico offers further material for observation. Vieques, Puerto Rico, was the site of an accidental civilian death at a U.S. Navy bombing range in 1999, leading to months of local protest, ultimately resulting in the expulsion of the Navy by referendum in 2001 and the exit of all U.S.

military presence.[73] The lobby was mobilized like never before, as the death united the island's "normally fractious political parties."[74] After months of negotiation while protesters occupied the Navy range, the Clinton administration agreed to a referendum on the issue.[75] The lobby's leading critic, Senator James M. Inhofe (R-OK), described the live-fire bombing opponents as "ungrateful, myopic and misinformed" but recognized that the lobby represented their people accurately. Inhofe said, "I know [Gov. Pedro Rossello's challenges] sounded good in Puerto Rico . . . as a typical politician he wants to be seen as a hero back home and the best way of doing that is by insulting me."[76] The lobby scored an unambiguous victory when the succeeding Bush administration acquiesced to the results of the referendum.[77] Fifteen years later, Inhofe still maintains this range should be reopened, but he has no support.[78]

The case of Representative Jay C. Kim (R-CA) presents a member becoming so close to an ethnic lobby that he blatantly crossed legal boundaries. In 1992, Kim was the first Korean American elected to Congress, but his campaign finances immediately came under investigation and were found illegal. The Department of Justice described his receiving contributions from various Asian foreign nationals as "the largest amount of criminal campaign finance violations ever committed by a Member of Congress," leading to Kim's guilty plea on multiple counts.[79] Kim nonetheless improbably sought re-election in 1998, lost, and lost again two years later. His sponsors were equally shameless. In the midst of his unsuccessful primary, a Korean language newspaper told its readers, "the Republic of Korea and President Kim Dae Jung need congressman Kim."[80] This led his opponent, future Representative Gary G. Miller (R-CA), to say:

> I thought he represented the USA. He needs to go back to Korea if that's what his focus is. I would understand if he said he represents the best interests of the Korean-American community. That's fine. But when an ad says the government of Korea . . . [needs] Jay Kim that bothers me a lot.[81]

The head of the Korean American Coalition, if not Representative Kim, understood the bad impression, saying: "If I were Jay Kim I would not approve that language. It creates the image that you're actually electing an agent for Korea. Korean Americans want someone to represent this country, not Korea."[82]

The demographic makeup of Congress can also drive the power of ethnic lobbies. The Congressional Black Caucus (CBC), the oldest and most prominent ethnic group, was founded in 1971 with thirteen House members and today has forty-three voting representatives, more than triple its original size.[83] The 1992 election brought the first wave of "majority-minority" congressional districts and a surge of minority legislators. The CBC reached thirty-eight House members (thirteen more than the previous Congress). This election also increased Hispanic House members from ten to seventeen (including notably an additional Cuban Republican from Miami).[84] After that election, there were fifty-five minorities in the House, up from thirty a decade earlier.[85] This, in turn, advanced the cause of ethnic lobbying, as dramatically more members self-identified with one or more ethnic groups. But, with increasingly polarized congressional districts, there is less cross-pollination of ethnic lobbies. Although there is less risk of getting too close to the "wrong" lobby, there is little incentive to reach across ethnic lobbies unless they are already aligned.

"Outside" members can adopt ethnic lobbies for their own purposes. Representative Gary L. Ackerman (D-NY) took an interest in India, becoming co-chair of the Congressional Caucus on India, which was founded in 1993 and grew to more than one hundred members of Congress. He was warmly lauded at a reception in his honor by the Indian Ambassador to the United States, upon his retirement.[86] Representative Eliot L. Engel (D-NY), top Democrat on the House Foreign Affairs Committee, was described more than a decade ago as "America's foremost politician on Albanian affairs."[87] Engel attributed his initial interest to the (small) Albanian population in his Bronx district.[88] Engel was so prominent on the subject that a street was named after him in Kosovo in July 2005 for his decade-plus efforts on the cause.[89]

In some cases, members of Congress can draw criticism for attempting to embrace lobbies outside their own ethnicity. Former Senator John F. Kerry (D-MA) benefited from the widespread assumption and his occasional assertion that he was Irish, the dominant ethnic group in Massachusetts. When he ran for president in 2004, the *Boston Globe*'s research discovered he was not Irish.[90] Former Senator Robert W. "Bob" Packwood (R-OR), before sexual scandal ended his career in 1995, drew heat for authoring pro-Israel political fundraising letters that falsely implied he was Jewish. He wrote that "we were there first" in "our own homeland," referring to Israel.[91] Although he was a prodigious fundraiser, his opponents and state media outlets denounced him.[92] Then-Senator Mark S. Kirk (R-IL) was so outspoken on Israel that critics claim he blurred his non-Jewish identity by posting his name in Hebrew and in the color of the Israeli flag on his 2010 campaign website.[93] Others have even questioned his loyalty to the United States. One critic argued, "Kirk is a pure Israel-firster. . . . [H]e brings home the bacon for Israel big time. Its wish is his command . . . Kirk is just pro-AIPAC and shaking the trees for all the campaign money he can get by his hate rhetoric about Arabs."[94] In an unsuccessful example of outreach, Representative Cohen attempted to join the Congressional Black Caucus after his election from a majority-minority district but was denied.[95] Similarly, Representative Beto O'Rourke (D-TX), whose district is El Paso, was denied entry into the Congressional Hispanic Caucus.[96]

Ethnic lobbying campaigns can come out of nowhere. As a staffer in the office of House Republican Conference Chairman J.C. Watts of Oklahoma, this author experienced our phones being overwhelmed one day in 2001 after talk show host Tavis Smiley urged his listeners to inundate the only black member of the House GOP leadership regarding a rumored threat to Historically Black Colleges and Universities (HBCUs). The genesis of this was unclear as Watts was a strong supporter of HBCUs and would become a paid lobbyist for multiple HBCUs after leaving Congress and would nonetheless give an immediate post-retirement announcement interview to Smiley.[97] While Watts's staff disputed the specifics and resented the bad day, the callers unquestionably made their point.

Watts offers a case study in the potential hold of an ethnic lobby. Elected as a conventional conservative in the GOP wave of 1994, he did not join the CBC or support much of its platform. In his early years, he disavowed highlighting his ethnicity, saying, "I didn't come to Congress to be a black leader or a white leader, but a leader."[98] His communication skills and telegenic presence made him a party favorite, resulting in receiving a primetime speaking slot at the 1996 National Convention, the State of the Union response in 1997, and being elected the head of the House GOP Conference in 1998, the party's number-four leadership position. But despite exchanging occasionally harsh public comments with CBC members, he ended up accepting their key views.[99] He supported affirmative action and still regularly criticizes Republicans for poor outreach.[100] He had warm relations with Representative Charles B. Rangel (D-NY) and Reverend Jesse Jackson, telling Rangel of his retirement plans before he went public (which Rangel promptly reported to the Democratic Congressional Campaign Committee). Watts would occasionally express bitterness at expectations placed upon him by the lobby, but he found it difficult to resist.[101]

Conclusion

The 2006 elections gave Democrats control of all of Congress and their promise to create "the most open and most ethical Congress in history" and to end the Republican "culture of corruption," in the words of Nancy Pelosi, was at the forefront.[102] Super-lobbyist Jack Abramoff's illegal influence-peddling and close relations with key Republican leaders led to widespread condemnation, the resignation of former House Majority

Leader Tom Delay (R-TX) and gave Democrats an opening. Ironically, a betrayed ethnic lobby, Native American tribes, helped unravel the Abramoff scandal alleging that his team had failed to represent them despite charging exorbitant fees.[103] Upon taking office, the new majority passed seemingly dramatic lobbying reforms in 2007, but the result has led to unintended consequences. Reforms could not alter the nature of the influence industry. The initial added scrutiny led to some cosmetic changes mentioned above, but business as usual has mostly returned.

Although the reforms were intended to stop the "revolving door" of public office to private gain, one investigation found that slightly more former members of Congress have gone into lobbying after leaving office than in the several years before.[104] Recent lobbying disclosure statements put the total number of lobbyists at almost 10,500, almost identical to the 1998 total of 10,405.[105] While total spending on lobbying doubled between 1998 and 2008, it has held roughly steady since, now at about $1.6 billion.[106] Former Senate Majority Leader Thomas A. "Tom" Daschle is well known for not having to register as a lobbyist because his activities fall below the minimum 20 percent of work activity required for registration, but his name brings access and influence.[107] Some critics argue that this and the disclosure requirements are so loose and barely policed so as to be worthless.[108] Reform efforts are regularly proposed but rarely advanced. Then freshman Representative Rod Blum (R-IA) introduced a lifetime ban on lobbying for members of Congress, following a similar effort by Senators Michael F. Bennet (D-CO) and Jon Tester (D-MT).[109] Passage of such a bill must be considered extremely unlikely and possibly constitutionally suspect.

Ethnicity is thicker than ideology, but it can also reinforce ideology. Lobbies that can successfully leverage these two elements have an added strength. The direct line between influence, issue mobilization, and the policy process remains contingent and varied, based on issue specifics. Presidential preemption, however, can still upend the strength of even longstanding lobbies. Ethnic lobbies thrive on access and generally succeed in getting an audience with a member of Congress. They do even better when a former member champions their cause. Policy success is not guaranteed, but access and the perception of influence are often enough to maintain some staying power. Win, lose, or draw, ethnic lobbies will return to reengage their issues. An ethnic lobby's work never ends.

Notes

1. David R. Mayhew, *Congress: The Electoral Connection*, 2nd ed. (New Haven, CT: Yale University Press, 2004).

2. While the Senate has caucuses, this is predominately a House phenomenon, as there are more caucuses than House members. Most members of the House of Representatives are in multiple caucuses. The National Guard Caucus, for example, boasts at least 185 House members. See http://palazzo.house.gov/ngrcc/membership.htm. As of August 2016, there were eighty-seven pages worth of caucuses, officially known as Congress Congressional Member Organizations (CMOs). See https://cha.house.gov/sites/republicans.cha.house.gov/files/documents/114CMOList%288.31.16%29.pdf

3. Eric Tucker, "Justice Dept. Criticized over Foreign Lobbying Enforcement," Associated Press, September 7, 2016, accessed at http://hosted.ap.org/dynamic/stories/U/us_foreign_lobbying?site=ap&section=home&template=default

4. Steven V. Roberts, "Hispanic Caucus Is Flexing Its Muscle," *New York Times*, October 10, 1983.

5. Eric Uslaner, "Cracks in the Armor? Interest Groups and Foreign Policy" in *Interest Group Politics*, 6th ed., eds. Allan J. Cigler and Burdett A. Loomis (Washington, DC: CQ Press, 2002), 356.

6. Dana Milbank, "How Paul Ryan Can Kick-Start Fixing Congress," *Washington Post*, November 6, 2015, accessed at https://www.washingtonpost.com/opinions/how-paul-ryan-can-kick-start-fixing-congress/2015/11/06/085e8554-8486-11e5-8ba6-cec48b74b2a7_story.html?utm_term=.ffa44febbb3f

7. https://ethics.house.gov/gifts/gift-exceptions-0/educational-events. "Educational events" with at least twenty-five attendees is permitted. This characterizes every lunch and reception.

8. Eric Lipton, Brooke Williams, and Nicholas Confessore, "Foreign Powers Buy Influence at Think Tanks," *New York Times*, September 6, 2014.

9. Andrew Perez, "Top Washington Lobbyist Slow to Disclose Relationship with Saudi Arabia," maplight.org/content/top-Washington-lobbyist-slow-to-disclose, June 6, 2016.

10. Adams and Fridman are both friendly former colleagues. Andrew Perez, "Top Washington Lobbyist Slow to Disclose Relationship with Saudi Arabia," maplight.org/content/top-Washington-lobbyist-slow-to-disclose, June 6, 2016.

11. John W. Huey Jr., "Power Lobbying," *Fortune*, December 8, 1997, accessed at http://archive.fortune.com/magazines/fortune/fortune_archive/1997/12/08/234897/index.htm, places AIPAC as the second most powerful lobby behind AARP. Richard E. Cohen and Peter Bell, "Congressional Insiders Poll," *National Journal*, March 5, 2005.

12. Peter Overby, "After Iran Deal Defeat, How Do Pro-Israel Lobbyists Regain Clout?" NPR.org, September 17, 2015.

13. Connie Bruck, "Friends of Israel, The lobbying group AIPAC Has Consistently Fought the Obama Administration on Policy. Is It Now Losing Influence?" *The New Yorker*, September 1, 2014.

14. Herb Keinon, "81 Congressmen to Visit Israel in Coming Weeks," *Jerusalem Post*, August 8, 2011, accessed: www.jpost.com/.../81-congressmen-to-visit-Israel-in-coming-weeks

15. Adam Kredo, "Israel's Ambassador: Move the U.S. Embassy to Jerusalem," *Washington Free Beacon*, June 5, 2014.

16. Karoun Demirjian and Carol Morello, "How AIPAC Lost the Iran Deal Fight," *Washington Post*, September 3, 2015.

17. Ibid.

18. Seth Mandel, "How AIPAC is Betraying Israel," *NY Post*, July 11, 2016.

19. Peter Overby, "AIPAC Walks Bipartisan Line While Israeli Politics Moves Sharply Right," NPR.org, September 17, 2015.

20. Demirjian and Morello, "How AIPAC Lost the Iran Deal Fight."

21. William M. Leo Grande, "The Cuba Lobby," *Foreign Policy*, April 12, 2013, accessed at foreignpolicy.com/2013/04/12/the-Cuba-lobby

22. Anna Kalinina, "Cuba and Congress: Who Will Change First?" *Foreign Policy in Focus*, August 9, 2010.

23. David Lauter and Mark Z. Barabak, "Obama's Cuba decision follows change in attitudes in Florida," *LA Times*, December 17, 2014.

24. Noah Feldman, "Obama takes on the Cuba lobby," *Chicago Tribune*, December 17, 2014.

25. Anthony Man and William E. Gibson, "Obama's Cuba policy doesn't mean Congress will change laws," *Orlando Sun Sentinel*, Dec 17, 2014. Notably, Representative Debbie Wasserman Schultz (D-FL), then chair of the Democratic National Committee, did not endorse the president's initiative.

26. Gabriel Debenedetti, "Who Will Help Greece? Not the Congressional Greek Caucus!" *New Republic*, July 26, 2011, accessed at https://newrepublic.com/article/92509/congress-greek-debt-crisis-hellenic-caucus

27. "American Hellenic Institute President Nick Larigakis: Congress should back ally Greece on 'Macedonia' name issue," Press Release, 2001.

28. Ileana Ros-Lehtinen, "What's In a Name; Macedonia's Unresolved Title Has Been an Obstacle to Balkan Stability," Hellenic Communication Service, July 27, 2006.

29. Gabriel Debenedetti, "Who Will Help Greece? Not the Congressional Greek Caucus!" *New Republic*, July 26, 2011, accessed at https://newrepublic.com/article/92509/congress-greek-debt-crisis-hellenic-caucus

30. "What Do the U.S. Midterm Elections Mean for Macedonia?" United Macedonian Diaspora, November 9, 2010.

31. H. Res. 639, "Expressing the Sense of the House of Representatives That the Former Yugoslav Republic of Macedonia Should Work Within the Framework of the United Nations Process with Greece to Achieve Longstanding United States and United Nations Policy Goals of Finding a Mutually Acceptable Composite Name, With a Geographical Qualifier and for All Uses for the Former Yugoslav Republic Of Macedonia," April 27, 2012, accessed at https://www.congress.gov/bill/112th-congress/house-resolution/639/cosponsors

32. Debenedetti, "Who Will Help Greece? Not the Congressional Greek Caucus!"

33. David Paul and Rachel Anderson Paul, *Ethnic Lobbies and U.S. Foreign Policy* (Boulder, CO: Lynne Rienner Publishers, 2009), 28.

34. Original study still accessible at mearsheimer.uchicago.edu/pdfs/Israel-Lobby.pdf

35. Michael Crowley, "Final Resolution; K Street Cashes In on the 1915 Armenian Genocide," *New Republic*, July 23, 2007.

36. "U.S. House Foreign Affairs Committee Passes Armenian Genocide Resolution," Pan Armenian Network, October 11, 2007, accessed at www.panarmenian.net/eng/world/news/23562

37. Quoted in Crowley, "Final Resolution; K Street Cashes In on the 1915 Armenian Genocide."

38. Glenn Kessler, "White House and Turkey Fight Bill on Armenia," *Washington Post*, October 10, 2007.

39. Jackie Kucinich, "Democrats torn over Turkey resolution," *The Hill*, October 17, 2007.

40. Crowley, "Final Resolution; K Street Cashes In on the 1915 Armenian genocide."

41. Ibid.

42. Ibid.

43. Ibid.

44. Nicole Gaouette and Laura Litvan, "Clinton Said to Plan Removing MEK from Terrorism List," *Bloomberg News*, September 21, 2012.

45. Scott Peterson, "Iranian group's big-money push to get off U.S. terrorist list," www.csmonitor.com, August 8, 2011.

46. Elizabeth Rubin, "An Iranian Cult and Its American Friends," *New York Times*, August 13, 2011, accessed at http://www.nytimes.com/2011/08/14/opinion/sunday/an-iranian-cult-and-its-american-friends.html

47. Peterson, "Iranian group's big-money push to get off U.S. terrorist list."

48. "Camp Liberty Cleared of Final Residents As 280 Are Flown to Albania," BriefingWire.com, September 10, 2016, http://www.briefingwire.com/pr/camp-liberty-cleared-of-final-residents-as-280-are-flown-to-albania

49. John Lancaster, "Activism Boosts India's Fortunes: Politically Vocal Immigrants Help tilt Policy in Washington," *Washington Post*, October 9, 1999, 1.

50. Mike McIntire, "Nuclear deal hones Indian-Americans' lobbying skills," *New York Times*, June 5, 2006.

51. Mira Kamdar, "Forget the Israel Lobby. The Hill's Next Big Player Is Made in India," *Washington Post*, September 30, 2007.

52. Sanjay Puri quoted in Kamdar, "Forget the Israel Lobby. The Hill's Next Big Player Is Made in India."

53. Tomás Valásek and Kathryn R. Schultz, "Hidden Costs of NATO Expansion; Expansion of the NATO military alliance is proceeding rapidly despite an overwhelming lack of public or congressional debate," *Foreign Policy in Focus*, May 1, 1997.

54. John F. Harris, "Open Mike Catches Canadian Leader's Cynicism about Clinton," *Seattle Times*, July 10, 1997, A24.

55. Kenneth R. Timmerman, "Dana Rohrabacher's Troubling Friends," FrontPageMagazine.com, January 26, 2004; Nicholas Fandos, "He's a Member of Congress. The Kremlin Likes Him So Much It Gave Him a Code Name," *New York Times*, November 21, 2017.

56. Charles R. Babcock, "Pakistan Lobbyist's Memo Alleges Shakedown by House Probe Leader," *Washington Post*, March 19, 1997, A1.

57. Chris Frates, "Pakistan's Man in Washington," *Politico*, May 6, 2011.

58. James Bamford, "It's Time for Obama to Send Home This Mass-Murdering Cuban Terrorist-in-Exile to Face His Punishment," *Foreign Policy*, July 7, 2016.

59. Scott Shane, "For Peter King, Lawmaker Examining Terror, a Pro-I.R.A. Past," *New York Times*, March 8, 2011.

60. "DioGuardi and Cloyes Meet the Congresswoman Ileana Ros-Lehtinen," gazetadielli.com, January 31, 2016.

61. "White House Lashes Out at Congress after 9/11 Bill Vote," Associated Press, September 29, 2016.

62. Taylor Luck, "To Counter Iranian Rival, Saudi Arabia Steps up Washington Lobbying," www.csmonitor.com, February 8, 2016.

63. Ibid.

64. Colby Itkowitz, "Which foreign countries spent the most to influence U.S. politics?" *Washington Post*, May 14, 2014.

65. Jim Ross, "Syria Poses No Threat to U.S., Rahall says," (Huntington, WV) *Herald Dispatch*, April 24, 2003.

66. Chuck Neubauer, "A Sibling Symbiosis in the Capitol," *LA Times*, June 17, 2004.

67. Catherine Ho, "Former Democratic Rep. Nick Rahall of West Virginia joins lobby shop Cassidy," *Washington Post*, March 7, 2016.

68. Brendan Bordelon, "Devin Nunes's One-Man War on the Pentagon," *National Review*, July 31, 2015.

69. Ibid.

70. Manuel Roig-Franzia, "Luis Gutierrez, Fierce Fighter for Immigration Reform," *Washington Post*, October 20, 2013.

71. Ibid.

72. Josh Stewart, "Dark Money Group's Spending Tops $714,000 against Puerto Rico Debt Relief Bill," SunlightFoundation.com, May 31, 2016.

73. "Vieques Voters Go to Polls Over Fate of Bombing Range," Tribune News Services, July 29, 2001.

74. Mike Williams, "Showdown Looms Over Bombing at Vieques," Cox News Service, May 2, 2000.

75. Ibid.

76. Ivan Roman, "Rossello Wins Praise with Vieques Stand," *Orlando Sentinel*, October 25, 1999.

77. Mike Allen and Sue Anne Pressley, "Puerto Rico Bombing to End in 2003; Navy to Seek New Site for Training Exercises," *Washington Post*, June 14, 2001, A1.

78. Senator James Inhofe, "Inhofe Calls on Congress to Look Into Reopening Military Base on Vieques," Press Release, April 12, 2016.

79. Tom Gorman, "Former Rep. Kim, Convicted in 1997, May Run Again," *LA Times*, December 4, 1999.

80. "Korean Newspaper Ad Urges Readers to Aid Kim," *LA Times*, May 16, 1998.

81. Ibid.

82. Ibid.

83. https://cbc-butterfield.house.gov

84. Adam Clymer, "The New Congress; Democrats Promise Quick Action on a Clinton Plan," *New York Times*, November 5, 1992. Redistricting of a decade later would add another Cuban Florida Republican, his brother.

85. Delia Grigg and Jonathan N. Katz, "The Impact of Majority-Minority Districts on Congressional Elections." Paper presentation, Midwest Political Science Association, Chicago, April 7–10, 2005. Ninety percent of minority members of Congress were from majority-minority districts in both years.

86. "India Bids Farewell to Friendly Congressman Gary Ackerman," India America Today News Service, July 21, 2012.

87. Jay Nordlinger, "Albania Votes," *National Review*, August 8, 2005, http://www.nationalreview.com/article/351965/albania-votes-jay-nordlinger

88. Sewell Chan, "Driving Down Congressman Engel Boulevard, in Kosovo," *New York Times*, May 2, 2008.

89. Ibid.

90. Michael Kranish, "Search for Kerry's Roots Finds Surprising History," *Boston Globe*, February 2, 2003.

91. Quoted in Richard H. Curtiss, "Senate Call for Packwood Expulsion Ended Protection of Israel Lobby," *Washington Report on Middle East Affairs* (Oct./Nov., 1995), 21, 101–102. Accessed at http://www.wrmea.org/1995-october-november/senate-call-for-packwood-expulsion-ended-protection-of-israel-lobby.html

92. Ibid.

93. Janet McMahon, "Pro-Israel PACs Already Working to Re-elect Sen. Mark Kirk (R-IL) in 2016," *Washington Report on Middle East Affairs* (May, 2015): 27–28. Accessed at http://www.wrmea.org/2015-may/election-watch-pro-israel-pacs-already-working-to-re-elect-sen.-mark-kirk-r-il-in-2016.html

94. M.J. Rosenberg, "Mark Kirk Is AIPAC's Million Dollar Baby," huffingtonpost.com, May 25, 2011.

95. Josephine Hearn, "Black Caucus: Whites Not Allowed," *Politico*, January 22, 2007.

96. Julián Aguilar, "El Paso Congressman Ineligible to Join Hispanic Caucus," *Texas Tribune*, July 24, 2013, https://www.texastribune.org/2013/07/24/city-el-paso-lacks-voice

97. J.C. Watts Companies, "Watts Consulting Group: Past and Current Clients," http://www.wattsconsultinggroup.com/aboutus/clients.htm; "J.C. Watts Speaks about His Decision to Retire from Congress in Interview with NPR's Tavis Smiley," NPR.org, July 2, 2002, www.npr.org/about/press/020702.watts.html

98. Sam Fulwood III, "Republicans Cast Watts as Leader, Healer," *LA Times*, February 22, 1999.

99. Watts referred to unnamed civil rights leaders as "race-hustling poverty pimps" but later apologized to Jesse Jackson. Quoted in Katharine Q. Seelye, "G.O.P., After Fumbling in '96, Turns to Orator for Response," *New York Times*, February 5, 1997. Watts himself was subject to racial criticism from all sides as he notes in his first book, with Chriss Winston, *What Color is a Conservative? My Life and My Politics* (New York: HarperCollins, 2002).

100. Carroll J. Doherty, "GOP Initiatives Hamper Efforts to Reach Out to Minority Groups," *CQ*, March 22, 1998. Goldwater Conservative Diary, "Why J.C. Watts is supporting Rand Paul's presidential bid," Red State, April 7, 2015, http://www.redstate.com/diary/freedomrepublican/2015/04/07/j-c-watts-supporting-rand-pauls-presidential-bid

101. See *What Color is a Conservative? My Life and My Politics* throughout for Watts demanding that his views be respected. Author's interpretation for "difficult to resist."

102. William Branigin, "Democrats Take Majority in House; Pelosi Poised to Become Speaker," *Washington Post*, November 8, 2006. This was based on a strategy to highlight GOP ethics shortcomings. See John Byrne, "Leaked Memo Indicates Democrats Will Focus on Abramoff as Keystone of 2006 Efforts to Retake Congress," *The Raw Story*, January 9, 2006, http://rawstory.com/news/2005/Leaked_memo_indicates_Democrats_will_focus_0109.html

103. Jennifer Hoar, "Indian Tribe Sues Abramoff, Reed," Associated Press, July 13, 2006, http://www.cbsnews.com/news/indian-tribe-sues-abramoff-reed

104. Isaac Arnsdorf, "The Lobbying Reform That Enriched Congress," *Politico*, July 3, 2016.

105. http://www.opensecrets.org/lobby

106. Ibid.

107. Arnsdorf, "The lobbying reform that enriched Congress."

108. Joe Schoffstall, "Clinton Bundler Faced No Punishment for Failing to Register Foreign Government Work," *Washington Free Beacon*, September 16, 2016.

109. "Rep. Rod Blum Introduces Lifetime Ban on Lobbying for Members of Congress," Press Release, April 14, 2015.

Appendix A

Vietnam/Vietnamese American-Relevant Legislation
That Came to a Floor Vote, 97th–113th Congresses

Congress	Bill	Title	Author	Party	State	District	Yea	Nay	Position on VN	Outcome
97	S2222	Immigration Reform and Control Act of 1982	Rep. Simpson	R	WY		80	19	Neutral	Referred
99	HR1555	International Security and Development Cooperation Act of 1985	Rep. Fascell	D	FL	19	247	177	Neutral	Other
99	S960	International Security and Development Cooperation Act of 1985	Sen. Lugar	R	IN		262	161	Neutral	Became
100	HR3100	International Security and Development Cooperation Act of 1987	Rep. Fascell	D	FL	19	286	122	*Unfavorable*	Other
100	HRes231	A resolution expressing the sense of the House of Representatives regarding the upcoming negotiations between General John Vessey and the Vietnamese to resolve the problem of Americans missing in Southeast Asia and other issues of humanitarian concern to the people of the United States and Vietnam	Rep. Ridge	R	PA	21	418	0	Neutral	Voted, agreed

100	SRes255	A resolution expressing the sense of the Congress with regard to the forthcoming negotiations by General John Vessey to resolve the fate of Americans missing in Southeast Asia, and other issues of humanitarian concern to the people of the United States and Vietnam	Sen. McCain	R	AZ		92	0	Neutral	Voted, agreed
101	HR2022	To establish certain categories of nationals of the Soviet Union and nationals of Indochina presumed to be subject to persecution and to provide for adjustment to refugee status of certain Soviet and Indochinese parolees	Rep. Morrison	D	CT	3	358	44	Neutral	Referred
101	HR2655	International Cooperation Act of 1989	Fascell	D	FL	19	314	101	Neutral	Referred
101	HConRes 254	Expressing the sense of Congress concerning negotiations for a political settlement in Cambodia	Rep. Solarz	D	NY	13	413	0	Neutral	Referred
102	HR2508	International Cooperation Act of 1991	Rep. Fascell	D	FL	19	159	262	Neutral	Other
102	S2532	FREEDOM Support Act	Sen. Pell	D	RI		232	164	*Unfavorable*	Became public law
103	Amendment 1263 to S.1281	Urging the President to lift the trade embargo on Vietnam expeditiously	Sen. Kerry	D	MA		62	38	Favorable	Voted, agreed

Congress	Bill	Title	Author	Party	State	District	Yea	Nay	Position on VN	Outcome
103	Amendment 1266 to S.1281	Requiring the President to report to Congress prior to lifting the trade embargo on Vietnam	Rep. Smith	R	NH		42	58	Unfavorable	Voted, failed
105	HR1757	Foreign Affairs Reform and Restructuring Act of 1998	Rep. Gilman	R	NY	20	51	49	Neutral	Other
105	S903	Foreign Affairs Reform and Restructuring Act of 1997	Sen. Helms	R	NC		90	5	Favorable	Calendared
105	Amendment S.3276 (Kerry) to S.2260	Motion to table	Sen. Gregg	R	NH		34	66	Unfavorable	Voted, failed
105	HJRes120	Disapproving the extension of the waiver authority contained in section 402(c) of the Trade Act of 1974 with respect to Vietnam	Rep. Rohrabacher	R	CA	45	163	260	Unfavorable	Tabled
106	HR2415	Bankruptcy Reform Act of 2000	Rep. Smith	R	NJ	4			Neutral	Other
106	HJRes58	Disapproving the extension of the waiver authority contained in section 402(c) of the Trade Act of 1974 with respect to Vietnam	Rep. Rohrabacher	R	CA	45	130	297	Unfavorable	Tabled
106	HJRes99	Disapproving the extension of the waiver authority contained in section 402(c) of the Trade Act of 1974 with respect to Vietnam	Rep. Rohrabacher	R	CA	45	91	332	Unfavorable	Tabled

106	HConRes295	Relating to continuing human rights violations and political oppression in the Socialist Republic of Vietnam 25 years after the fall of South Vietnam to Communist forces	Rep. Rohrabacher	R	CA	45	415	3	Unfavorable	Referred
106	HR4811	Kentucky National Forest Land Transfer Act of 2000	Rep. Callahan	R	AL	1	65	27	Neutral	Became public law
107	HJRes101	Disapproving the extension of the waiver authority contained in section 402(c) of the Trade Act of 1974 with respect to Vietnam	Rep. Rohrabacher	R	CA	45	91	338	Unfavorable	Tabled
107	HJRes51	Approving the extension of nondiscriminatory treatment with respect to the products of the Socialist Republic of Vietnam	Rep. Armey	R	TX	26	88	12	Favorable	Became public law
107	HR2833	Viet Nam Human Rights Act	Rep. Smith	R	NJ	4	410	1	Unfavorable	Calendared in the Senate
107	HJRes55	Disapproving the extension of the waiver authority contained in section 402(c) of the Trade Act of 1974 with respect to Vietnam	Rep. Rohrabacher	R	CA	45	91	324	Unfavorable	Tabled
108	HR1587	Vietnam Human Rights Act of 2004	Rep. Smith	R	NJ	4	323	45	Unfavorable	Referred

Congress	Bill	Title	Author	Party	State	District	Yea	Nay	Position on VN	Outcome
108	HRes427	Expressing the sense of the House of Representatives regarding the courageous leadership of the Unified Buddhist Church of Vietnam and the urgent need for religious freedom and related human rights in the Socialist Republic of Vietnam	Rep. Sanchez	D	CA	47	409	13	Unfavorable	Tabled, agreed
108	HConRes378	Calling on the Government of the Socialist Republic of Vietnam to immediately and unconditionally release Father Thaddeus Nguyen Van Ly, and for other purposes	Rep. Smith	R	NJ	4	424	1	Unfavorable	Referred
109	HConRes320	Calling on the Government of the Socialist Republic of Vietnam to immediately and unconditionally release Dr. Pham Hong Son and other political prisoners and prisoners of conscience, and other purposes	Rep. Smith	R	NJ	4	425	1	Unfavorable	Referred
109	HRes228	Honoring the contributions of Vietnamese Americans to American society over the past three decades	Rep. Davis	R	VA	11	416	0	Neutral	Other, agreed
109	HR5602	To authorize the extension of nondiscriminatory treatment (normal trade relations treatment) to the products of Vietnam	Rep. Ramstad	R	MN	3	228	161	Favorable	Other, failed to meet 2/3 rule

109	HR6406	To modify temporarily certain rates of duty and make other technical amendments to the trade laws, to extend certain trade preference programs, and for other purposes	Rep. Thomas	R	CA	22	212	184	Favorable	Other, appended to other amendments and became law
110	HR3096	Vietnam Human Rights Act of 2007	Rep. Smith	R	NJ	4	414	3	Unfavorable	Referred
110	HRes243	Calling on the Government of the Socialist Republic of Vietnam to immediately and unconditionally release Father Nguyen Van Ly, Nguyen Van Dai, Le Thi Cong Nhan, Le Quoc Quan, and other political prisoners and prisoners of conscience, and for other purposes	Rep. Smith	R	NJ	4	404	0	Unfavorable	Other
113	HR1897	Vietnam Human Rights Act of 2013	Rep. Smith	R	NJ	4	405	3	Unfavorable	Referred
113	S744	Border Security, Economic Opportunity, and Immigration Modernization Act	Sen. Schumer	D	NY		68	32	Neutral	Hearings held

Notes: Shading represents those selected for regression analysis. Excludes authorization and appropriations bills. "Position on Vietnam" determined by inclusion of language in the bill deemed to be favorable, neutral, or unfavorable to the government of Vietnam.

Appendix B

The Influence of Vietnamese-American Constituencies on Contested Floor Votes on Vietnam-Related Measures, 103rd–109th Congresses

	Measures Favorable to Vietnam				Measures Unfavorable to Vietnam							
	103rd S.1263 (a)	107th HJRes51	109th HR5602	109th HR6406	103rd S.1266 (a)	105th S.2260 (a) Gregg Motions to table S.3276 (Kerry)	105th HJRes120	106th HJRes58	106th HJRes99	107th HJRes101	107th HJRes55	108th HR1587
	Kerry	Armey	Ramstad	Thomas	R. Smith		Rohra-bacher	Rohra-bacher	Rohra-bacher	Rohra-bacher	Rohra-bacher	C. Smith
Floor vote	62–38	88–12	228–161	212–184	42–58	34–66	163–260	130–297	91–332	91–338	91–324	323–345
% Vietnamese in constituency	371.32 *	337.72	-5.05	-6.51	-448.91 *	-150.86	39.97 *	29.69 **	29.95 **	38.60 ***	43.98 ***	31.58
Ideology (DW-NOMINATE 1)	-2.29 ***	-4.38 *	0.60 *	0.41 ^	3.46 ***	4.13 ***	2.26 ***	1.78 ***	1.65 ***	1.24 ***	1.30 ***	0.49
White	1.13	3.99 *	1.10 ***	0.33	-1.29	-3.47 ***	-0.22	-0.52	-0.47	0.12	-0.94 *	-0.57
Military service	0.67	0.27	-0.46 ^	-0.51 *	-0.51	-1.47 **	0.26	0.18	0.05	0.29	0.39	-0.34
Foreign affairs committee	0.17	0.26	-0.15	0.03	-0.97	0.33	-0.14	0.22	0.19	0.97 **	0.93 **	0.09
Electoral margin	2.80 *	0.27	-0.38	-0.19	-2.82 *	-2.95	-0.30	-0.10	-0.57	0.39	-0.09	0.43
Constant	-2.22	-4.47	-0.35	0.03	2.80	3.62 *	-0.67 *	-0.81 *	-1.12 *	-3.07 ***	-1.10 **	2.19 ***
Wald chi2 (df = 6)	19.80	14.99	31.21	10.52	25.89	36.84	66.46	45.45	36.06	35.08	29.84	6.05
N	100	100	389	396	100	100	423	427	423	429	415	368

(a) Amendments
^ p < .10, * p < .05, ** p < .01, *** p < .001

Sources:
Roll call votes (dependent variables): Taken from 103rd, 105th, 106th, 107th, 108th, and 109th Roll Call Data (http://www.voteview.com/dwnl.htm)
% Vietnamese (Census and American Community Survey data for appropriate Congress): Minnesota Population Center. National Historical Geographic Information System: Version 11.0 [Database]. Minneapolis: University of Minnesota. 2016. http://doi.org/10.18128/D050.V11.0)
Party and ideology: Taken from 103rd, 105th, 106th, 107th, 108th, and 109th Roll Call Data and DW-NOMINATE Scores for 1–113th Congresses datafiles (http://www.voteview.com/dwnl.htm)
White: Coded by author using Biographical Directory of the United States Congress (http://bioguide.congress.gov/biosearch/biosearch.asp) and cross-checked by Vital Statistics on Congress (https://www.brookings.edu/research/vital-statistics-on-congressdata-on-the-u-s-congress-a-joint-effort-from-b
Military service: 103rd: Inter-university Consortium for Political and Social Research, and Carroll McKibbin. Roster of United States Congressional Officeholders and Biographical Characteristics of Members of the United States Congress, 1789–1996: Merged Data. ICPSR07803-v10. Ann Arbor, MI: Inter-u
Foreign affairs committee: Charles Stewart III and Jonathan Woon. Congressional Committee Assignments, 103rd to 114th Congresses, 19932017: [House, Senate] [August 19, 2016, July 28, 2016]. (http://web.mit.edu/17.251/www/data_page.html)
Electoral margin: 1998 and 2002: Derived from uselectionatlas.org: 1986–90; 1992, 1996, 2000, 2004, 2006 derived from official results (http://www.fec.gov/pubrec/electionresults.shtml)

Contributors

Kirk J. Beattie is Professor of Political Science at Simmons College. He has taught at Harvard, Wellesley, the Fletcher School of Law and Diplomacy, and the University of Michigan. He is a recipient of numerous national scholarships, including a Fulbright grant, a Fulbright-Hays grant, an International Rotary Foundation Fellowship, an American Research Center in Egypt grant, and a Center for Arabic Study Abroad fellowship. He is the author of *Congress and the Shaping of the Middle East, Egypt During the Sadat Years* and *Egypt During the Nasser Years*.

Colton C. Campbell is Professor of National Security Strategy at the National War College (NWC). He has worked in the offices of Senate Democratic Leader Harry Reid (D-NV), Senator Bob Graham (D-FL), and Representative Mike Thompson (D-CA). Prior to joining the NWC, he was an analyst in American national government at the Congressional Research Service and an Associate Professor of Political Science at Florida International University. He has authored or edited several books on Congress, most recently *Congress and Civil-Military Relations* and *Congress and the Politics of National Security*.

Christian Collet is Senior Associate Professor at International Christian University. Prior to joining International Christian University, he worked as an opinion research consultant and held appointments at Viet Nam National University under the U.S. Fulbright Program and at Doshisha University in Kyoto. He spent the 2012–2013 academic year at the Walter H. Shorenstein Asia Pacific Research Center at Stanford University. His work has appeared in *The Journal of Politics, Public Opinion Quarterly, Perspectives on Politics, Japanese Journal of Political Science, Social Science Japan Journal, PS, Amerasia Journal and Race/Ethnicity: Multidisciplinary Global Contexts* and several edited volumes. He is the co-editor of *The*

Transnational Politics of Asian Americans and is currently engaged in projects concerning the role of nationalism on the political incorporation of Vietnamese Americans, the dynamics of public opinion in Sino-Japanese relations, and the impact of sports on nationalism.

Chuck Cushman is Dean of Academics at the College of International Security Affairs, National Defense University. Previously he was a senior fellow at Georgetown University's Government Affairs Institute. Before that he spent a decade at the Graduate School of Political Management at George Washington University, where he taught courses on political history, politics and public policy, national security policymaking, and Congress's role in defense policy. Prior to that, he was the defense and foreign affairs legislative assistant to Representative David Price (D-NC). He is a graduate of the United States Military Academy and served nine years in the U.S. Army as an armor officer. He is the author of *An Introduction to the US Congress* and a forthcoming book on Congress and national security policymaking.

William Danvers is the Special Representative for International Affairs at the World Bank. Prior to this, he was a Senior Fellow at the Center for American Progress (CAP), where he worked on a range of national security issues. Before joining CAP, he served as Deputy Secretary-General of the Organisation for Economic Co-operation and Development, served as Director of Congressional Affairs at the CIA for then DCIA Leon Panetta, and worked for Secretary of State John Kerry as his Deputy Chief of Staff. In the Clinton administration, he worked for Ambassador Strobe Talbott on post-Soviet relations with Russia at the Department of State. He has served as special assistant to the president for national security affairs and as senior director for legislative affairs at the National Security Council. He has several years of experience working in the House of Representatives as a foreign policy aide and press secretary, as a legislative aide for Senator Joe Lieberman (D-CT), and as staff director of the Senate Foreign Relations Committee.

David A. Dulio is Professor of Political Science and Director of the Center for Civic Engagement at Oakland University. Dulio teaches courses on campaigns and elections, Congress, political parties, interest groups, and other areas of American politics. He has published ten books, including *Campaigns from the Ground Up*, *Diversity in Contemporary American Politics and Government*, and *Michigan Government, Politics and Policy*. He has written dozens of articles and book chapters on subjects ranging from the role of professional consultants in U.S. elections to campaign finance. He is also a former American Political Science Congressional Fellow on Capitol Hill where he worked in the U.S. House of Representatives Republican Conference for Representative J.C. Watts, Jr. (R-OK).

William Curtis Ellis is Chair and Associate Professor of History, Humanities, and Government at Oral Roberts University (ORU). Prior to joining Oral Roberts University, he was Assistant Professor at Auburn University at Montgomery, a staff aide in the Virginia General Assembly and the Virginia Lt. Governor's Office, and an American Political Science Association Congressional Fellow where he worked on the House Committee on Education and Labor. His research focuses on Congress exploring the impact of race and ethnicity on the congressional agenda, the relationship between institutions and agenda control, as well as the ever-changing face of campaign financing in congressional elections. His scholarship has been published in outlets such as *Polity* and *Social Science Quarterly*, as well as in contributions to the 2012 and 2014 editions of *The Roads to Congress* book series.

Patrick Griffin is Adjunct Professorial Lecturer in the Department of Government at American University. He served in the White House as assistant to the president for legislative affairs, 1994–1996. In addition to his service in the Clinton administration, his private sector experience includes founding the Washington, DC, government relations firm, Griffin, Johnson, Madigan, Peck, Boland, Dover & Stewart, where he continues to serve as president. Griffin also was senior vice president and managing director for the government relations division of Burson-Marsteller. In the U.S. Senate he held the position of Secretary for the Democrats, and the positions of professional staff member on the Senate Democratic Policy Committee and the Senate Budget Committee. He also served as a domestic policy advisor at the U.S. Department of Health, Education, and Welfare and as an assistant professor of education at the University of Wisconsin-Milwaukee.

Patrick J. Haney is Professor of Political Science and Associate Dean in the College of Arts and Science at Miami University. He has published several books, including *U.S. Foreign Policy: Back to the Water's Edge*, *The Cuban Embargo: The Domestic Politics of an American Foreign Policy*, and *Organizing for Foreign Policy Crises: Presidents, Advisers, and the Management of Decision-Making*. He also has published numerous articles and chapters on U.S. Foreign Policy, Cuban Americans, and domestic politics.

He is on the editorial board of *Foreign Policy Analysis, International Studies Perspectives,* and the *Oxford Encyclopedia of Foreign Policy Analysis.*

Khalil Mousa Marrar is Assistant Professor of Political Science at Governors State University where he teaches courses in history, religion, and political science at various institutions. While specializing in the Israeli-Palestinian conflict, his research interests include international relations, American culture, foreign policy, political organizations, and terrorism. He has served in editorial positions at the Arab Studies Quarterly and the Association of Arab-American University Graduates. He is the author of *The Arab Lobby and US Foreign Policy: The Two-State Solution* and *Middle East Conflicts: The Basics.*

Gregory C. McCarthy served as a congressional staffer for nearly sixteen years, in both the House and Senate, committee and personal offices, ending with the House Foreign Affairs Committee in 2014. His congressional offices included: Senator James M. "Jim" Inhofe (R-OK), Chairman Henry J. Hyde (R-IL), Chairman Ileana Ros-Lehtinen (R-FL), and Representative Dana Rohrabacher (R-CA). He has also been an active duty officer and Pentagon civilian. He holds a PhD in American Politics from Catholic University of America.

James A. Thurber is University Distinguished Professor of Government and Founder (1979) and Former Director (1979–2016) of the Center for Congressional and Presidential Studies at American University. He is founder and director American University's Public Affairs and Advocacy Institute, the annual Workshop on Ethics and Lobbying, the European Public Affairs and Advocacy Institute in Washington, DC, and Brussels, and is working with the OECD on international lobbying reform. He was a member of the American Bar Association's Task Force on Lobbying Law Reform. He is the author of numerous books and more than eighty articles and chapters on Congress, interest groups and lobbying, and campaigns and elections, most recently *American Gridlock: The Sources, Character and Impact of Political Polarization* and *Rivals for Power: Presidential-Congressional Relations* (with Jordan Tama).

Walter Clark Wilson is Associate Professor of Political Science and Geography at the University of Texas, San Antonio. His areas of specialization are Latino politics and representation and Congress and legislative studies. He has published numerous articles and chapters on Latino representation in Congress. His work has appeared in *Polity, Legislative Studies Quarterly,*

American Review of Politics, Social Science Quarterly, Journal of Legislative Studies, and *Politics, Groups and Identities*.

Julien Zarifian is Associate Professor at Cergy-Pontoise University, France. He received his PhD in Geopolitics from the French Institute of Geopolitics, Paris 8 University, in 2010. His research involves U.S. foreign policies in Eurasia, and the role of ethnic lobbies and of memory issues in U.S. political and geopolitical life. He is on the editorial board of *Politique Américaine* and *Études Arméniennes Contemporaines*. He has published more than thirty articles and chapters on U.S. foreign policy with particular emphasis on the role of different ethnic groups, such as Armenian Americans. In 2017–2018, he was a Fulbright Visiting Scholar at the University of Southern California.

Index

AAA (Armenian Assembly of America), 120–22, 124, 125, 131, 133nnn16, 18, 26

AAI. *See* Arab American Institute (AAI)

AARP (American Association for Retired Persons), *26* (table), 73, 107

Abramoff, Jack, 237–38

Abrams, Elliott, 67–68

Ackerman, Gary L., 236

ACLU (American Civil Liberties Union), 105

Adams, David, 226, 239n10

Adams, Gerry, 51

ADC. *See* American-Arab Anti-Discrimination Committee (ADC)

Adelson, Sheldon, 76

ADL. *See* Anti-Defamation League (ADL)

Afghanistan, 5, 28

AIPAC (American-Israel Public Affairs Committee)
and constituent mobilization, 82–83
ideology of, *70* (table)
Iran nuclear deal and, 1–2, 50, 55, 86, 227
and Jerusalem Embassy Act, 227
Jewish Americans and, 1, 50, 82, 139

lobbying by, 34, 50–51, 73, 74, 76, 77–79, 80, 81–82, 83–87, 104, 226, 236
power of, 11, 34, 73, 226–27, 239n11
and U.S. foreign policy influence, 50–51, 82, 139
and youth recruitment, 89n36

Akhmetshin, Rinat, 3

Albanians, 233, 236

Algeria, 10

al-Qaeda, 106

Ambrosio, Thomas, 123

American-Arab Anti-Discrimination Committee (ADC), 12, 91, 99–100, 101, 104–5

American Committee for the Independence of Armenia, 121

American G.I. Forum, 142, 151–52, *154* (table), 156

American-Israel Public Affairs Committee. *See* AIPAC (American-Israel Public Affairs Committee)

American Israel Education Fund (AIEF), 77–78

American Jewish Committee (AJC), 73, 83

"The Americans" (television show), 43

Americans for Peace Now (APN), 36, 73, 81, 84, 86, 87

261